lonely planet

Italian

Phrasebook & Dictionary

T0003196

Acknowledgments
Product Editors Damian Kemp, Bruce Evans
Book Designer Fergal Condon
Language Writers Pietro Iagnocco, Karina Coates, Susie Walker,
Mirna Cicioni, Anna Beltrami
Cover Image Researcher Gwen Cotter

Published by Lonely Planet Global Limited
CRN 554153

9th Edition – June 2023
ISBN 978 1 78868 087 5
Text © Lonely Planet 2023
Cover Image Visitor in the Reggia di Venaria Reale museum in Turin.
ArtOfPhotos/Shutterstock ©
Printed in China   10 9 8 7 6 5 4 3 2 1

Contact lonelyplanet.com/contact

MIX
Paper from
responsible sources
FSC™ C021741
www.fsc.org

Look out for the following icons throughout the book:

 'Shortcut' Phrase
Easy-to-remember alternative to the full phrase

 Q&A Pair
'Question-and-answer' pair – we suggest a response to the question asked

 Look For
Phrases you may see on signs, menus etc

 Listen For
Phrases you may hear from officials, locals etc

 Language Tip
An insight into the foreign language

 Culture Tip
An insight into the local culture

How to read the phrases:
- Coloured words and phrases throughout the book are phonetic guides to help you pronounce the foreign language.
- Lists of phrases with tinted background are options you can choose to complete the phrase above them.

These abbreviations will help you choose the right words and phrases in this book:

f feminine	**m** masculine	**sg** singular
inf informal	**pl** plural	
lit literal	**pol** polite	

Contents

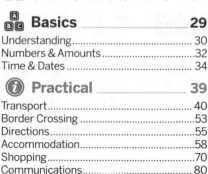

PAGE 184

Menu Decoder
Dishes and ingredients explained –
order with confidence and try new foods.

PAGE 204

Two-Way Dictionary
Quick reference vocabulary guide –
3500 words to help you communicate.

Italian

italiano ee·ta·*lya*·no

Who speaks Italian?

OFFICIAL LANGUAGE
ITALY
SAN MARINO
VATICAN CITY
SWITZERLAND
ISTRIA (CROATIA & SLOVENIA)

Widely Understood Eritrea – Malta – Monaco

Why Bother

When even a simple sentence sounds like an aria, it's difficult to resist striking up a conversation. Besides, all you need for *la dolce vita* is to be able to tell your Moschino from your *macchiato* and your Fellini from your *fettuccine*!

Distinctive Sounds

The rolled r, stronger than in English; most other consonants can have a more emphatic pronunciation too (in which case they're written as double letters).

65 MILLION
speak Italian as their
first language

20 MILLION
speak Italian as their
second language

Italian in the World

Thanks to widespread migration and the enormous popularity of Italian culture and cuisine – from 'spaghetti Western' to opera – Italian is often a language of choice in schools all over the world, despite the fact that Italy never established itself as a colonial power.

Italian in Italy

Italians are very proud of their language's rich history and influence – rightly so, since it claims the closest relationship with the language spoken by the Romans. For example, Italy is one of the few countries in Europe where dubbing of foreign-language movies is preferred to subtitling.

False Friends

Warning: many Italian words look like English words but have a different meaning altogether, eg *camera* *ka·me·ra* is a room, not a camera (which is *macchina fotografica ma·kee·na fo·to·gra·fee·ka* in Italian).

Language Family

Romance (developed from Latin, the language of the Roman Empire). Close relatives include Spanish, Portuguese, French and Romanian.

Must-Know Grammar

Italian has a formal and informal word for 'you' (*Lei* lay and *tu* too respectively); the verbs have a different ending for each person, like the English 'I do' vs 'he/she does'.

Donations to English

Numerous – most of us are familiar with *ciao, pasta, bella, maestro, mafia*...

5 Phrases to Learn Before You Go

 1 **What's the local speciality?**
Qual'è la specialità di questa regione?
kwa·*le* la spe·cha·lee·*ta* dee *kwes*·ta re·jo·ne

A bit like the rivalry between medieval Italian city-states, these days the country's regions compete in specialty foods and wines.

 2 **Which combined tickets do you have?**
Quali biglietti cumulativi avete?
kwa·lee bee·*lye*·tee koo·moo·la·*tee*·vee a·*ve*·te

Make the most of your euro by getting combined tickets to various sights; they are available in all major Italian cities.

 3 **Where can I buy discount designer items?**
C'è un outlet in zona? che oon owt·let in zo·na

Discount fashion outlets are big business in major cities – get bargain-priced seconds, samples and cast-offs for *la bella figura*.

 4 **I'm here with my husband/boyfriend.**
Sono qui con il mio marito/ragazzo.
so·no kwee kon eel *mee*·o ma·*ree*·to/ra·ga·tso

Solo women travellers may receive unwanted attention in some parts of Italy; if ignoring fails have a polite rejection ready.

 5 **Let's meet at 6pm for pre-dinner drinks.**
Ci vediamo alle sei per un aperitivo.
chee ve·*dya*·mo a·le say per oon a·pe·ree·*tee*·vo

At dusk, watch the main *piazza* get crowded with people sipping colourful cocktails and snacking the evening away: join your new friends for this authentic Italian ritual!

10 Phrases to Sound Like a Local

| What's up? | **Cosa c'é?** | *ko*·za che |

| All OK? | **Tutto a posto?** | *too*·ta *pos*·to |

| It's OK. | **Va bene.** | va *be*·ne |

| Great! | **Fantastico!** | fan·*tas*·tee·ko |

| That's true. | **È vero.** | e *ve*·ro |

| Sure. | **Certo.** | *cher*·to |

| No way! | **Per niente!** | per *nyen*·te |

| You're kidding! | **Scherzi!** | *sker*·tsee |

| If only! | **Magari!** | ma·*ga*·ree |

| Really? | **Davvero?** | da·*ve*·ro |

ABOUT Italian

Pronunciation

The Italian sound system will be familiar to most English-speakers: almost all of the sounds you'll hear exist in English. You might notice slight differences, particularly with the vowel sounds, but there's nothing to stop you from having a go and being understood. Standard Italian pronunciation is given in this book – the same form that's used in education and the media.

Vowel Sounds

Italian vowel sounds are generally shorter than in English. They normally do not run together to form vowel sound combinations (diphthongs), though it can often sound that way to English-speakers. There are four vowel sounds that roughly correspond to diphthongs in English (ai, ay, ow, oy).

SYMBOL	ENGLISH EQUIVALENT	ITALIAN EXAMPLE	TRANSLITERATION
a	father	pane	*pa·ne*
ai	aisle	mai	mai
ay	say	vorrei	*vo·ray*
e	red	letto	*le·to*
ee	bee	vino	*vee·no*
o	pot	molto	*mol·to*
oo	took	frutta	*froo·ta*
ow	cow	ciao, autobus	chow, *ow·to·boos*
oy	boy	poi	poy

Consonant Sounds

SYMBOL	ENGLISH EQUIVALENT	ITALIAN EXAMPLE	TRANSLITERATION
b	big	bello	*be·*lo
ch	chilli	centro	*chen·*tro
d	din	denaro	de·*na·*ro
dz	lids	mezzo, zaino	*me·*dzo, *dzai·*no
f	fun	fare	*fa·*re
g	go	gomma	*go·*ma
j	jam	cugino	koo·*jee·*no
k	kick	cambio, quanto	*kam·*byo, *kwan·*to
l	loud	linea	*lee·*ne·a
ly	million	figlia	*fee·*lya
m	man	madre	*ma·*dre
n	no	numero	noo·*me·*ro
ny	canyon	bagno	*ba·*nyo
p	pig	pronto	*pron·*to
r	run (strong and rolled)	ristorante	rees·to·*ran·*te
s	so	sera	*se·*ra
sh	show	capisce	ka·*pee·*she
t	tin	teatro	te·*a·*tro
ts	hits	grazie, sicurezza	*gra·*tsye, see·koo·re·*tsa
v	van	viaggio	vee·*a·*jo
w	win	uomo	*wo·*mo
y	yes	italiano	ee·tal·*ya·*no
z	zoo	casa	*ka·*za

As well as the pronunciation described above, Italian consonant sounds have an additional form: a stronger, almost emphatic pronunciation. The actual sounds are basically the same, though meaning can be altered between a normal consonant sound and this double consonant sound. It's referred to as a 'double consonant' because usually, if the word is written with a double letter, that's the cue to use the stronger form.

Here are some examples where this 'double consonant' effect can make a difference:

sonno	*son·no*	sleep
sono	*so·no*	I am
pappa	*pap·pa*	baby food
papa	*pa·pa*	pope

Unlike the above examples, the pronunciation guides in this book don't distinguish between the two forms. Refer to the written Italian beside each transliteration as the cue to making the consonant sounds a little stronger. Even if you never distinguish them, you'll always be understood in context – your audience will work out if you're talking about the pope or baby food!

Reading & Writing

~ ITALIAN ALPHABET ~

A a a	**B b** bee	**C c** chee
D d dee	**E e** e	**F f** *e·fe*
G g jee	**H h** *a·ka*	**I i** ee
L l *e·le*	**M m** *e·me*	**N n** *e·ne*
O o o	**P p** pee	**Q q** koo
R r *e·re*	**S s** *e·se*	**T t** tee
U u oo	**V v** voo	**Z z** *tse·ta*

The relationship between Italian sounds and their spelling is straightforward and consistent. The table below will help you read the Italian that you come across in your travels.

~ SPELLBOUND ~

c, g, sc	before *a, o, u* and *h* they sound hard like the 'k' in 'kick', 'g' in 'go' and 'sc' in 'scooter' respectively; before *e* and *i* they sound soft like the 'ch' in 'chilli', 'j' in 'jam' and 'sh' in 'show' respectively	bianco, gomma, fresco; centro, gelato, ascensore
ci, gi, sci	before *a, o* and *u*, the 'i' is not pronounced	ciao, giallo, prosciutto
h	never pronounced	traghetto
j, w, k, x, y	only found in foreign words that have been adopted by Italian	jogging, weekend, kosher, fax, yogurt
z	pronounced as 'dz' or as 'ts'	zaino, grazie
s	pronounced as 'z' between vowels; pronounced as 's' elsewhere	casa; sì, essere, scatola
gli, gn	pronounced as the 'll' in 'million' and 'ny' in 'canyon' respectively	figlia, bagno

Word Stress

In Italian, you generally emphasise the second-last syllable in a word. However, when a written word has an accent marked on a vowel, the stress is on that syllable. The characteristic singsong quality of an Italian sentence is created by pronouncing the syllables evenly and rhythmically, then swinging down on the last word. The stressed syllable is always italicised in our pronunciation guides, so you can't go wrong!

ABOUT Italian

Grammar

This chapter is designed to explain the main grammatical structures you need in order to make your own sentences. Look under each heading – listed in alphabetical order – for information on functions which these grammatical categories express in a sentence. For example, demonstratives are used for giving instructions, so you'll need them to tell the taxi driver where your hotel is etc.

Adjectives & Adverbs

Describing People/Things · Doing Things

Adjectives generally come after the noun in Italian. However, adjectives expressing quantity (eg 'much', 'few') always precede the noun.

black cat	gatto nero (lit: cat black-**m-sg**) *ga·to ne·ro*
many cats	molti gatti (lit: many-**m-pl** cats) *mol·tee ga·tee*

The adjective endings change depending on whether the noun is masculine or feminine, singular or plural (see **gender** and **plurals**).

	~ SINGULAR ~		~ PLURAL ~	
m	bello	*be*·lo	belli	*be*·lee
f	bella	*be*·la	belle	*be*·le

Adjectives ending in -*e* in the singular – eg *felice* fe·*lee*·che (happy) – take the ending -*i* in the plural, regardless of the noun's gender:

| **happy cats** | gatti felici (lit: cats happy-m-pl) |
| | *ga*·tee fe·*lee*·chee |

Many adverbs in Italian are derived from adjectives by adding the ending -*mente* ·*men*·te to the singular feminine form of the adjective (ie the form ending in -*a*), just like you add the ending '-ly' to the adjective in English. In Italian, adverbs are generally placed after the verb they refer to.

a slow train	un treno lento
	(lit: a-m-sg train slow-m-sg)
	oon *tre*·no *len*·to
to speak slowly	parlare lentamente
	(lit: to-speak slowly)
	par·*la*·re len·ta·*men*·te

Articles

Naming People/Things

There are four words for the definite article (ie equivalents of 'the' in English) in Italian. Which one you use depends on the gender and number of the noun (see **gender** and **plurals**).

~ DEFINITE ARTICLES ~			
m sg	**the train**	il treno	eel *tre*·no
m pl	**the trains**	i treni	ee *tre*·nee
f sg	**the receipt**	la ricevuta	la ree·che·*voo*·ta
f pl	**the receipts**	le ricevute	le ree·che·*voo*·te

Note that the forms *lo* lo and *gli* lyee are used before masculine nouns starting with 's' plus a consonant, or with *z-*, *gn-*, *pn-*, *ps-*, *x-* or *y-*. The form *l'* is used before masculine and feminine nouns starting with a vowel (*l'* is joined in pronunciation with the noun).

m sg	**the backpack**	lo zaino	lo *dzai*·no
m pl	**the backpacks**	gli zaini	lyee *dzai*·nee
f sg	**the exit**	l'uscita	loo·*shee*·ta
f pl	**the exits**	le uscite	le oo·*shee*·te

The definite article in Italian is joined with some prepositions when it's used after them, eg *di* dee (of) + *il* eel becomes *del* del, and *a* a (to) + *la* la becomes *alla* a·la. See also **prepositions**.

Italian has two words for the indefinite article (ie 'a/an'), depending on the noun's gender (*un* oon/*una* oo·na). Two other forms are used depending on the first letter of the next word: *uno* oo·no (for masculine nouns starting with 's' plus a consonant, or with *z-*, *gn-*, *pn-*, *ps-*, *x-* or *y-*) and *un'* oon (for feminine nouns starting with a vowel).

~ INDEFINITE ARTICLES ~

m sg	**a sandwich**	un panino	oon pa·*nee*·no
	a stadium	uno stadio	oo·no *sta*·dyo
f sg	**an apple**	una mela	oo·na *me*·la
	a friend	un'amica	oon·a·*mee*·ka

Be

Describing People/Things • Making Statements

There are two equivalents of the English verb 'be' in Italian – *essere* *e*·se·re and *stare* *sta*·re – which are used depending on the context. For negative forms with 'be', see **negatives**.

~ USE OF ESSERE (TO BE) ~

permanent characteristics of persons/things	Sei molto bella. *say mol·to be·la*	You're very beautiful.
occupations or nationality	Sono dall'Inghilterra. *so·no da·leen·geel·te·ra*	I am from England.
time or location of events	È l'una. *e loo·na*	It's one o'clock.
mood of a person	Sei felice? *say fe·lee·che*	Are you happy?
possession	Non è mio. *non e mee·o*	It's not mine.

~ USE OF STARE (TO BE) ~

temporary characteristics of persons/things	Sará malato. *sa·ra ma·la·to*	He will be sick.
time or location of events	Stai a casa? *stai a ka·za*	Are you at home?

~ ESSERE (TO BE) – PRESENT TENSE ~

I	am	io	sono	yo	*so·no*
you sg inf	are	tu	sei	too	*say*
you sg pol	are	Lei	è	lay	*e*
he/ she/ it	is	lui/ lei	è	looy/ lay	*e*
we	are	noi	siamo	noy	*sya·mo*
you pl inf	are	voi	siete	voy	*syo·te*
you pl pol	are	Loro	sono	lo·ro	*so·no*
they	are	loro	sono	lo·ro	*so·no*

~ STARE (TO BE) – PRESENT TENSE ~

I	am	io	sto	yo	sto
you sg inf	**are**	tu	stai	too	stai
you sg pol	**are**	Lei	sta	lay	sta
he/she/it	**is**	lui/lei	sta	looy/lay	sta
we	**are**	noi	stiamo	noy	*stya·mo*
you pl inf	**are**	voi	state	voy	*sta·te*
you pl pol	**are**	Loro	stanno	lo·ro	*sta·no*
they	**are**	loro	stanno	lo·ro	*sta·no*

Demonstratives

Giving Instructions • Indicating Location • Pointing Things Out

To point something out, just use the phrase *È* ... e ... (it-is ...):

It's a local custom.   È una tradizione locale.
(lit: it-is a-**f-sg** custom local-**f-sg**)
e *oo·na* tra·dee·*tsyo*·ne lo·*ka*·le

To refer to or to point out a person or object, use one of the following demonstratives before the noun. Each of these words changes form depending on the gender and number of the noun it refers to. See also **gender** and **plurals**.

~ DEMONSTRATIVES ~

	m sg			m pl	
this	questo	*kwe*·sto	**these**	questi	*kwe*·stee
that	quel/ quello	kwel/ *kwe*·lo	**those**	quei/ quegli/ quelli	kway/ *kwe*·lyee/ *kwe*·lee
	f sg			f pl	
this	questa	*kwe*·sta	**these**	queste	*kwe*·ste
that	quella	*kwe*·la	**those**	quelle	*kwe*·le

Demonstratives can also be used on their own:

How much is this?   Quanto costa questo?
                         (lit: how-much costs this-m-sg)
                         kwan·to kos·ta kwe·sto

Gender

Naming People/Things

In Italian, all nouns are either masculine or feminine. You can recognise the noun's gender by the article, demonstrative, possessive or any other adjective used with the noun, as they all change form to agree with the noun's gender. The gender of words is also indicated in the dictionary, but here are some general rules:

» A word is masculine/feminine if it refers to a man/woman.
» Words ending in -o, -ore or a consonant are usually masculine.
» Words ending in -a or -ione are generally feminine.

The masculine and feminine forms of words are indicated with the abbreviations m and f throughout this phrasebook where relevant. See also the box **masculine & feminine** (p130).

Have

Possessing

Possession can be indicated in various ways in Italian (see also **possessives**). One way is by using the verb *avere a·ve·re* (have). For negative forms with 'have', see **negatives**.

~ AVERE (TO HAVE) – PRESENT TENSE ~					
I	**have**	io	ho	yo	o
you sg inf	**have**	tu	hai	too	ai
you sg pol	**have**	Lei	ha	lay	a
he/ she/ it	**has**	lui/ lei	ha	looy/ lay	a
we	**have**	noi	abbiamo	noy	a·*bya*·mo
you pl inf	**have**	voi	avete	voy	a·*ve*·te
you pl pol	**have**	Loro	hanno	*lo*·ro	*a*·no
they	**have**	loro	hanno	*lo*·ro	*a*·no

You can also use the phrases *c'è* che (there is) and *ci sono* chee *so*·no (there are) to say or ask if something is available:

Is there hot water?   C'è acqua calda?
(lit: there-is water hot-**f-sg**)
che a·kwa *kal*·da

Negatives

Negating

To make a negative statement in Italian, just add the word *non* non (not) before the main verb of the sentence. Unlike English, Italian uses double negatives.

I don't understand.   Non capisco.
(lit: not I-understand)
non ka·*pee*·sko

I don't understand anything.   Non capisco niente.
(lit: not I-understand nothing)
non ka·*pee*·sko *nyen*·te

Personal Pronouns

Making Statements • Naming People/Things

Personal pronouns ('I', 'you' etc) change form in Italian depending on whether they're the subject or the object in a sentence. It's the same in English, which has 'I' and 'me' as the subject and object pronouns respectively (eg 'I see her' vs 'She sees me'). Note, however, that the subject pronoun is usually omitted in Italian as the subject is understood from the corresponding verb form.

I'm a student.

Sono studente.
(lit: I-am student)
so·no stoo·den·tee

~ SUBJECT PRONOUNS ~

I	io	yo	**we**	noi	noy
you sg inf	tu	too	**you** pl inf	voi	voy
you sg pol	Lei	lay	**you** pl pol	Loro	lo·ro
he/ she/ it	lui/ lei	looy/ lay	**they**	loro	lo·ro

When talking to people familiar to you or younger than you, it's usual to use the informal form of 'you', *tu* too, rather than the polite form, *Lei* lay. Phrases in this book use the form of 'you' that is appropriate to the situation you're likely to encounter as a traveller. Where both forms are used, they are indicated by the abbreviations pol and inf. See also the box **addressing people** (p107).

ABOUT ITALIAN GRAMMAR

ABOUT ITALIAN GRAMMAR

~ OBJECT PRONOUNS ~

me	mi	mee	us	ci	chee
you sg inf	ti	tee	**you** pl inf	vi	vee
you sg pol	La/ Le	la/ le	**you** pl pol	Li/ Loro m Le/ Loro f	lee/ *lo*·ro m le/ *lo*·ı o f
him it	lo/ gli	lo/ lyee	**them**	li/ loro m le/ loro f	lee/ *lo*·ro m le/ *lo*·ro f
her it	la/ le	la/ le			

In the table above, the forms separated by a slash are direct/indirect object pronouns.

The direct and indirect object pronouns differ only for the third person ('he', 'she', 'it', 'they') and the polite 'you' form.

I've seen him.	Lo ho visto. (lit: him I-have seen) lo o *vee*·sto
I've talked to him.	Gli ho parlato. (lit: to-him I-have talked) lyee o par·*la*·to

The object pronouns generally come before the verb. The indirect object pronoun comes before the direct object pronoun.

I'll give it to you.	Ti lo darò. (lit: to-you-sg-inf it I-will-give) tee lo da·*ro*

Plurals

Naming People/Things

General rules for forming plurals in Italian are pretty simple: words ending in -*a* in the singular end in -*e* in the plural, and words ending in -*o* or -*e* in the singular end in -*i* in the plural. See also the box **irregular plurals** (p97).

~ SINGULAR ~			~ PLURAL ~		
a person	una persona	*oo·na per·so·na*	**three people**	tre persone	*tre per·so·ne*
a ticket	un biglietto	*oon bee·lye·to*	**two tickets**	due biglietti	*doo·e bee·lye·tee*
a country	un paese	*oon pa·e·se*	**five countries**	cinque paesi	*cheen·kwe pa·e·see*

Possessives

Possessing

A common way of indicating possession is by using possessive adjectives before the noun they refer to. Like other adjectives, they agree with the noun in number and gender, and they are preceded by the definite article (see **articles**).

It's my ticket.　　　　È il mio biglietto.
　　　　　　　　　　　　(lit: it-is the-**m·sg** my-**m·sg** ticket)
　　　　　　　　　　　　e eel mee·o bee·lye·to

In Italian, possessive adjectives (ie 'my', 'your' etc) and possessive pronouns (ie 'mine', 'yours' etc) are the same – if what is being talked about is clear from the context, the noun can be omitted:

It's mine.　　　　　　È il mio.
　　　　　　　　　　　　(lit: it-is the-**m·sg** mine-**m·sg**)
　　　　　　　　　　　　e eel mee·o

ABOUT ITALIAN GRAMMAR

~ POSSESSIVE ADJECTIVES & PRONOUNS ~

my/ mine	il mio i miei la mia le mie	eel *mee*·o ee *mye*·ee la *mee*·a le *mee*·e	**our/ ours**	il nostro i nostri la nostra le nostre	eel *nos*·tro ee *nos*·tree la *nos*·tra le *nos*·tre
your/ yours sg inf	il tuo i tuoi la tua le tue	eel *too*·o ee *two*·ee la *too*·a le *too*·e	**your/ yours** pl inf	il vostro i vostri la vostra le vostre	eel *vos*·tro ee *vos*·tree la *vos*·tra le *vos*·tre
your/ yours sg pol	il Suo i Suoi la Sua le Sue	eel *soo*·o ee *swo*·ee la *soo*·a le *soo*·e	**your/ yours** pl pol	il Loro i Loro la Loro le Loro	eel *lo*·ro ee *lo*·ro la *lo*·ro le *lo*·ro
his/ her(s)/ its	il suo i suoi la sua le sue	eel *soo*·o ee *swo*·ee la *soo*·a le *soo*·e	**their/ theirs**	il loro i loro la loro le loro	eel *lo*·ro ee *lo*·ro la *lo*·ro le *lo*·ro

The four alternatives given in the table above are used with
m sg, m pl, f sg and f pl nouns.

Ownership can also be expressed with the verb *avere* a·*ve*·re
(see **have**) or the construction '*di* dee (of) + noun/pronoun':

It's Lorenzo's backpack.	È lo zaino di Lorenzo. (lit: it-is the-m-sg backpack of Lorenzo) e lo *dzai*·no dee lo·*ren*·dzo
Whose seat is this?	Di chi è questo posto? (lit: of who is this-m-sg place) dee kee e *kwe*·sto *pos*·to

Prepositions

Giving Instructions • Indicating Location • Pointing Things
Out

Like English, Italian uses prepositions to explain where things
are in time or space. Common prepositions are listed on the
following page; more can be found in the **dictionary**.

When certain prepositions are followed by a definite article, they are contracted into a single word (see **articles**).

~ PREPOSITIONS ~

after	dopo	*do*·po	**in (place)**	in	een
at (time)	a	a	**of**	di	dee
before	prima	*pree*·ma	**to**	a	a
from	da	da	**with**	con	kon

Questions

Asking Questions • Negating

The easiest way of forming 'yes/no' questions in Italian is to add the phrase è vero e *ve*·ro (literally 'is-it true') to the end of a statement, similar to 'isn't it?' in English.

This seat is free, isn't it?	Questo posto è libero, è vero? (lit: this-m-sg seat is free-m-sg is-it true) *kwe*·sto po·sto e *lee*·be·ro e *ve*·ro

You can also turn a statement into a question by putting the verb before the subject of the sentence, just like in English.

Is this seat free?	È libero questo posto? (lit: is free-m-sg this-m-sg seat) e *lee*·be·ro *kwe*·sto po·sto

As in English, there are also question words for more specific questions. These words go at the start of the sentence.

~ QUESTION WORDS ~

how	come	*ko*·me	**where**	dove	*do*·ve
what	che cosa	ke *ko*·za	**who**	chi	kee
when	quando	*kwan*·do	**why**	perché	per·*ke*

Verbs

Doing Things

There are three verb categories in Italian – those whose infinitive (dictionary form) ends in *-are, -ere* or *-ire,* eg *parlare* par·*la*·re (talk), *scrivere skree*·ve·re (write), *capire* ka·*pee*·re (understand). Tenses are formed by adding various endings for each person to the verb stem (the part of the verb that remains after removing *-are, -ere* or *-ire* from the infinitive), and for most verbs these endings follow regular patterns according to the verb category. The verb endings for the present, past and future tenses are presented in the following tables.

As in any language, there are also irregular verbs in Italian. The most important ones are *essere, stare* and *avere* (see **be** and **have**). For negative forms of verbs, see **negatives**.

| **I speak, write and understand Italian.** | Parlo, scrivo e capisco italiano. (lit: I-speak, I-write and I-understand Italian) *par*·lo *skree*·vo e ka·*pee*·sko ee·ta·*lya*·no |

Note that before the endings for the present tense, some verbs ending in *-ire* (eg *capire*) also change their verb stem slightly.

~ PRESENT TENSE ~

		parlare	**scrivere**	**capire**
I	io	parlo	scrivo	capisco
you sg inf	tu	parli	scrivi	capisci
you sg pol	Lei	parla	scrive	capisce
he/she	lui/lei	parla	scrive	capisce
we	noi	parliamo	scriviamo	capiamo
you pl inf	voi	parlate	scrivete	capite
you pl pol	Loro	parlano	scrivono	capiscono
they	loro	parlano	scrivono	capiscono

The main past tense in Italian, used for a completed action, is a compound tense, which means it is made up of an auxiliary verb – either *essere* e·se·re (be) or *avere* a·ve·re (have) – in the present tense, plus a form of the main verb, called 'past participle'. The past participle is formed by replacing the infinitive endings -*are*, -*ere* or -*ire* with -*ato*, -*uto* or -*ito* respectively. Some past participles are irregular. See also **be** and **have**.

	~ INFINITIVE ~		~ PAST PARTICIPLE ~	
love	amare	a·ma·re	amato	a·ma·to
believe	credere	kre·de·re	creduto	kre·doo·to
follow	seguire	se·gee·re	seguito	se·gee·to

Past participles taking *essere* agree in gender and number with the subject, while those taking *avere* agree with the object.

I went there.	Sono andato/andata là. **m/f**
	(lit: I-am gone-**m-sg**/-**f-sg** there)
	so·no an·da·to/an·da·ta la
I saw her yesterday.	La ho vista ieri.
	(lit: her I-have seen-**f-sg** yesterday)
	la o vee·sta ye·ree

~ FUTURE TENSE ~

		parlare	**scrivere**	**capire**
I	io	parlerò	scriverò	capirò
you sg inf	tu	parlerai	scriverai	capirai
you sg pol	Lei	parlerà	scriverà	capirà
he/she	lui/lei	parlerà	scriverà	capirà
we	noi	parleremo	scriveremo	capiremo
you pl inf	voi	parlerete	scriverete	capirete
you pl pol	Loro	parleranno	scriveranno	capiranno
they	loro	parleranno	scriveranno	capiranno

You can also express future plans by using the present tense with some indication of time referring to the future:

Tomorrow we're going to Rome.

Domani andiamo a Roma.
(lit: tomorrow we-go to Rome)
do·*ma*·nee an·*dya*·mo a *ro*·ma

Word Order

Making Statements

Italian has a basic word order of subject–verb–object, just like English. However, the subject pronoun (eg 'I' or 'you') is usually omitted in Italian as the subject is understood from the corresponding verb form (see **verbs**) – so the second example below is more common.

We're waiting for the bus.

Noi aspettiamo l'autobus.
(lit: we wait the-**m-sg**-bus)
noy as·pe·*tya*·mo *low*·to·boos

We're waiting for the bus.

Aspettiamo l'autobus.
(lit: we-wait the-**m-sg**-bus)
as·pe·*tya*·mo *low*·to·boos

See also **negatives** and **questions**.

Basics

Understanding

KEY PHRASES

Do you speak English?	Parla/Parli inglese? pol/inf	*par*·la/*par*·lee een·*gle*·ze
I don't understand.	(Non) Capisco.	(non) ka·*pee*·sko
What does ... mean?	Che cosa vuol dire ...?	ke *ko*·za vwol *dee*·re ...

Q Do you speak English?	Parla/Parli inglese? pol/inf *par*·la/*par*·lee een·*gle*·ze
Q Does anyone speak English?	C'è qualcuno che parla inglese? che kwal·*koo*·no ke *par*·la een·*gle*·ze
A I speak English.	Parlo inglese. *par*·lo een·*gle*·ze
I need an interpreter who speaks English.	Ho bisogno di un interprete che parla l'inglese. o bee·*so*·nyo dee oon een·*ter*·pre·te ke *par*·la leen·*gle*·ze
Q Do you understand?	Capisce/Capisci? pol/inf ka·*pee*·she/ka·*pee*·shee
A I (don't) understand.	(Non) Capisco. (non) ka·*pee*·sko
I (don't) speak Italian.	(Non) Parlo italiano. (non) *par*·lo ee·ta·*lya*·no
I speak a little.	Parlo un po'. *par*·lo oon po

I'd like to practise Italian.	Vorrei fare pratica con l'italiano. vo·*ray* fa·re pra·tee·ka kon lee·ta·*lya*·no
I'd like to learn some of your local dialects.	Vorrei imparare qualche dialetto regionale. vo·*ray* eem·pa·*ra*·re *kwal*·ke dee·a·*le*·to re·jo·*na*·le
Would you like me to teach you some English?	Vuole che le insegni un po' d'inglese? *vwo*·le ke le een·*se*·nyee oon po deen·*gle*·ze
What does ... mean?	Che cosa vuol dire ...? ke *ko*·za vwol dee·re ...
How do you pronounce this?	Come si pronuncia questo? *ko*·me see pro·*noon*·cha *kwe*·sto
How do you write ...?	Come si scrive ...? *ko*·me see skree·ve ...
Could you please repeat that?	Può/Puoi ripeterlo, per favore? **pol/inf** pwo/pwoy ree·*pe*·ter·lo per fa·*vo*·re
Could you please write it down?	Può/Puoi scriverlo, per favore? **pol/inf** pwo/pwoy skree·ver·lo per fa·*vo*·re
Could you please speak more slowly?	Può/Puoi parlare più lentamente, per favore? **pol/inf** pwo/pwoy par·*la*·re pyoo len·ta·*men*·te per fa·*vo*·re

✂	**Slowly, please!**	Più lentamente, per favore!	pyoo len·ta·*men*·te per fa·*vo*·re

Numbers & Amounts

KEY PHRASES

How much?	Quanto/a? m/f	kwan·to/a
some	alcuni/e m/f	al·koo·nee/al·koo·ne
less/more	di meno/più	dee me·no/pyoo

Cardinal Numbers

0	zero	dze·ro
1	uno	oo·no
2	due	doo·e
3	tre	tre
4	quattro	kwa·tro
5	cinque	cheen·kwe
6	sei	say
7	sette	se·te
8	otto	o·to
9	nove	no·ve
10	dieci	dye·chee
11	undici	oon·dee·chee
12	dodici	do·dee·chee
13	tredici	tre·dee·chee
14	quattordici	kwa·tor·dee·chee
15	quindici	kween·dee·chee
16	sedici	se·dee·chee
17	diciassette	dee·cha·se·te

18	diciotto	dee·*cho*·to
19	diciannove	dee·cha·*no*·ve
20	venti	*ven*·tee
21	ventuno	ven·*too*·no
30	trenta	*tren*·ta
40	quaranta	kwa·*ran*·ta
50	cinquanta	cheen·*kwan*·ta
60	sessanta	se·*san*·ta
70	settanta	se·*tan*·ta
80	ottanta	o·*tan*·ta
90	novanta	no·*van*·ta
100	cento	*chen*·to
200	duecento	doo·e·*chen*·to
1000	mille	*mee*·le
2000	duemila	doo·e·*mee*·la
1,000,000	un milione	oon mee·*lyo*·ne

Ordinal Numbers

1st	primo/a m/f	*pree*·mo/a
2nd	secondo/a m/f	se·*kon*·do/a
3rd	terzo/a m/f	*ter*·tso/a

Useful Amounts

How much?	Quanto/a? m/f	*kwan*·to/a
How many?	Quanti/e? m/f	*kwan*·tee/*kwan*·te
less	di meno	dee *me*·no
more	di più	dee pyoo
some	alcuni/e m/f	al·*koo*·nee/al·*koo*·ne

For more amounts, see **self-catering** (p176).

Time & Dates

KEY PHRASES

What time is it?	Che ora è?	ke o·ra e
At what time?	A che ora...?	a ke o·ra ...
What date?	Che data?	ke *da*·ta

Telling the Time

When telling the time in Italian, 'It is ...' is expressed by *Sono le so*·no le followed by a number. However, 'one o'clock' is *È l'una* e *loo*·na, and 'midday' is *È mezzogiorno* e me·dzo·*jor*·no. Note that in Italy the 24-hour clock is commonly used.

Q **What time is it?**	Che ora è? ke o·ra e
A **It's one o'clock.**	È l'una. e *loo*·na
A **It's (two) o'clock.**	Sono le (due). *so*·no le (*doo*·e)
A **Quarter past (one).**	(L'una) e un quarto. (*loo*·na) e oon *kwar*·to
A **Half past (one).**	(L'una) e mezza. (*loo*·na) e *me*·dza
A **Quarter to (eight).**	(Le otto) meno un quarto. (le *o*·to) *me*·no oon *kwar*·to
in the morning	di mattina dee ma·*tee*·na
in the afternoon	di pomeriggio dee po·me·*ree*·jo
in the evening	di sera dee *se*·ra

at night	di notte	dee *no*·te
midday	mezzogiorno	me·dzo·*jor*·no
midnight	mezzanotte	me·dza·*no*·te
🅠 At what time ...?	A che ora ...?	a ke *o*·ra ...
🅐 At one.	All'una.	a·*loo*·na
🅐 At (7.57pm).	Alle (19.57).	*a*·le (dee·cha·*no*·ve e cheen·kwan·ta·*se*·te)

The Calendar

Monday	lunedì m	loo·ne·*dee*
Tuesday	martedì m	mar·te·*dee*
Wednesday	mercoledì m	mer·ko·le·*dee*
Thursday	giovedì m	jo·vo·*dee*
Friday	venerdì m	ve·ner·*dee*
Saturday	sabato m	*sa*·ba·to
Sunday	domenica f	do·*me*·nee·ka
January	gennaio m	je·*na*·yo
February	febbraio m	fo·*bra*·yo
March	marzo m	*mar*·tso
April	aprile m	a·*pree*·le
May	maggio m	*ma*·jo
June	giugno m	*joo*·nyo
July	luglio m	*loo*·lyo
August	agosto m	a·*gos*·to
September	settembre m	se·*tem*·bre

October	ottobre m	o·*to*·bre
November	novembre m	no·*vem*·bre
December	dicembre m	dee·*chem*·bre
summer	estate f	es·*ta*·te
autumn	autunno m	ow·*too*·no
winter	inverno m	een·*ver*·no
spring	primavera f	pree·ma·*ve*·ra

What date?	Che data? ke *da*·ta
💬 **What date is it today?**	Che giorno è oggi? ke *jor*·no e o·jee
🅰 **It's (3 March).**	È (il terzo) marzo. e (eel *ter*·tso *mar*·tso)

Present

now	adesso a·*de*·so
this morning	stamattina sta·ma·*tee*·na
this afternoon	oggi pomeriggio o·jee po·me·*ree*·jo
today	oggi o·jee
tonight	stasera sta·*se*·ra
this month	questo mese *kwe*·sto *me*·ze
this week	questa settimana *kwe*·sta se·tee·*ma*·na
this year	quest'anno kwe·*sta*·no

Past

day before yesterday	l'altro ieri *lal·*tro *ye·*ree
yesterday	ieri *ye·*ree
yesterday morning	ieri mattina *ye·*ree ma·*tee·*na
yesterday afternoon	ieri pomeriggio *ye·*ree po·me·*ree·*jo
yesterday evening	ieri sera *ye·*ree *se·*ra
last night	ieri notte *ye·*ree *no·*te
last week	la settimana scorsa la se·tee·*ma·*na *skor·*sa
last month	il mese scorso eel *me·*ze *skor·*so
last year	l'anno scorso *la·*no *skor·*so
(three days) ago	(tre giorni) fa (tre *jor·*nee) fa
since (May)	da (maggio) da (*ma·*jo)

Future

day after tomorrow	dopodomani do·po·do·*ma·*nee
tomorrow	domani do·*ma·*nee
tomorrow morning	domani mattina do·*ma·*nee ma·*tee·*na

🔊 LISTEN FOR

You'll often hear the centuries referred to as follows, particularly when talking about periods in history and art:

Il Duecento	eel doo·e·*chen*·to	13th century (lit: the 200)
Il Trecento	eel tre·*chen*·to	14th century (lit: the 300)
Il Quattrocento	eel kwa·tro·*chen*·to	15th century (lit: the 400)
Il Cinquecento	eel cheen·kwe·*chen*·to	16th century (lit: the 500)

tomorrow afternoon	domani pomeriggio do·*ma*·nee po·me·*ree*·jo
tomorrow evening	domani sera do·*ma*·nee *se*·ra
next week	la settimana prossima la se·tee·*ma*·na *pro*·see·ma
next month	il mese prossimo eel *me*·ze *pro*·see·mo
next year	l'anno prossimo *la*·no *pro*·see·mo
in (six days)	fra (sei giorni) fra (say *jor*·nee)
until (June)	fino a (giugno) *fee*·no a (*joo*·nyo)

Practical

Transport

KEY PHRASES

When's the next bus?	A che ora passa il prossimo autobus?	a ke o·ra pa·sa eel pro·see·mo ow·to·boos
One ticket to ..., please.	Un biglietto per ..., per favore.	oon bee·lye·to per ..., per fa·vo·re
Can you tell me when we get to ...?	Mi sa dire quando arriviamo a ...?	mee sa dee·re kwan·do a·ree·vya·mo a ...
Please take me to (this address).	Mi porti a (questo indirizzo), per piacere.	mee por·tee a (kwe·sto een·dee·ree·tso) per pya·che·re

Getting Around

At what time does the ... leave/arrive?	A che ora parte/arriva ...? a ke o·ra par·te/a·ree·va ...

boat	la nave	la na·ve
bus	l'autobus	low·to·boos
ferry	il traghetto	eel tra·ge·to
hydrofoil	l'aliscafo	la·lees·ka·fo
metro	la metropolitana	la me·tro·po·lee·ta·na
plane	l'aereo	la·e·re·o
train	il treno	eel tre·no

Can we get there by public transport?	Possiamo arrivarci con i mezzi pubblici? po·*sya*·mo a·ree·*var*·chee kon ee *me*·dzee *poo*·blee·chee
At what time's the first bus?	A che ora passa il primo autobus? a ke *o*·ra *pa*·sa eel *pree*·mo *ow*·to·boos
At what time's the last bus?	A che ora passa l'ultimo autobus? a ke *o*·ra *pa*·sa *lool*·tee·mo *ow*·to·boos
At what time's the next bus?	A che ora passa il prossimo autobus? a ke *o*·ra *pa*·sa eel *pro*·see·mo *ow*·to·boos
That's my seat.	Quel posto è mio. kwel *pos*·to e *mee*·o
Is this seat free?	È libero questo posto? e *lee*·be·ro *kwe*·sto *pos*·to
✂ **Is it free?**	È libero? e *lee*·be·ro

For phrases on disabled access, see **senior & disabled travellers** (p99).

Buying Tickets

Where can I buy a ticket?	Dove posso comprare un biglietto? *do*·ve *po*·so kom·*pra*·re oon bee·*lye*·to
Do I need to book?	Bisogna prenotare (un posto)? bee·*zo*·nya pre·no·*ta*·re (oon *pos*·to)

PRACTICAL TRANSPORT

🔊 LISTEN FOR

Deve cambiare a (Parma).	*de*·ve kam·*bya*·re a (*par*·ma)	You'll have to change at (Parma).
Il treno è cancellato.	eel *tre*·no e kan·che·*la*·to	The train is cancelled.
La prossima fermata è ...	la *pro*·see·ma fer·*ma*·ta e ...	The next stop is ...
Questa fermata è ...	*kwe*·sta fer·*ma*·ta e ...	We're arriving at ...

Can I get a stand-by ticket?	Posso essere messo/a in lista d'attesa? m/f *po*·so e·se·re *me*·so/a een *lee*·sta da·*te*·sa
What time do I have to check in?	A che ora devo presentarmi per l'accettazione? a ke o·ra *de*·vo pre·zen·*tar*·mee per la·che·ta·*tsyo*·ne
I'd like a sleeping berth.	Vorrei una cuccetta, per favore. vo·*ray* oo·na koo·*che*·ta per fa·*vo*·re
I'd like to ... my ticket, please.	Vorrei ... il mio biglietto, per favore. vo·*ray* ... eel *mee*·o bee·*lye*·to per fa·*vo*·re

cancel	cancellare	kan·che·*la*·re
change	cambiare	kam·*bya*·re
collect	ritirare	ree·tee·*ra*·re
confirm	confermare	kon·fer·*ma*·re

Buying a Ticket

When does the ... leave?

A che ora parte il/la prossimo/a ...? m/f
a ke o·ra par·te eel/la pro·see·mo/a ...

 boat
nave f
na·ve

 bus
autobus m
ow·to·boos

 train
treno m
tre·no

One ... ticket, please.

Un biglietto di..., per favore.
oon bee·lye·to dee... per fa·vo·re

 one-way
sola andata
so·la an·da·ta

 return
andata e ritorno
an·da·ta e ree·tor·no

I'd like a/an ... seat.

Vorrei un posto ...
vo·ray oon pos·to ...

aisle
sul corridoio
sool
ko·ree·do·yo

window
vicino al finestrino
vee·chee·no al
fee·nes·tree·no

Which platform does it depart from?

Da quale binario parte?
da kwa·le bee·na·ryo par·te

One ... ticket (to Rome), please.	Un biglietto ... (per Roma), per favore. oon bee·*lye*·to ... (per *ro*·ma) per fa·*vo*·re

1st-class	di prima classe	dee *pree*·ma *kla*·se
2nd-class	di seconda classe	dee se·*kon*·da *kla*·se
child's	per bambini	per bam·*bee*·nee
one-way	di sola andata	dee *so*·la an·*da*·ta
return	di andata e ritorno	dee an·*da*·ta e ree·*tor*·no
student's	per studenti	per stoo·*den*·tee

I'd like an aisle seat, please.	Vorrei un posto sul corridoio, per favore. vo·*ray* oon *pos*·to sool ko·ree·*do*·yo per fa·*vo*·re
I'd like a window seat, please.	Vorrei un posto vicino al finestrino, per favore. vo·*ray* oon *pos*·to vee·*chee*·no al fee·nes·*tree*·no per fa·*vo*·re

For phrases about getting through customs and immigration, see **border crossing** (p53).

> ## *Si fermi qui, per favore.*
> see *fer*·mee kwee per fa·*vo*·re
> ### *Please stop here.*

Luggage

My luggage hasn't arrived.	Non è arrivato il mio bagaglio. non e a·ree·*va*·to eel *mee*·o ba·*ga*·lyo
My luggage has been damaged.	Il mio bagaglio è stato danneggiato. eel *mee*·o ba·*ga*·lyo e *sta*·to da·ne·*ja*·to
My luggage has been stolen.	Il mio bagaglio è stato rubato. eel *mee*·o ba·*ga*·lyo e *sta*·to roo·*ba*·to
I'd like a luggage locker.	Vorrei un armadietto per il bagaglio. vo·*ray* oon ar·ma·*dye*·to per eel ba·*ga*·lyo

Bus, Tram & Metro

Which bus goes to (Rome)?	Quale autobus va a (Roma)? *kwa*·le *ow*·to·boos va a (*ro*·ma)
Where's the bus stop?	Dov'è la fermata dell'autobus? do·*ve* la fer·*ma*·ta del *ow*·to·boos
What's the next stop?	Qual è la prossima fermata? kwa·*le* la *pro*·see·ma fer·*ma*·ta
I want to get off here/at ...	Voglio scendere qui/a ... *vo*·lyo *shen*·de·re kwee/a ...

PRACTICAL TRANSPORT

🔍 **LOOK FOR**

Fermata del Tram	fer·*ma*·ta del tram	Tram Stop
Fermata dell'autobus	fer·*ma*·ta de·*low*·to·boos	Bus Stop
Stazione della Metropolitana	sta·*tsyo*·ne *de*·la me·tro·po·lee·*ta*·na	Metro Station
Uscita	oo·*shee*·ta	Way Out

How many stops to (the museum)?	Quante fermate mancano (al museo)? *kwan*·te fer·*ma*·te man·ka·no (al moo·ze·o)
Can you tell me when we get to (the market)?	Mi sa dire quando arriviamo (al mercato)? mee sa *dee*·re *kwan*·do a·ree·*vya*·mo (al mer·*ka*·to)

For bus numbers, see **numbers & amounts** (p32).

Train

What station is this?	Che stazione è questa? ke sta·*tsyo*·ne e *kwe*·sta
What's the next station?	Qual'è la prossima stazione? kwa·*le* la *pro*·see·ma sta·*tsyo*·ne
Does this train stop at (Milan)?	Questo treno si ferma a (Milano)? *kwe*·sto *tre*·no see *fer*·ma a (mee·*la*·no)

Is it a direct route?	È un itinerario diretto? e oon ee·tee·ne·ra·ryo dee·re·to
How long does the trip take?	Quanto ci vuole? *kwan·to chee vwo·le*
Where's the dining car?	Dov'è il vagone ristorante? do·ve eel va·go·ne rees·to·ran·te
Which carriage is 1st class?	Quale carrozza è di prima classe? *kwa·le ka·ro·tsa e dee pree·ma kla·se*
Which carriage is for (Rome)?	Quale carrozza è per (Roma)? *kwa·le ka·ro·tsa e per (ro·ma)*
Do I need to change trains?	Devo cambiare treno? *de·vo kam·bya·re tre·no*

🔊 LISTEN FOR

diretto	dee·re·to	direct – no need to change trains
espresso	es·pre·so	express – stops only at major stations
Eurostar Italia (ES)	e·oo·ro·star ee·ta·lya	very fast
Inter City	een·ter see·tee	runs between large cities
locale	lo·ka·le	local – usually stops at all stations
rapido	ra·pee·do	fast – runs between large cities

PRACTICAL TRANSPORT

Borgo (B.go)	*bor*·go	district
Corso (C.so)	*kor*·so	main street/avenue
Largo (L.go)	*lar*·go	little square
Piazza (P.za)	*pya*·tsa	square
Strada (Str.)	*stra*·da	street
Via (V.)	*vee*·a	road/street
Viale (V.le)	vee·*a*·le	avenue/boulevard
Vicolo (V.lo)	*vee*·ko·lo	alley/lane

Taxi

I'd like a taxi at (9am).	Vorrei un tassì alle (nove di mattina). vo·*ray* oon ta·*see a*·le (*no*·ve dee ma·*tee*·na)
Is this taxi free?	È libero questo tassì? e *lee*·be·ro *kwe*·sto ta·*see*
✂ **Is it free?**	È libero? e *lee*·be·ro
How much is it to ...?	Quant'è per ...? kwan·*te* per ...
Please put the meter on.	Usi il tassametro, per favore. oo·zee eel ta·*sa*·me·tro per fa·*vo*·re
Please take me to (this address).	Mi porti a (questo indirizzo), per piacere. mee *por*·tee a (*kwe*·sto een·dee·*ree*·tso) per pya·*che*·re
✂ **To ...**	A ... a ...

Please slow down.	Rallenti, per favore.	ra·*len*·tee per fa·*vo*·re
Please stop here.	Si fermi qui, per favore.	see *fer*·mee kwee per fa·*vo*·re
Please wait here.	Mi aspetti qui, per favore.	mee as·*pe*·tee kwee per fa·*vo*·re

Car & Motorbike

I'd like to hire a/an ...	Vorrei noleggiare ...	vo·*ray* no·le·*ja*·re ...

4WD	un fuoristrada	oon fwo·ree·*stra*·da
automatic (car)	una macchina automatica	oo·na ma·*kee*·na ow·to·*ma*·tee·ka
car	una macchina	oo·na ma·*kee*·na
manual (car)	una macchina manuale	oo·na ma·*kee*·na ma·noo·*a*·le
motorbike	una moto	oo·na *mo*·to

How much is it daily?	Quanto costa al giorno?	*kwan*·to *kos*·ta al *jor*·no
How much is it weekly?	Quanto costa alla settimana?	*kwan*·to *kos*·ta a la se·tee·*ma*·na
Does that include insurance?	E' compresa l'assicurazione?	e kom·*pre*·sa la·see·koo·ra·*tsyo*·ne
Does that include mileage?	E' compreso il chilometraggio?	e kom·*pre*·so eel kee·lo·me·*tra*·jo

PRACTICAL TRANSPORT

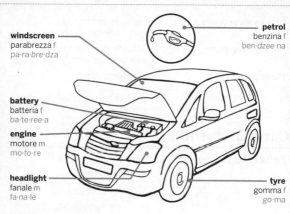

windscreen
parabrezza f
pa·ra·*bre*·dza

petrol
benzina f
ben·*dzee*·na

battery
batteria f
ba·te·*ree*·a

engine
motore m
mo·*to*·re

headlight
fanale m
fa·*na*·le

tyre
gomma f
go·ma

What's the city/country speed limit?	Qual'è il limite di velocità in città/campagna? kwa·*le* eel *lee*·mee·te dee ve·lo·chee·*ta* een chee·*ta*/ kam·*pa*·nya
Is this the road to (Venice)?	Questa strada porta a (Venezia)? *kwe*·sta *stra*·da *por*·ta a (ve·*ne*·tsya)
Where's a service station?	Dov'è una stazione di servizio? do·*ve* oo·na sta·*tsyo*·ne dee ser·*vee*·tsyo
(How long) Can I park here?	(Per quanto tempo) Posso parcheggiare qui? (per *kwan*·to *tem*·po) *po*·so par·ke·*ja*·re kwee
I need a mechanic.	Ho bisogno di un meccanico. o bee·*zo*·nyo dee oon me·*ka*·nee·ko

LOOK FOR

benzina f **con/ senza piombo**	ben·*dzee*·na kon/ *sen*·tsa *pyom*·bo	leaded/unleaded petrol
gasauto m	ga·*zow*·to	LPG
gasolio/diesel m	ga·*zo*·lyo/*dee*·zel	diesel

I had an accident.	Ho avuto un incidente. o a·*voo*·to oon een·chee·*den*·te
The car/motorbike has broken down.	La macchina/moto si è guastata. la *ma*·kee·na/*mo*·to see e gwas·*ta*·ta

Bicycle

Can we get there by bike?	Possiamo arrivarci in bicicletta? po·*sya*·mo a·ree·*var*·chee een bee·chee·*kle*·ta
Where can I hire a bicycle?	Dove posso noleggiare una bicicletta? *do*·ve *po*·so no·le·*ja*·re oo·na bee·chee·*kle*·ta
How much per day?	Quanto costa al giorno? *kwan*·to *kos*·ta al *jor*·no
How much per hour?	Quanto costa all'ora? *kwan*·to *kos*·ta a·*lo*·ra
I'd like to have my bicycle repaired.	Vorrei fare riparare la mia bicicletta. vo·*ray fa*·re ree·pa·*ra*·re la *mee*·a bee·chee·*kle*·ta
I have a puncture.	Ho una gomma bucata. o *oo*·na *go*·ma boo·*ka*·ta

LOOK FOR

Alt	alt	Stop
Attenzione	a·ten·*tsyo*·ne	Caution
Autostrada	ow·to·*stra*·da	Freeway
Dare la Precedenza	*da*·re la pre·che·*den*·tsa	Give Way
Deviazione	de·vya·*tsyo*·ne	Detour
Divieto di Accesso	dee·*vye*·to dee a·*che*·so	No Entry
Divieto di Sorpasso	dee·*vye*·to dee sor·*pa*·so	No Overtaking
Divieto di Sosta	dee·*vye*·to dee *sos*·ta	No Parking
Entrata	en·*tra*·ta	Entrance
Lavori in Corso	la·*vo*·ree een *kor*·so	Roadworks
Parcheggio	par·*ke*·jo	Parking
Passo Carrabile	*pa*·so ka·*ra*·bee·le	Keep Clear
Pedaggio	pe·*da*·jo	Toll
Pericolo	pe·*ree*·ko·lo	Danger
Rallentare	ra·len·*ta*·re	Slow Down
Rimozione Forzata	ree·mo·*tsyo*·ne for·*tsa*·ta	Tow-Away Zone
Senso Unico	*sen*·so oo·nee·ko	One Way
Uscita	oo·*shee*·ta	Exit

Are there cycling paths?	Ci sono piste ciclabili? chee *so*·no *pee*·ste chee·*kla*·bee·lee
Can I take my bike on the train?	Posso portare la bicicletta in treno? *po*·so por·*ta*·re la bee·chee·*kle*·ta een *tre*·no

Border Crossing

KEY PHRASES

I'm here for ... days.	Sono qui per ... giorni.	*so·*no kwee per ... *jor·*nee
I'm staying at ...	Alloggio a ...	a·*lo·*jo a ...
I have nothing to declare.	Non ho niente da dichiarare.	non o *nyen·*te da dee·kya·*ra·*re

Passport Control

I'm here ...		Sono qui ... *so* no kwee
in transit	in transito	een *tran·*see·to
on business	per affari	per a·*fa·*ree
on holiday	in vacanza	een va·*kan·*tsa
to study	per motivi di studio	per mo·*tee·*vee dee *stoo·*dyo
to visit relatives	per visitare parenti	per vee·zee·*ta·*re pa·*ren·*tee

I'm here for (six) days.	Sono qui per (sei) giorni. *so* no kwee per (say) *jor·*nee
I'm here for (three) weeks.	Sono qui per (tre) settimane. *so·*no kwee per (tre) se·tee·*ma·*ne
I'm here for (two) months.	Sono qui per (due) mesi. *so·*no kwee per (*doo·*e) *me·*zee

🔊 LISTEN FOR

Il Suo visto, per favore.	eel *soo*·o *vees*·to per fa·*vo*·re	Your visa, please.
Viaggia da solo/a? m/f	vee·*a*·ja da *so*·lo/a	Are you travelling on your own?

I have a residency/work permit.	Ho un permesso di soggiorno/lavoro. o oon per·*me*·so dee so·*jor*·no/la·*vo*·ro
I'm going to (Perugia).	Vado a (Perugia). *va*·do a (pe·*roo*·ja)
I'm staying at the ...	Alloggio al ... a·*lo*·jo al ...

At Customs

I have nothing to declare.	Non ho niente da dichiarare. non o *nyen*·te da dee·kya·*ra*·re
I have something to declare.	Ho delle cose da dichiarare. o *de*·le *ko*·ze da dee·kya·*ra*·re
Do you have this form in English?	Avete questo modulo in inglese? a·*ve*·te *kwe*·sto *mo*·doo·lo een een·*gle*·ze

🔍 LOOK FOR

Controllo Passaporti	kon·*tro*·lo pa·sa·*por*·tee	Passport Control
Dogana	do·*ga*·na	Customs
Immigrazione	ee·mee·gra·*tsyo*·ne	Immigration

Directions

KEY PHRASES

Where's ...?	Dov'è ...?	do·ve ...
What's the address?	Qual'è l'indirizzo?	kwa·le leen·dee·ree·tso
How far is it?	Quant'è distante?	kwan·te dees·tan·te

I'm looking for (the public toilets).	Cerco (i servizi igienici). *cher·ko (ee ser·vee·tsee ee·je·nee·chee)*
Q Which way's (the post office)?	Dove si trova (l'ufficcio postale)? *do·ve see tro·va (loo·fee·cho pos·ta·le)*
Q Where's (the bank)?	Dov'è (la banca)? *do·ve (la ban·ka)*
A It's ...	È ... *e ...*
How do I get there?	Come ci si arriva? *ko·me chee see a·ree·va*
How far is it?	Quant'è distante? *kwan·te dees·tan·te*
Can you show me (on the map)?	Può mostrarmi (sulla pianta)? *pwo mos·trar·mee (soo·la pyan·ta)*
What's the address?	Qual'è l'indirizzo? *kwa·le leen·dee·ree·tso*

Turn at the corner.	Giri all'angolo. *jee·ree a·lan·go·lo*
Turn at the traffic lights.	Giri al semaforo. *jee·ree al se·ma·fo·ro*
Turn left.	Giri a sinistra. *jee·ree a see·nee·stra*
Turn right.	Giri a destra. *jee·ree a de·stra*
It's (100) metres.	È a (cento) metri. *e a (chen·to) me·tree*
It's (30) minutes.	È a (trenta) minuti. *e a (tren·ta) mee·noo·tee*

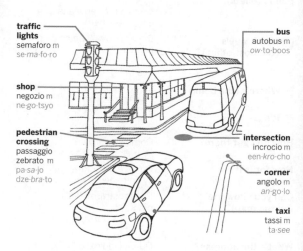

traffic lights
semaforo m
se·ma·fo·ro

shop
negozio m
ne·go·tsyo

pedestrian crossing
passaggio zebrato m
pa·sa·jo dze·bra·to

bus
autobus m
ow·to·boos

intersection
incrocio m
een·kro·cho

corner
angolo m
an·go·lo

taxi
tassi m
ta·see

🔊 LISTEN FOR

a destra	a *de*·stra	right
a sinistra	a see·*nee*·stra	left
accanto a ...	a·*kan*·to a ...	next to ...
all'angolo	a·*lan*·go·lo	on the corner
davanti a ...	da·*van*·tee a ...	in front of ...
di fronte a ...	dee *fron*·te a ...	opposite ...
dietro ...	*dye*·tro ...	behind ...
là	la	there
lontano	lon·*ta*·no	far away
qui	kwee	here
sempre diritto	*sem*·pre dee·*ree*·to	straight ahead
vicino (a ...)	vee·*chee*·no (a ...)	near (to ...)

by bus	con l'autobus kon *low*·to·boos
by taxi	con il tassì ko·*neel* ta·*see*
by train	con il treno ko·*neel* tre·no
on foot	a piedi u *pye*·dee

PRACTICAL DIRECTIONS

Accommodation

KEY PHRASES

Where's a hotel?	Dov'è un albergo?	do·*ve* oo·nal·*ber*·go
Do you have a room?	Avete una camera?	a·*ve*·te *oo*·na *ka*·me·ra
How much is it per night?	Quanto costa per una notte?	*kwan*·to *kos*·ta per *oo*·na *no*·te
Is breakfast included?	La colazione è compresa?	la ko·la·*tsyo*·ne e kom·*pre*·sa
What time is checkout?	A che ora si deve lasciar libera la camera?	a ke o·*ra* see *de*·ve la·*shar lee*·be·ra la *ka*·me·ra

Finding Accommodation

Can you recommend a place?	Può consigliare qualche posto? pwo kon·see·*lya*·re *kwal*·ke *pos*·to
Where's a/an ...?	Dov'è ...? do·*ve* ...

campsite	un campeggio	oon kam·*pe*·jo
guesthouse	una pensione	*oo*·na pen·*syo*·ne
hotel	un albergo	oo·nal·*ber*·go
inn	una locanda	*oo*·na lo·*kan*·da
youth hostel	un ostello della gioventù	oo·nos·*te*·lo *de*·la jo·ven·*too*

For phrases on how to get there, see **directions** (p55).

Booking Ahead & Checking In

I'd like to book a room, please.	Vorrei prenotare una camera, per favore.
	vo·ray pre·no·ta·re oo·na ka·me·ra per fa·vo·re

✂ | **Are there rooms?** | Avete camere libere? | a·ve·te ka·me·ray lee·be·ray |

Do you have a single room?	Avete una camera singola?
	a·ve·te oo·na ka·me·ra seen·go·la
Do you have a twin room?	Avete una camera doppia a due letti?
	a·ve·te oo·na ka·me·ra do·pya a doo·e le·tee
How much is it per night/ week?	Quanto costa per una notte/settimana?
	kwan·to kos·ta per oo·na no·te/se·tee·ma·na
How much is it per person?	Quanto costa per persona?
	kwan·to kos·ta per per·so·na
I have a reservation.	Ho una prenotazione.
	o oo·na pre·no·ta·tsyo·ne
Is breakfast included?	La colazione è compresa?
	la ko·la·tsyo·ne e kom·pre·sa
Is there parking?	C'è il parcheggio?
	chay eel par·ke·jo
Is there wireless internet access here?	Qui c'è il collegamento Wi-Fi?
	kwee chay eel ko·le·ga·men·to wai·fai

PRACTICAL ACCOMMODATION

PRACTICAL ACCOMMODATION

🔊 LISTEN FOR

Ha una prenotazione?	a oo·na pre·no·ta·tsyo·ne	Do you have a reservation?
Mi dispiace, è completo.	mee dees·pya·che e kom·ple·to	I'm sorry, we're full.
Per quante notti?	per kwan·te no·tee	For how many nights?

For (three) nights/weeks.	Per (tre) notti/settimane. per (tre) no·tee/se·tee·ma·ne
From (July 2) to (July 6).	Dal (due luglio) al (sei luglio). dal (doo·e loo·lyo) al (say loo·lyo)
Can I see it?	Posso vederla? po·so ve·der·la
It's fine. I'll take it.	Va bene. La prendo. va be·ne la pren·do

For methods of payment, see **money & banking** (p87).

Requests & Queries

When's breakfast served?	A che ora è la prima colazione? a ke o·ra e la pree·ma ko·la·tsyo·ne
Where's breakfast served?	Dove si prende la prima colazione? do·ve see pren·de la pree·ma ko·la·tsyo·ne
Please wake me at (seven).	Mi svegli (alle sette), per favore. mee sve·lyee (a·le se·te) per fa·vo·re

Booking a Room

Do you have a ... room?

Avete una camera ...?
a·ve·te oo·na ka·me·ra ...

double
doppia
do·pya

single
singola
seen·go·la

How much is it per ...?

Quanto costa per ...?
kwan·to kos·ta per ...

night
una notte
oo·na no·te

person
persona
per·so·na

Is breakfast included?

La colazione è compresa?
la ko·la·tsyo·ne e kom·pre·sa

Can I see the room?

Posso vederla?
po·so ve·der·la

I'll take it.

La prendo.
la pren·do

I won't take it.

Non la prendo.
non la pren·do

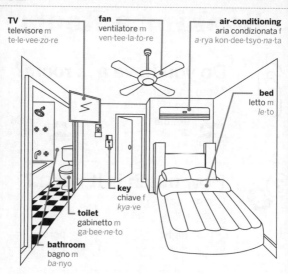

TV
televisore m
te·le·vee·zo·re

fan
ventilatore m
ven·tee·la·to·re

air-conditioning
aria condizionata f
a·rya kon·dee·tsyo·na·ta

bed
letto m
le·to

key
chiave f
kya·ve

toilet
gabinetto m
ga·bee·ne·to

bathroom
bagno m
ba·nyo

Can I get another ...?	Può darmi un altro/a ... m/f
	pwo *dar*·mee oon·*al*·tro/a ...
Can I use the ...?	Posso usare ...?
	po·so oo·*za*·re ...

internet	l'Internet	*leen*·ter·net
kitchen	la cucina	la koo·*chee*·na
laundry	la lavanderia	la la·van·de·*ree*·a
telephone	il telefono	eel te·*le*·fo·no

Do you have an elevator?	C'è un ascensore?
	che oo·na·shen·*so*·re

Do you have a laundry service?	C'è il servizio lavanderia? che eel ser·*vee*·tsyo la·van·de·*ree*·a
Do you have a safe?	C'è una cassaforte? che *oo*·na ka·sa·*for*·te
Do you arrange tours here?	Si organizzano le gite qui? see or·ga·*nee*·dza·no le *jee*·te kwee
Do you change money here?	Si cambiano i soldi qui? see *kam*·bya·no ee *sol*·dee kwee
Can I leave a message for someone?	Posso lasciare un messaggio per qualcuno? *po*·so la·*sha*·re oon me·*sa*·jo per kwal·*koo*·no
Is there a message for me?	C'è un messaggio per me? che oon me·*sa*·jo per me

Ho una prenotazione

o oo·na pre·no·ta·*tsyo*·ne

I have a reservation

I'm locked out of my room.	Mi sono chiuso/a fuori dalla mia camera. **m/f** mee *so*·no *kyoo*·zo/a *fwo*·ree *da*·la *mee*·a *ka*·me·ra
The (bathroom) door is locked.	La porta (del bagno) è chiusa a chiave. la *por*·ta (del *ba*·nyo) e *kyoo*·za a *kya*·ve

Complaints

The room is too ...	La camera è troppo ... la *ka*·me·ra e *tro*·po ...	

cold	fredda	*fre*·da
dark	scura	*skoo*·ra
light/bright	luminosa	loo·mee·*no*·za
small	piccola	*pee*·ko·la

This ... isn't clean.	Questo/a ... non è pulito/a. **m/f** *kwe*·sto/a ... no·*ne* poo·*lee*·to/a
There's no hot water.	Non c'è acqua calda. non chay *ak*·wa *kal*·da
The ... doesn't work.	... non funziona. ... non foon·*tsyo*·na

air-con	L'aria condizionata	*la*·rya kon·dee·tsyo·*na*·ta
fan	Il ventilatore	eel ven·tee·la·*to*·re
heater	La stufa	la *stoo*·fa
toilet	Il gabinetto	eel ga·bee·*ne*·to

For more things you might have in your room, see the **dictionary**.

Answering the Door

Who is it?	Chi è? kee e
Just a moment.	Un momento. oon mo·men·to
Come in.	Avanti. a·van·tee
Come back later, please.	Torni più tardi, per favore. tor·nee pyoo tar·dee per fa·vo·re

Checking Out

What time is checkout?	A che ora si deve lasciar libera la camera? a ke o·ra see de·ve la·shar lee·be·ra la ka·me·ra
Can I have a late checkout?	Posso liberare la camera più tardi? po·so lee·be·ra·re la ka·me·ra pyoo tar·dee
Can I leave my luggage here?	Posso lasciare il mio bagaglio qui? po·so la·sha·re eel mee·o ba·ga·lyo kwee
Can you call a taxi for me (for 11 o'clock)?	Può chiamarmi un tassì (per le undici)? pwo kya·mar·mee oon ta·see (per le oon·dee·chee)
Could I have my deposit, please?	Posso avere la caparra, per favore? po·so a·ve·re la ka·pa·ra per fa·vo·re

PRACTICAL ACCOMMODATION

🔊 LISTEN FOR

La chiave è alla reception.	la *kya*·ve e *a*·la ray·sep·*shon*	The key is at reception.
Qual'è il Suo numero di camera?	kwa·*le* eel *soo*·o *noo*·me·ro dee *ka*·me·ra	What's your room number?
Ha usato il frigobar?	a oo·*za*·to eel *free*·go·bar	Did you use the mini-bar?

Could I have my passport, please?	Posso avere il mio passaporto, per favore? *po*·so a·*ve*·re eel *mee*·o pa·sa·*por*·to per fa·*vo*·re
Could I have my valuables, please?	Posso avere i miei oggetti di valore, per favore? *po*·so a·*ve*·re ee myay o·*je*·tee dee va·*lo*·re per fa·*vo*·re
I'll be back on (Tuesday).	Torno (martedì). *tor*·no (mar·te·*dee*)
I had a great stay, thank you.	Sono stato/a benissimo/a, grazie. **m/f** *so*·no *sta*·to/a be·*nee*·see·mo/a *gra*·tsye

Camping

Can I camp here?	Si può campeggiare qui? see pwo kam·pe·*ja*·re kwee
Where's the nearest campsite?	Dov'è il campeggio più vicino? do·*ve* eel kam·*pe*·jo pyoo vee·*chee*·no

Where's the nearest shop?	Dov'è il negozio più vicino?	do·ve eel ne·go·tsyo pyoo vee·chee·no
Where's the nearest shower facility?	Dov'è il servizio doccia più vicino?	do·ve eel ser·vee·tsyo do·cha pyoo vee·chee·no
Where's the nearest toilet block?	Dove sono i servizi igienici più vicini?	do·ve so·no ee ser·vee·tsee ee·je·nee·chee pyoo vee·chee·nee
Is the water drinkable?	L'acqua è potabile?	la·kwa e po·ta·bee·le
Do you have ...?	Avete ...?	a·ve·te ...

a site	un sito	oon see·to
electricity	la corrente	la ko·ren·te
shower facilities	servizio doccia	ser·vee·tsyo do·cha
tents for hire	tende da noleggiare	ten·de da no·le·ja·re

How much is it per ...?	Quant'è per ...?	kwan·te per

caravan	roulotte	roo·lot
person	persona	per·so·na
tent	tenda	ten·da
vehicle	veicolo	ve·ee·ko·lo

Renting

I'm here about the ... for rent.	Sono qui per il/la ... che date in affitto. m/f	*so·*no kwee per eel/la ... ke *da·*te ee·na·*fee·*to
Do you have a/an ... for rent?	Avete ... d'affittare?	a·*ve·*te ... da·fee·*ta·*re

apartment	un appartamento	oo·na·par·ta·*men·*to
cabin	una cabina	*oo·*na ka·*bee·*na
house	una casa	*oo·*na *ka·*za
room	una camera	*oo·*na *ka·*me·*ra
villa	una villa	*oo·*na *vee·*la

(partly) furnished	(in parte) ammobiliato/a m/f	(een *par·*te) a·mo·bee·*lya·*to/a
unfurnished	non ammobiliato/a m/f	no·na·mo·bee·*lya·*to/a
How much is it for (one) week?	Quant'è per (una) settimana?	kwan·*te* per (*oo·*na) se·tee·*ma·*na
How much is it for (two) months?	Quant'è per (due) mesi?	kwan·*te* per (*doo·*e) *me·*zee
Are bills extra?	Sono extra le bollette?	*so·*no *ek·*stra le bo·*le·*te

Staying with Locals

Can I stay at your place?	Posso stare da Lei/te? pol/inf	*po·*so *sta·*re da lay/te

Thanks for your hospitality.	Grazie per la Sua/tua ospitalità. pol/inf *gra*·tsye per la *soo*·a/*too*·a os·pee·ta·lee·*ta*
Is there anything I can do to help?	Posso aiutare in qualche modo? *po*·so a·yoo·*ta*·re een *kwal*·ke *mo*·do
I have my own mattress.	Ho il mio proprio materasso. o eel *mee*·o *pro*·pryo ma·te·*ra*·so
I have my own sleeping bag.	Ho il mio proprio sacco a pelo. o eel *mee*·o *pro*·pryo *sa*·ko a *pe*·lo
Can I ...?	Posso ...? *po*·so ...

bring anything for the meal	portare qualcosa per il pasto	por·*ta*·re kwal·*ko*·za per eel *pas*·to
do the dishes	lavare i piatti	la·*va*·re ee *pya*·lee
set/clear the table	apparecchiare/ sparecchiare	a·pa·re·*kya*·re/ spa·re·*kya*·re
take out the rubbish	gettare la spazzatura	je·*ta*·re la spa·tsa·*too*·ra

For compliments to the chef, see **eating out** (p168).

Shopping

KEY PHRASES

I'd like to buy ...	Vorrei comprare ...	vo·*ray* kom·*pra*·re ...
Can I look at it?	Posso dare un'occhiata?	*po*·so *da*·re oo·no·*kya*·ta
Can I try it on?	Potrei provarmelo/a? m/f	po·*tray* pro·*var*·me·lo/a
How much is it?	Quanto costa?	*kwan*·to *kos*·ta
That's too expensive.	È troppo caro/a. m/f	e *tro*·po *ka*·ro/a

Looking For ...

Where's (a travel agency)?	Dov'è (un'agenzia di viaggi)? do·*ve* (oo·na·jen·*tsee*·a dee vee·*a*·jee)
Where can I buy (bread)?	Dove posso comprare (pane)? *do*·ve *po*·so kom·*pra*·re (*pa*·ne)

For more on shops and services, see the **dictionary**.

Making a Purchase

I'd like to buy ...	Vorrei comprare ... vo·*ray* kom·*pra*·re ...
I'm just looking.	Sto solo guardando. sto *so*·lo gwar·*dan*·do

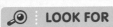 LOOK FOR

Aperto	a·*per*·to	Open
Chiuso	*kyoo*·zo	Closed
Spingere	*speen*·je·re	Push
Tirare	tee·*ra*·re	Pull

What is this made of?	Questo con che cosa è fatto? *kwe*·sto kon ke *ko*·za e *fa*·to
How much is this?	Quanto costa questo? *kwan*·to *kos*·ta *kwes*·to
✂ **How much?**	Quanto? *kwan*·to
Can you write down the price?	Può scrivere il prezzo? pwo *skree*·ve·re eel *pre*·tso
Do you have any others?	Ne avete altri? ne a·*ve*·te *al*·tree
Can I look at it?	Posso dare un'occhiata? *po*·so *da*·re oo·no *kya*·ta
Could I have it wrapped, please?	Può incartarlo, per favore? pwo een·kar·*tar*·lo per fa·*vo*·re
Does it have a guarantee?	Ha la garanzia? a la ga·ran·*tsee*·a
Can you order it for me?	Me lo può ordinare, per favore? me lo pwo or·dee·*na*·re per fa·*vo*·re
Can I pick it up later?	Posso ritirarlo più tardi? *po*·so ree·tee·*rar*·lo pyoo *tar*·dee
It's faulty.	È difettoso. e dee·fe·*to*·zo

It's broken.	È rotto. e *ro*·to
Do you accept credit/ debit cards?	Accettate la carta di credito/debito? a·che·*ta*·te la *kar*·ta dee *kre*·dee·to/*de*·bee·to
Could I have a bag, please?	Può darmi un sacchetto, per favore? pwo *dar*·mee oon sa·*ke*·to per fa·*vo*·re
I don't need a bag, thanks.	Non mi serve la busta, grazie. non mee *ser*·ve la *boos*·ta *gra*·tsye
Could I have a receipt, please?	Può darmi una ricevuta, per favore? pwo *dar*·mee *oo*·na ree·che·*voo*·ta per fa·*vo*·re

✂	**Receipt, please.**	La ricevuta, per favore.	la ree·che·*voo*·ta per fa·*vo*·re

I'd like my money back, please.	Vorrei un rimborso, per favore. vo·*ray* oon reem·*bor*·so per fa·*vo*·re
I'd like to change this, please.	Vorrei cambiare questo/a, per favore. m/f vo·*ray* kam·*bya*·re *kwe*·sto/a per fa·*vo*·re

◀) **LISTEN FOR**

Posso aiutarla?	*po*·so a·yoo·*tar*·la	Can I help you?
No, non ne abbiamo.	no non ne a·*bya*·mo	No, we don't have any.

Making a Purchase

I'd like to buy ...
Vorrei comprare...
vo·ray kom·*pra*·re ...

How much is it?
Quanto costa?
kwan·to kos·ta

-------- OR --------

Can you write down the price?
Può scrivere il prezzo?
pwo *skree*·ve·re eel *pre*·tso

Do you accept credit cards?
Accettate la carta di credito?
a·che·*ta*·te la *kar*·ta dee *kre·dee*·to

Could I have a ..., please?
Può darmi ..., per favore?
pwo *dar*·mee ... per fa·*vo*·re

receipt
una ricevuta
oo·na
ree·che·*voo*·ta

bag
un sacchetto
oon sa·*ke*·to

I'd like to return this, please.	Vorrei restituire questo/a, per favore. m/f vo·*ray* res·tee·*twee*·re *kwe*·sto/a per fa·*vo*·re

Bargaining

That's too expensive.	È troppo caro/a. m/f e *tro*·po *ka*·ro/a
The price is very high.	Il prezzo è molto alto. eel *pre*·tso e *mol*·to *al*·to
Can you lower the price?	Può farmi lo sconto? pwo *far*·mee lo *skon*·to
Do you have something cheaper?	Ha qualcosa di meno costoso? a kwal·*ko*·za dee *me*·no kos·*to*·zo
I'll give you ...	Le offro ... le *o*·fro ...

Clothes

Can I try it on?	Potrei provarmelo/a? m/f po·*tray* pro·*var*·me·lo/a
It doesn't fit.	Non va bene. non va *be*·ne

CULTURE TIP

Shop Etiquette

In style-conscious Italy, though shop window displays may look good enough to eat, they're absolutely not to be touched. Disrupting a window display could jeopardise a shop's *bella figura be*·la fee·*goo*·ra – that all-important Italian preoccupation with creating a good impression.

PRACTICAL SHOPPING

affare m	a·*fa*·re	bargain
affarista m	a·fa·*ree*·sta	bargain hunter
fregatura f	fre·ga·*too*·ra	rip-off
occasioni f pl	o·ka·*zyo*·nee	specials
saldi m pl	*sal*·dee	sales

My size is large.	Sono una taglia forte. *so·no oo·na ta·lya for·te*
My size is medium.	Sono una taglia media. *so·no oo·na ta·lya me·dya*
My size is small.	Sono una taglia piccola. *so·no oo·na ta·lya pee·ko·la*

For clothing items see the **dictionary**, and for sizes see **numbers & amounts** (p32).

Repairs

Can I have my backpack repaired here?	Posso far aggiustare il mio zaino qui? *po·so far a·joo·sta·re eel mee·o dzai·no kwee*
Can I have my camera repaired here?	Posso far aggiustare la mia macchina fotografica qui? *po·so far a·joo·sta·re la mee·a ma·kee·na fo·to·gra·fee·ka kwee*
When will it be ready?	Quando sarà pronto? *kwan·do sa·ra pron·to*

Books & Reading

Is there an English-language bookshop?	C'è una libreria specializzata in lingua inglese? che *oo*·na lee·bre·*ree*·a spe·cha·lee·*dza*·ta een *leen*·gwa een·*gle*·ze
Is there an (English-language) entertainment guide?	C'è una guida agli spettacoli (in inglese)? che *oo*·na *gwee*·da a·lyee spe·*ta*·ko·lee (ee·ncen·*gle*·ze)
Do you have a book by (Alberto Moravia)?	C'è un libro di (Alberto Moravia)? che oon *lee*·bro dee (al·*ber*·to mo·*ra*·vee·a)

Music & DVD

I'd like a CD/DVD.	Vorrei un CD/DVD. vo·*ray* oon chee·*dee*/ dee·voo·*dee*
I'd like headphones.	Vorrei delle cuffia. vo·*ray* de·le *koo*·fya
I heard a band called (Marlene Kuntz).	Ho sentito un gruppo chiamato (Marlene Kuntz). o sen·*tee*·to oon *groo*·po kya·*ma*·to (mar·*le*·ne koonts)
What's his/her best recording?	Qual'è la sua migliore incisione? kwa·*le* la *soo*·a mee·*lyo*·re een·chee·*zyo*·ne
Can I listen to this?	Potrei ascoltare questo? po·*tray* as·kol·*ta*·re *kwe*·sto
Will this work on any DVD player?	Funzionerà con tutti i lettori di DVD? foon·tsyo·ne·*ra* kon *too*·tee ee le·*to*·ree dee dee·voo·*dee*

Video & Photography

I need a cable to connect my camera to a computer.	Mi serve un cavo per collegare la mia macchina a un computer. mee *ser*·ve oon *ka*·vo per ko·le·*ga*·re la *mee*·a ma·kee·na a oon komp·*yoo*·ter
I need a cable to recharge this battery.	Mi serve un cavo per ricaricare questa batteria. mee *ser*·ve oon *ka*·vo per ree·ka·ree·*ka*·re *kwe*·sta ba·te·*ree*·a
Do you have memory cards for this camera?	Avete schede di memoria per questa macchina fotografica? a·*ve*·te *ske*·de dee me·*mo*·rya per *kwe*·sta ma·kee·na fo·to·*gra*·fee·ka
Do you have batteries for this camera?	Avete batterie per questa macchina fotografica? a·*ve*·te ba·te·*ree*·e per *kwe*·sta ma·kee·na fo·to·*gra*·fee·ka
Can you print digital photos?	Potete stampare foto digitali? po·*te*·te stam·*pa*·re *fo*·to dee·jee·*ta*·lee

PRACTICAL SHOPPING

LANGUAGE TIP

Addressing People
The plural polite form has become virtually obsolete in modern Italian. If you want to show respect to more than one person, use *voi* voy. See also **personal pronouns** in the **grammar** chapter (p21).

Can you transfer my photos from camera to CD?	Potete trasferire le mie foto dalla macchina su un CD? po·*te*·te tra·sfe·*ree*·re le *mee*·e *fo*·to *da*·la ma·*kee*·na soo oon chee·*dee*
I need a ... film for this camera.	Vorrei un rullino ... per questa macchina fotografica. vo·*ray* oon roo·*lee*·no ... per *kwe*·sta ma·*kee*·na fo·to·*gra*·fee·ka

B&W	in bianco e nero	een *byan*·ko e *ne*·ro
colour	a colori	a *ko*·lo·ree
slide	per diapositive	per dya·po·zee·*tee*·ve
(100) speed	da (cento) ASA	da (*chen*·to) *a*·za

Could you develop this film?	Potrebbe sviluppare questo rullino? po·*tre*·be svee·loo·*pa*·re *kwe*·sto roo·*lee*·no

For more photographic equipment, see the **dictionary**.

Souvenirs

antiques	pezzi m d'antiquariato *pe*·tsee dan·tee·kwa·*rya*·to
blown glass	vetro m soffiato *ve*·tro so·*fya*·to
ceramics/pottery	ceramiche f pl che·*ra*·mee·ke
embroidery	ricamo m ree·*ka*·mo
glassware	vetrame m ve·*tra*·me

handicrafts	ogetti m pl d'artigianato o·*je*·tee dar·tee·ja·*na*·to
jewellery	gioielli m pl jo·ye·lee
lace	merletto m mer·*le*·to
leather goods	pelletterie f pl pe·le·te·*ree*·e
marbled paper	carta f marmorizzata *kar*·ta mar·mo·ree·*tsa*·ta
masks	maschere f pl *ma*·ske·re
paper goods	articoli m pl di carta ar·*tee*·ko·lee dee *kar*·ta
woodcarvings	legno m intagliato *le*·nyo con·ta·*lya*·to

Ne avete altri?
ne a·*ve*·te *al*·tree

Do you have any others?

Communications

KEY PHRASES

Where's the local internet cafe?	Dove si trova l'Internet point?	*do*·ve see *tro*·va *leen*·ter·net poynt
I'd like to check my email.	Vorrei controllare il mio email.	vo·*ray* kon·tro·*la*·re eel *mee*·o e·mayl
I'd like a SIM card.	Vorrei un SIM card.	vo·*ray* oon seem kard

Post Office

I want to send a ...		Vorrei mandare ... vo·*ray* man·*da*·re ...
letter	una lettera	*oo*·na *le*·te·ra
parcel	un pacchetto	oon pa·*ke*·to
postcard	una cartolina	*oo*·na kar·to·*lee*·na

I want to buy an envelope.	Vorrei comprare una busta. vo·*ray* kom·*pra*·re *oo*·na *boo*·sta
I want to buy stamps.	Vorrei comprare dei francobolli. vo·*ray* kom·*pra*·re day fran·ko·*bo*·lee

🔊 LISTEN FOR

dichiarazione f **doganale**	dee·kya·ra·*tsyo*·ne do·ga·*na*·le	customs declaration
indirizzo m **postale**	een·dee·*ree*·tso po·*sta*·le	postal address
posta f **prioritaria**	*pos*·ta pryo·ree·*ta*·rya	express mail
posta f **raccomandata**	*pos*·ta ra·ko·man·*da*·ta	registered mail

Please send it by airmail (to Denmark).	Lo mandi via aerea (in Danimarca), per favore. lo *man*·dee vee·a a·e·re·a (een da·nee·*mar*·ka) per fa·*vo*·re
It contains ...	Contiene ... kon·*tye*·ne ...
Where's the poste restante section?	Dov'è il fermo posta? do·*ve* eel *fer*·mo *pos*·ta
Is there any mail for me?	C'è posta per me? che *pos*·ta per me

Phone

🅠 **What's your phone number?**	Qual'è il Suo/tuo numero di telefono? pol/inf kwa·*lo* eel soo·o/too·o *noo*·me·ro dee te·*le*·fo·no
🅐 **The number is ...**	Il numero è ... eel *noo*·me·ro e ...
🅐 **I don't have a contact number.**	Non ho un numero fisso. non o oon *noo*·me·ro *fee*·so

Where's the nearest public phone?	Dov'è il telefono pubblico più vicino? do·*ve* eel te·*le*·fo·no *poo*·blee·ko pyoo vee·*chee*·no
I'd like to know the number for ...	Vorrei sapere il numero di ... vo·*ray* sa·*pe*·re eel *noo*·me·ro dee ...
I want to make a/an ...	Vorrei fare una chiamata ... vo·*ray* fa·re oo·na kya·*ma*·ta ...

call to (Belgium)	ın (Belgio)	een (*bel*·jo)
internet call	via Internet	*vee*·a een·ter·net
local call	urbana	oor·*ba*·na
reverse-charge/ collect call	a carico del destinatario	a *ka*·ree·ko del des·tee·na·*ta*·ryo

I want to buy a phone card.	Vorrei comprare una scheda telefonica. vo·*ray* kom·*pra*·re oo·na *ske*·da te·le·fo·nee·ka
How much does a (three)-minute call cost?	Quanto costa una telefonata di (tre) minuti? *kwan*·to *kos*·ta oo·na te·le·fo·*na*·ta dee (tre) mee·*noo*·tee
What's the area/country code for ...?	Qual'è il prefisso per ...? kwa·*le* eel pre·*fee*·so per ...
It's engaged.	La linea è occupata. la *lee*·ne·a e o·koo·*pa*·ta
I've been cut off.	È caduta la linea. e ka·*doo*·ta la *lee*·ne·a
The connection's bad.	La linea non è buona. la *lee*·ne·a no·*ne bwo*·na

Hello.	Pronto. *pron·to*
It's ...	Sono ... *so·no ...*
Can I speak to ...?	Posso parlare con ...? *po·so par·la·re kon ...*
Can I leave a message?	Posso lasciare un messaggio? *po·so la·sha·re oon me·sa·jo*
Please tell him/her I called.	Gli/Le dica che ho telefonato, per favore. *lyee/le dee·ka ke o te·le·fo·na·to per fa·vo·re*
I'll call back later.	Richiamerò più tardi. *ree·kya·me·ro pyoo tar·dee*

For telephone numbers, see **numbers & amounts** (p32).

> ### *Qui c'è il collegamento Wi-Fi?*
> kwee chay eel ko·le·ga·men·to wai·fai
>
> ### *Is there wi-fi here?*

🔊 LISTEN FOR

Con chi parlo?	kon kee *par*·lo	Who's calling?
Con chi vuole parlare?	kon kee *vwo*·le par·*la*·re	Who do you want (to speak to)?
Sì, è qui.	see e kwee	Yes, he/she is here.
Glielo/Gliela passo.	*lye*·lo/*lye*·la *pa*·so	I'll put him/her on.
Mi dispiace, (lui/lei) non c'è.	mee dees·*pya*·che (*loo*·ee/lay) non che	I'm sorry, he/she is not here.
Mi dispiace, ha sbagliato numero.	mee dees·*pya*·che a sba·*lya*·to *noo*·me·ro	Sorry, wrong number.

Mobile/Cell Phone

What are the rates?	Quali sono le tariffe? *kwa*·lee *so*·no le ta·*ree*·fe	
I'd like a/an ...	Vorrei ... vo·*ray* ...	

adaptor plug	un adattatore	oo·na·da·ta·*to*·re
charger for my phone	un caricabatterie	oon ka·ree·ka·ba·te·*ree*·e
mobile/cell phone for hire	un cellulare da noleggiare	oon che·loo·*la*·re da no·le·*ja*·re
recharge card for ...	una ricarica telefonica per ...	*oo*·na re·*ka*·ree·ka te·le·*fo*·nee·ka per ...
SIM card for your network	un SIM card per la vostra rete telefonica	oon seem kard per la *vos*·tra *re*·te te·le·*fo*·nee·ka

The Internet

Where's the local internet cafe?	Dove si trova l'Internet point? *do*·ve see *tro*·va leen·ter·net poynt
Do you have public internet access here?	Qui c'è il collegamento a Internet? kwee chay eel ko·le·ga·*men*·to a een·ter·net
Is there wireless internet access here?	Qui c'è il collegamento Wi-Fi? kwee chay eel ko·le·ga·*men*·to wai·fai
Can I connect my laptop here?	Posso collegare il mio portatile? *po*·so ko·le·*ga*·re eel *mee*·o por·ta·*tee*·le
Do you have headphones (with a microphone)?	Avete una cuffia (con microfono)? a·*ve*·te oo·na *koo*·fya (kon mee·*kro*·fo·no)
I'd like to ...	Vorrei ... vo·*ray* ...

burn a CD	masterizzare un CD	mas·te·ree·*tsa*·re oon chee·dee
check my email	controllare il mio email	kon·tro·*la*·re eel *mee*·o e·mayl
download my photos	scaricare le mie foto	ska·ree·*ka*·re le *mee*·e fo·to
use a printer	usare una stampante	oo·*za*·re oo·na stam·*pan*·te
use a scanner	scandire	skan·*dee*·re
use Skype	usare Skype	oo·*za*·re skaip

How much per hour?	Quanto costa all'ora? *kwan*·to *kos*·ta a·*lo*·ra
How much per page?	Quanto costa a pagina? *kwan*·to *kos*·ta a *pa*·jee·na
How do I log on?	Come posso accedere? *ko*·me *po*·so a·*che*·de·re
It's crashed.	Si è bloccato. see e blo·*ka*·to
I've finished.	Ho finito. o fee·*nee*·to
Can I connect my ... to this computer?	Posso collegare ... a questo computer? *po*·so ko·le·*ga*·re ... a *kwe*·sto kom·*pyoo*·ter

camera	la mia macchina fotografica	la *mee*·a *ma*·kee·na fo·to·*gra*·fee·ka
iPod	il mio iPod	eel *mee*·o *ai*·pod
media player (MP3)	il mio lettore MP3	eel *mee*·o le·*to*·re e·me·pee·tre
portable hard drive	il mio hard drive portatile	eel *mee*·o hard draiv por·*ta*·tee·le
PSP	la mia consolle PSP portatile	la *mee*·a kon·*so*·le pee·*e*·se·pee por·*ta*·tee·le
USB flash drive (memory stick)	la mia chiavetta USB	la *mee*·a kya·*ve*·ta oo·*e*·se·bee

Money & Banking

KEY PHRASES

How much is this?	Quanto costa questo?	kwan·to kos·ta kwe·sto
What's the exchange rate?	Quant'è il cambio?	kwan·te eel kam·byo
Where's the nearest ATM?	Dov'è il Bancomat più vicino?	do·ve eel ban·ko·mat pyoo vee·chee·no
I'd like to exchange money.	Vorrei cambiare denaro.	vo·ray kam·bya·re de·na·ro
Can I have smaller notes?	Mi può dare banconote più piccole?	mee pwo da·re ban·ko·no·te pyoo pee·ko·le

Paying the Bill

Q How much is this?	Quanto costa questo? kwan·to kos·ta kwe·sto
A It's free.	È gratuito. e gra·too·ee·to
A It's ... euros.	È ... euro. e ... e·oo·ro
Can you write down the price?	Può scrivere il prezzo? pwo skree·ve·re eel pre·tso
Do you accept credit/ debit cards?	Accettate la carta di credito/debito? a·che·ta·te la kar·ta dee kre·dee·to/de·bee·to

I'd like a receipt, please.	Vorrei una ricevuta, per favore. vo·*ray* oo·na ree·che·*voo*·ta per fa·*vo*·re
I'd like a refund, please.	Vorrei un rimborso, per favore. vo·*ray* oon reem·*bor*·so per fa·*vo*·re
I'd like my change, please.	Vorrei il mio resto, per favore. vo·*ray* eel *mee*·o *res*·to per fa·*vo*·re
There's a mistake in the bill.	C'è un errore nel conto. che oon e·*ro*·re nel *kon*·to
I don't want to pay the full price.	Non voglio pagare il prezzo intero. non *vo*·lyo pa·*ga*·re eel *pre*·tso een·*te*·ro
Do I need to pay upfront?	Devo pagare in anticipo? *de*·vo pa·*ga*·re ee·nan·*tee*·chee·po

Banking

What time does the bank open?	A che ora apre la banca? a ke o·ra a·pre la *ban*·ka
Do you change money here?	Si cambiano i soldi qui? see *kam*·bya·no ee *sol*·dee kwee
Where can I ...?	Dove posso ...? *do*·ve *po*·so ...
I'd like to ...	Vorrei ... vo·*ray* ...

arrange a transfer	trasferire soldi	tras·fe·*ree*·re *sol*·dee
cash a cheque	riscuotere un assegno	ree·*skwo*·te·re oo·na·se·nyo
change a travellers cheque	cambiare un assegno di viaggio	kam·*bya*·re oo·na·se·nyo dee vee·*a*·jo
change money	cambiare denaro	kam·*bya*·re de·*na*·ro
get a cash advance	prelevare con carta di credito	pre·le·*va*·re kon *kar*·ta dee *kre*·dee·to
get change for this note	cambiare questa banconota	kam·*bya*·re *kwe*·sta ban·ko·*no*·ta
withdraw money	fare un prelievo	*fa*·re oon pre·*lye*·vo

Where's the nearest automatic teller machine?	Dov'è il Bancomat più vicino? do·*ve* eel *ban*·ko·mat pyoo vee·*chee*·no
Where's the nearest foreign exchange office?	Dov'è il cambio più vicino? do·*ve* eel *kam*·byo pyoo vee·*chee*·no
What's the commission?	Quant'è la commissione? kwan·*te* la ko·mee·*syo*·ne
What's the exchange rate?	Quant'è il cambio? kwan·*te* eel *kam*·byo
The automatic teller machine took my card.	Il Bancomat ha trattenuto la mia carta di credito. eel *ban*·ko·mat a tra·te·*noo*·to la *mee*·a *kar*·ta dee *kre*·dee·to

🔊 LISTEN FOR

Il Suo passaporto.	eel soo·o pa·sa·por·to	Your passport.
Vuole firmare o usare il suo PIN?	vwo·le feer·ma·re o oo·sa·re eel soo·o peen	Do you want to sign or use your PIN?
Può firmare qui, per favore?	pwo feer·ma·re kwee per fa·vo·re	Please sign here.
C'è un problema con il Suo conto.	che oon pro·ble·ma ko·neel soo·o kon·to	There's a problem with your account.
Non possiamo farlo.	non po·sya·mo far·lo	We can't do that.

I've forgotten my PIN.	Ho dimenticato il mio codice PIN. o dee·men·tee·ka·to eel mee·o ko·dee·che peen
Can I use my credit card to withdraw money?	Si può usare la carta di credito per fare prelievi? see pwo oo·za·re la kar·ta dee kre·dee·to per fa·re pre·lye·vee
Can I have smaller notes?	Mi può dare banconote più piccole? mee pwo da·re ban·ko·no·te pyoo pee·ko·le
Has my money arrived yet?	È arrivato il mio denaro? e a·ree·va·to eel mee·o de·na·ro
How long will it take to arrive?	Quanto tempo ci vorrà per il trasferimento? kwan·to tem·po chee vo·ra per eel tras·fe·ree·men·to

Business

KEY PHRASES

I'm attending a conference.	Sono qui per una conferenza.	*so*·no kwee per *oo*·na kon·fe·*ren*·tsa
I have an appointment with ...	Ho un appuntamento con ...	o oon· a·poon·ta·*men*·to kon ...
Can I have your business card?	Potrei avere il suo biglietto da visita?	po·*tray* a·*ve*·re eel *soo*·o bee·*lye*·to da *vee*·zee·ta

Where's the conference/ meeting?	Dov'è la conferenza/ riunione? do·*ve* la kon·fe·*ren*·tsa/ ree·oo·*nyo*·ne

I'm attending a ...	Sono qui per ... *so*·no kwee per ...

conference	una conferenza	*oo*·na kon·fe·*ren*·tsa
course	un corso	oon *kor*·so
meeting	una riunione	*oo*·na ree·oo·*nyo*·ne
trade fair	una fiera commerciale	*oo*·na *fye*·ra ko·mer·*cha*·le

I'm here with my company.	Sono qui con la mia azienda. *so*·no kwee kon la *mee*·a a·*dzyen*·da

I'm here with my colleague.	Sono qui con il/la mio/a collega. m/f so·no kwee kon eel/la mee·o/a ko·le·ga
Q Can I have your business card?	Potrei avere il suo biglietto da visita? po·tray a·ve·re eel soo·o bee·lye·to da vee·zee·ta
A Here's my business card.	Ecco il mio biglietto da visita. e·ko eel mee·o bee·lye·to da vee·zee·ta
I have an appointment with ...	Ho un appuntamento con ... o oo·na·poon·ta·men·to kon ...
I'm expecting a call.	Aspetto una telefonata. a·spe·to oo·na te·le·fo·na·ta
I need a computer.	Ho bisogno di un computer. o bee·zo·nyo dee oon kom·pyoo·ter
I need a connection to the internet.	Ho bisogno di una connessione Internet. o bee·zo·nyo dee oo·na ko·ne·syo·ne een·ter·net
I need an interpreter.	Ho bisogno di un/un'interprete. m/f o bee·zo·nyo dee oo·neen·ter·pre·te

CULTURE TIP · **Business Etiquette**
Italian business culture is formal and hierarchical. First names aren't used between executives and subordinates, and using the right titles (see p106) may help you clinch that deal. Business isn't usually discussed over a meal. As a visitor you'll be expected to be *in orario* een o·ra·ryo (on time), but don't get touchy about being kept waiting.

Sightseeing

KEY PHRASES

I'd like a guide.	Vorrei una guida.	vo·*ray* oo·na *gwee*·da
Can I take a photograph?	Posso fare una foto?	*po*·so *fa*·re oo·na *fo*·to
When's the museum open?	Quando è aperto il museo?	*kwan*·do e a·*per*·to eel moo·*ze*·o

I'd like a/an ...	Vorrei ... vo·*ray* ...	
audio set	un auricolare	oo·now·ree·ko·*la*·re
guide (person)	una guida	oo·na *gwee*·da
guidebook in English	una guida in inglese	oo·na *gwee*·da een·neen·*gle*·ze
local map	una cartina della zona	oo·na kar·*tee*·na de·la *dzo*·na

Do you have information on ... sights?	Avete delle informazioni su posti ...? a·*ve*·te de·le een·tor·ma·*tsyo*·nee soo *pos*·tee ...	
architectural	architettonici	ar·kee·te·*to*·nee·chee
historical	storici	*sto*·ree·chee
local	locali	lo·*ka*·lee
natural	di bellezza naturale	dee be·*le*·tsa na·too·*ra*·le

I'd like to see ...	Vorrei vedere ... vo·*ray* ve·*de*·re ...
I'd like to hire a local guide.	Vorrei ingaggiare una guida del posto. vo·*ray* een·ga·*ja*·re *oo*·na *gwee*·da del *po*·sto
What's that?	Cos'è? ko·*ze*
How old is it?	Quanti anni ha? *kwan*·tee *a*·nee a
Could you take a photograph of me?	Può farmi una foto? pwo *far*·mee *oo*·na *fo*·to
Can I take a photograph (of you)?	Posso fare una foto (di Lei/tu)? pol/inf *po*·so *fa*·re *oo*·na *fo*·to (dee lay/too)

Getting In

What time does it open/ close?	A che ora apre/chiude? a ke *o*·ra *a*·pre/*kyoo*·de
What's the admission charge?	Quant'è il prezzo d'ingresso? kwan·*te* eel *pre*·tso deen·*gre*·so
Is there a discount for ...?	C'è uno sconto per ...? che *oo*·no *skon*·to per ...

children	bambini	bam·*bee*·nee
families	famiglie	fa·*mee*·lye
groups	gruppi	*groo*·pee
older people	persone anziane	per·*so*·ne an·*tsya*·ne
students	studenti	stoo·*den*·tee

Tours

Can you recommend a tour?	Può consigliare una gita turistica? pwo kon·see·*lya*·re oo·na *jee*·ta too·*ree*·stee·ka
When's the next tour?	A che ora parte la prossima gita? a ke o·ra *par*·te la *pro*·see·ma *jee*·ta
When's the next day trip?	A che ora parte la prossima escursione in giornata? a ke o·ra *par*·te la *pro*·see·ma es·koor·*syo*·ne een jor·*na*·ta
When's the next excursion?	A che ora parte la prossima escursione? a ke o·ra *par*·te la *pro*·see·ma es·koor *syo*·ne
Is accommodation included?	È incluso l'alloggio? e een·*kloo*·zo la·*lo*·jo
Is food included?	È incluso il vitto? e een·*kloo*·zo eel *vee*·to
Is transport included?	È incluso il trasporto? e een·*kloo*·zo eel tras·*por*·to
Are there organised walking tours?	Ci sono visite guidate a piedi? chee so·no vee·zee·te gwee·*da*·te a *pye*·dee
I'd like to do cooking/language classes.	Vorrei fare un corso di cucina/lingua. vo·*ray* fa·re oon *kor*·so dee koo·*chee*·na/*leen*·gwa
The guide has paid.	La guida ha pagato. la *gwee*·da a pa·*ga*·to

How long is the tour?	Quanto dura la gita?
	kwan·to doo·ra la jee·ta
What time should we be back?	A che ora dovremmo ritornare?
	a ke o·ra dov·re·mo ree·tor·na·re
I've lost my group.	Ho perso il mio gruppo.
	o per·so eel mee·o groo·po

Museums & Galleries

When's the gallery open?	Quando è aperta la galleria?
	kwan·do e a·per·ta la ga·le·ree·a
When's the museum open?	Quando è aperto il museo?
	kwan·do e a·per·to eel moo·ze·o
What do you think of ...?	Cosa ne pensa/pensi di ...? pol/inf
	ko·za ne pen·sa/pen·see dee ...
It's a/an (futurist art) exhibition.	Cosa ne pensa/pensi di ...? pol/inf
	ko·za ne pen·sa/pen·see dee ...

> ## Quanto dura la gita?
> *kwan·to doo·ra la jee·ta*
> ### How long is the tour?

> **LANGUAGE TIP**
>
> ### Irregular Plurals
>
> Italian has some irregular plural forms – here are some examples:
>
> | | | |
> |---|---|---|
> | **il dio** m sg | eel *dee*·o | the god |
> | **i dei** m pl | ee day | the gods |
> | **la ala** f sg | la *a*·la | the wing |
> | **le ali** f pl | le *a*·lee | the wings |
>
> Some words even change gender in the plural:
>
> | | | |
> |---|---|---|
> | **il labbro** m sg | eel *la*·bro | the lip |
> | **le labbra** f pl | le *la*·bra | the lips |
>
> See also **plurals** in the **grammar** chapter (p23).

Q What kind of art are you interested in?

Che tipo di arte Le/ti interessa? pol/Inf
ke *tee*·po dee *ar*·te le/tee een·te·*re*·sa

A I'm interested in ... art/architecture.

Mi interessa l'arte/ l'architettura ...
mee een·te·*re*·sa *lar*·te/ lar·kee·te·*too*·ra ...

---

baroque	barocca	ba·*ro*·ka
Byzantine	bizantina	bee·dzan·*tee*·na
modernist	modernista	mo·der·*nee*·sta
Renaissance	rinascimentale	ree·na·shee·men·*ta*·le
Romanesque	romanica	ro·*ma*·nee·ka

PRACTICAL SIGHTSEEING

🔍 LOOK FOR

Gabinetti	ga·bee·*ne*·tee	Toilets
Ingresso Gratuito	een·*gre*·so gra·*too*·ee·to	Free Admission
Messa in Corso	*me*·sa een *kor*·so	Service in Progress
Non Calpestare l'Erba	non kal·pe·*sta*·re *ler*·ba	Keep Off the Grass
Non Entrare	no·nen·*tra*·re	No Entry
Proibito	pro·ee·*bee*·to	Prohibited
Servizi Pubblici	ser·*vee*·tsee poo·blee·chee	Public Toilets
Uscita di Sicurezza	oo·*shee*·ta dee see·koo·*re*·tsa	Emergency Exit
Vietato	vye·*ta*·to	Prohibited
Vietato Consumare Cibi o Bevande	vye·*ta*·to kon·soo·*ma*·re *chee*·bee o be·*van*·de	No Eating or Drinking Allowed
Vietato Fotografare	vye·*ta*·to fo·to·gra·*fa*·re	Do Not Take Photographs
Vietato Toccare	vye·*ta*·to to·*ka*·re	Do Not Touch

Senior & Disabled Travellers

KEY PHRASES

I need assistance.	Ho bisogno di assistenza.	o bee·zo·nyo dee a·sees·ten·tsa
Is there wheelchair access?	C'è un'entrata per sedie a rotelle?	che oo·nen·tra·ta per se·dye a ro·te·le
Are there toilets for the disabled?	Ci sono gabinetti per disabili?	chee so·no ga·bee·ne·tee per dee·za·bee·lee

I'm disabled.	Sono disabile. so·no dee·za·bee·le
I need assistance.	Ho bisogno di assistenza. o bee·zo·nyo dee a·sees·ten·tsa
Are guide dogs permitted?	Sono ammessi i cani guida? so·no a·me·see ee ka·nee gwee·da
Is there wheelchair access?	C'è un'entrata per sedie a rotelle? che oo·nen·tra·ta per se·dye a ro·te·le
How many steps are there?	Quanti gradini ci sono? kwan·tee gra·dee·nee chee so·no
How wide is the entrance?	Quant'è larga l'entrata? kwan·te lar·ga len·tra·ta
Is there a lift?	C'è un ascensore? che oo·na·shen·so·re

🔍 LOOK FOR

Riservato ai Disabili	ree·ser·*va*·to ai dee·*za*·bee·lee	Reserved for People with a Disability

Is there somewhere I can sit down?	C'è un posto dove sedersi? che oon *pos*·to *do*·ve se·*der*·see
Are there toilets for the disabled?	Ci sono gabinetti per disabili? chee *so*·no ga·bee·*ne*·tee per dee·*za*·bee·lee
Are there rails in the bathroom?	Ci sono corrimani nel bagno? chee *so*·no ko·ree·*ma*·nee nel *ba*·nyo
Are there parking spaces for the disabled?	Ci sono parcheggi per disabili? chee *so*·no par·*ke*·jee per dee·*za*·bee·lee
Could you call me a taxi for the disabled?	Può chiamarmi un tassì per i disabili? pwo kya·*mar*·mee oon ta·*see* per ee dee·*za*·bee·lee
Could you help me cross the street?	Può aiutarmi ad attraversare la strada? pwo a·yoo·*tar*·mee a·da·tra·*ver*·sa·re la *stra*·da
crutches	stampelle f pl stam·*pe*·le
ramp	rampa f *ram*·pa
walking frame	deambulatore m de·am·boo·la·*to*·re
walking stick	bastone m ba·*sto*·ne

Travel with Children

KEY PHRASES

Are children allowed?	I bambini sono ammessi?	ee bam·*bee*·nee *so*·no a·*me*·see
Is there a child discount?	C'è uno sconto per bambini?	che *oo*·no *skon*·to per bam·*bee*·nee
Is there a baby change room?	C'è un bagno con fasciatoio?	che oon *ba*·nyo kon fa·sha·*to*·yo

Is there a/an ...?	C'è ...? che ...	
baby change room	un bagno con fasciatoio	oon *ba*·nyo kon fa·sha·*to*·yo
(English-speaking) babysitter	un/una babysitter (che parli inglese) m/f	oon/*oo*·na be·bee·*see*·ter (ke *par*·lee een·*gle*·ze)
child discount	uno sconto per bambini	*oo*·no *skon*·to per bam·*bee*·nee
child-minding service	un servizio di babysitter	oon ser·*vee*·tsyo dee be·bee·*see*·ter
children's menu	un menù per bambini	oon me·*noo* per bam·*bee*·nee
family discount	uno sconto per famiglia	*oo*·no *skon*·to per fa·*mee*·lya
playground nearby	un parco giochi da queste parti	oon *par*·ko *jo*·kee da *kwe*·ste *par*·tee

| **I need a ...** | Ho bisogno di ... |
| | o bee·*zo*·nyo dee ... |

child seat	un seggiolino	oon se·jo·*lee*·no
	per bambini	per bam·*bee*·nee
cot	una culla	*oo*·na *koo*·la
potty	un vasino	oon va·*zee*·no
stroller	un passeggino	oon pa·se·*jee*·no

| **Do you sell ...?** | Vendete ...? |
| | ven·*de*·te ... |

baby wipes	salviettine	sal·vye·*tee*·ne
	detergenti	de·ter·*jen*·tee
	per bambini	per bam·*bee*·nee
disposable nappies/ diapers	pannolini	pa·no·*lee*·nee
	usa-e-getta	*oo*·sa·e·*je*·ta
milk formula	latte in polvere	*la*·te een *pol*·ve·re
painkillers for infants	anti- dolorifici	an·tee· do·lo·*ree*·fee·chee
	per bambini	per bam·*bee*·nee

| **Do you mind if I breastfeed (him/her) here?** | Le dispiace se allatto il/la bimbo/a qui? m/f |
| | le dees·*pya*·che se a·*la*·to eel/la *beem*·bo/a kwee |

| **Are children allowed?** | I bambini sono ammessi? |
| | ee bam·*bee*·nee *so*·no a·*me*·see |

| **Is this suitable for (two)-year-old children?** | Questo è adatto per bambini di (due) anni? |
| | *kwe*·sto e a·*da*·to per bam·*bee*·nee dee (*doo*·e) *a*·nee |

If your child is sick, see **health** (p150).

Social

Meeting People

KEY PHRASES

My name is ...	Mi chiamo ...	mee *kya*·mo ...
I'm from ...	Vengo ...	*ven*·go ...
I work in ...	Lavoro nel campo de ...	la·*vo*·ro nel *kam*·po de ...
I'm ... years old.	Ho ... anni.	o ... *a*·nee
And you?	E Lei/tu? pol/inf	e lay/too

Basics

Yes.	Sì. see
No.	No. no
Please.	Per favore. per fa·*vo*·re
Thank you (very much).	Grazie (mille). *gra*·tsye (*mee*·le)
You're welcome.	Prego. *pre*·go
Sorry.	Mi dispiace. mee dees·*pya*·che
Excuse me. **(for attention/apology)**	Mi scusi. pol mee *skoo*·zee Scusami. inf *skoo*·za·mee
Excuse me. **(if going past)**	Permesso. per·*me*·so

Greetings

Although *ciao* chow is a common greeting, it's best not to use it when addressing strangers. Also note that in Italy the word *buonasera* bwo·na·*se*·ra (good evening) may be heard any time from early afternoon onwards.

Hello.	Buongiorno./ bwon·*jor*·no/ Salve. pol *sal*·ve
Hi.	Ciao. inf chow
Good day/morning/ afternoon.	Buongiorno. bwon·*jor*·no
Good evening.	Buonasera. bwo·na·*se*·ra
Good night.	Buonanotte. bwo·na·*no*·te
See you.	Ci vediamo. chee ve·*dya*·mo
See you later.	A più tardi. a pyoo *tar*·dee
Goodbye.	Arrivederci. pol a·ree·ve·*der*·chee
Bye.	Ciao. inf chow
Q How are you?	Come sta? sg pol *ko*·me sta Come stai? sg inf *ko*·me stai Come state? pl pol&inf *ko*·me *sta*·te
A Fine.	Bene. *be*·ne
A And you?	E Lei/tu? pol/inf e lay/too

Q What's your name?	Come si chiama? pol
	ko·me see kya·ma
	Come ti chiami? inf
	ko·me tee kya·mee
A My name is ...	Mi chiamo ...
	mee kya·mo ...
I'm pleased to meet you.	Piacere.
	pya·che·re
I'd like to introduce you to ...	Le/Ti presento ... pol/inf
	le/tee pre·zen·to ...

✂ This is ...	Questo/Questa è... m/f	kwe·sto/kwes·ta e ...

Titles & Addressing People

Italians will greatly appreciate your efforts to try to speak their language and you'll leave an even better impression if you use the correct titles and forms of address. So when in Rome ...

Mr/Sir	Signore
	see·nyo·re
Mrs/Madam	Signora
	see·nyo·ra
Miss/Ms	Signorina
	see·nyo·ree·na
Doctor (anyone with a university degree)	Dottore/Dottoressa m/f
	do·to·re/do·to·re·sa
Professor (high-school or university lecturer)	Professore/ Professoressa m/f
	pro·fe·so·re/ pro·fe·so·re·sa
Director or Manager (anybody that runs anything)	Direttore/Direttrice m/f
	dee·re·to·re/dee·re·tree·che

> **LANGUAGE TIP**
>
> **Addressing People**
> Italian has two forms for the singular 'you'. With family, friends, children or peers use the informal form *tu* too. When addressing strangers, older people, or people you've just met, use the polite form *Lei* lay. When your newly made friends feel it's time to start using the informal form, they might suggest:
>
> | **Let's use the 'tu' form.** | Diamoci del tu. | *dya*·mo·chee del too |
> |---|---|---|
>
> See also **personal pronouns** in the **grammar** chapter (p21).

Making Conversation

Do you live here?	Lei è di qui? pol lay e dee kwee Tu sei di qui? inf too say dee kwee
Where are you going?	Dove va/vai? pol/inf *do*·ve va/vai
What are you doing?	Che fa/fai? pol/inf ke fa/fai
That's (beautiful), isn't it!	È (bello/a), no? m/f e (*be*·lo/a) no
How long are you here for?	Quanto tempo si fermerà? pol *kwan*·to *tem*·po see fer·*me*·ra Quanto tempo ti fermerai? inf *kwan*·to *tem*·po tee fer·me·*rai*
Q Are you here on holiday?	È/Sei qui in vacanza? pol/inf e/say kwee een va·*kan*·tsa
A I'm here for a holiday.	Sono qui in vacanza. *so*·no kwee een va·*kan*·tsa

| **A** I'm here on business. | Sono qui per affari.
so·no kwee per a·fa·ree |
| **A** I'm here to study. | Sono qui per motivi
di studio.
*so·no kwee per mo·tee·vee
dee stoo·dyo* |

Nationalities

| **Q** Where are you from? | Da dove viene/vieni? pol/inf
da do·ve vye·ne/vye·nec |
| **A** I'm from ... | Vengo ...
ven·go ... |

Australia	dall'Australia	*dal·ow·stra·lya*
Canada	dal Canada	*dal ka·na·da*
England	dall'Inghilterra	*da·leen·geel·te·ra*
New Zealand	dalla Nuova Zelanda	*da·la nwo·va ze·lan·da*
the USA	dagli Stati Uniti	*da·lyee sta·tee oo·nee·tee*

For more countries, see the **dictionary**.

Age

Q How old are you?	Quanti anni ha/hai? pol/inf *kwan·tee a·nee a/ai*
A I'm ... years old.	Ho ... anni. *o ... a·nee*
Q How old is your son?	Quanti anni ha Suo/tuo figlio? pol/inf *kwan·tee a·nee a soo·o/too·o fee·lyo*

Q How old is your daughter?	Quanti anni ha Sua/tua figlia? pol/inf *kwan·tee a·nee a soo·a/too·a fee·lya*
A He/She is ... years old.	Ha ... anni. *a ... a·nee*

For your age, see **numbers & amounts** (p32).

Occupations & Studies

Q What's your occupation?	Che lavoro fa/fai? pol/inf *ke la·vo·ro fa/fai*
A I'm a manual worker.	Sono manovale. *so·no ma·no·va·le*
A I'm an office worker.	Sono impiegato/a. m/f *so·no eem·pye·ga·to/a*
A I'm a tradesperson.	Sono operaio/a. m/f *so·no o·pe·ra·yo/a*
A I work in administration.	Lavoro nel campo dell'amministrazione. *la·vo·ro nel kam·po de·la·mee·nee·stra·tsyo·ne*
A I'm retired.	Sono pensionato/a. m/f *so·no pen·syo·na·to/a*
A I'm unemployed.	Sono disoccupato/a. m/f *so·no dee·zo·koo·pa·to/a*
A I'm self-employed.	Lavoro in proprio. *la·vo·ro een pro·pryo*

CULTURE TIP

Conversation Do's & Don'ts
Italians are great communicators, so you shouldn't have too much trouble striking up a conversation. Talking about the Mafia, Mussolini or the Vatican, however, could see the conversation come to a premature halt. Try topics such as Italian architecture, films, food and soccer.

Q **What are you studying?**	Cosa studia/studi? pol/inf *ko*·za stoo·dya/stoo·dee
A **I'm studying arts/humanities.**	Sto studiando lettere. sto stoo·*dyan*·do *le*·te·re
A **I'm studying business.**	Sto studiando commercio. sto stoo·*dyan*·do ko·*mer*·cho
A **I'm studying engineering.**	Sto studiando ingegneria. sto stoo·*dyan*·do een·je·nye·*ree*·a

For more occupations and studies, see the **dictionary**.

Family

Q **Do you have (children)?**	Ha/Hai (bambini)? pol/inf a/ai (bam·*bee*·nee)
A **I have (a partner).**	Ho (un/una compagno/a). m/f o (oon/*oo*·na kom·*pa*·nyo/a)
Q **Do you live with (your family)?**	Abita con (la Sua famiglia)? pol *a*·bee·ta kon (la *soo*·a fa·*mee*·lya) Abiti con (la tua famiglia)? inf *a*·bee·tee kon (la *too*·a fa·*mee*·lya)
A **I live with (my parents).**	Abito con (i miei genitori). *a*·bee·to kon (ee myay je·nee·*to*·ree)

CULTURE TIP

Well-Wishing

An Italian will typically wish you good luck with the expression *In bocca al lupo!* een *bo*·ka·*loo*·po, which is literally translated as 'In the mouth of the wolf!'. Make sure your answer is *Crepi!* *kre*·pee (literally 'Die!'), to ward off bad luck.

🔊 LISTEN FOR

Figuriamoci!	fee·goo·*rya*·mo·chee	Yeah, right!
Incredibile!	een·kre·*dee*·bee·le	Unbelievable!
Non è vero!	non e *ve*·ro	That's not true!
Scherzi!	*sker*·tsee	You're kidding!
Taci!	*ta*·chee	Shut up!

Q Are you married?	È sposato/a? m/f pol e spo·*za*·to/a Sei sposato/a? m/f inf say spo·*za*·to/a
A I live with someone.	Convivo. kon·*vee*·vo
A I'm ...	Sono ... *so*·no ...

married	sposato/a m/f	spo·*za*·to/a
separated	separato/a m/f	se·pa·*ra*·to/a
single (man)	celibe	*che*·lee·be
single (woman)	nubile	*noo*·bee·le

For more kinship terms, see the **dictionary**.

Talking with Children

What's your name?	Come ti chiami? *ko*·me tee *kya*·mee
How old are you?	Quanti anni hai? *kwan*·tee *a*·nee ai
What grade are you in?	Quale classe fai? *kwa*·le *kla*·se fai

CULTURE TIP

Body Language
Italians are emotionally demonstrative, so expect to see lots of cheek-kissing among acquaintances, embraces between good friends and lingering handshakes. Both men and women may walk along arm-in-arm. Pushing and shoving in busy places is not considered rude.

Be aware that respectful behaviour is expected in churches. Women should ideally cover their heads and avoid exposing too much flesh – wearing shorts or skimpy tops is considered disrespectful.

Do you like school?	Ti piace la scuola? tee *pya*·che la *skwo*·la
Do you like sport?	Ti piace lo sport? tee *pya*·che lo sport
What do you do after school?	Cosa fai dopo la scuola? *ko*·za fai *do*·po la *skwo*·la
Do you learn English?	Stai imparando l'inglese? stai eem·pa·*ran*·do leen·*gle*·ze
Do you have a pet at home?	Hai un animale domestico a casa? ai oon a·nee·*ma*·le do·*mes*·tee·ko a *ka*·za

Farewells

Q What's your ...?	Qual'è il Suo/tuo ...? pol/inf kwa·*le* eel *soo*·o/*too*·o ...
A Here's my (email) address.	Ecco il mio indirizzo (di email). *e*·ko eel *mee*·o een·dee·*ree*·tso (dee e·mayl)

🔊 LISTEN FOR

Assolutamente no!	a·so·loo·ta·*men*·te no	No way!
Forse.	*for*·se	Maybe.
Non c'è problema.	non che pro·*ble*·ma	No problem.
Sto bene.	sto *be*·ne	I'm OK.

Here's my mobile number.	Ecco il mio numero di cellulare. *e·ko eel mee·o noo·me·ro dee che·loo·la·re*
If you ever visit (England), come and visit us.	Caso mai venissi in (Inghilterra), vieni a trovarci. *ka·zo mai ve·nee·see een (leen·geel·te·ra) vye·ne a tro·var·chee*
If you ever visit (England), you can stay with me.	Caso mai venissi in (Inghilterra), puoi stare da me. *ka·zo mai ve·nee·see een (leen·geel·te·ra) pwoy sta·re da me*
It's been great meeting you.	È stato veramente un piacere conoscerti. *e sta·to ve·ra·men·te oon pya·che·re ko no·sher·tee*
Are you on Facebook?	Lei è su Facebook? pol *lay e soo fays·book* Sei su Facebook? inf *say soo fays·book*
Keep in touch!	Teniamoci in contatto! *te·nya·mo·chee een kon·ta·to*

For more on addresses, see **directions** (p55).

SOCIAL

MEETING PEOPLE

SOCIAL INTERESTS

Interests

KEY PHRASES

What do you do in your spare time?	Cosa fai nel tuo tempo libero?	*ko·za fai nel too·o tem·po lee·be·ro*
Do you like ...?	Ti piace/ piacciono ...? sg/pl	tee *pya·che/ pya·cho·no ...*
I (don't) like ...	(Non) Mi piace/ piacciono ... sg/pl	(non) mee *pya·che/ pya·cho·no ...*

Common Interests

What do you do in your spare time?	Cosa fai nel tuo tempo libero? *ko·za fai nel too·o tem·po lee·be·ro*
Q Do you like ...?	Ti piace/piacciono ...? sg/pl tee *pya·che/pya·cho·no ...*
A I (don't) like ...	(Non) Mi piace/ piacciono ... sg/pl (non) mee *pya·che/ pya·cho·no ...*

art	l'arte sg	*lar·te*
card games	i giochi di carte pl	*ee jo·kee dee kar·te*
cooking	cucinare sg	*koo·chee·na·re*
travelling	viaggiare sg	*vee·a·ja·re*

For more hobbies and sporting interests, see **sports** (p135) and the **dictionary**.

Music

Do you like to ...?	Ti piace ...? tee *pya*·che ...	
dance	ballare	ba·*la*·re
go to concerts	andare ai concerti	an·*da*·re ai kon·*cher*·tee
listen to music	ascoltare la musica	as·kol·*ta*·re la *moo*·zee·ka
play an instrument	suonare uno strumento	swo·*na*·re oo·no stroo·*men*·to
sing	cantare	kan·*ta*·re

What bands do you like?	Quali gruppi ti piacciono? *kwa*·lee *groo*·pee tee *pya*·cho·no
What music do you like?	Quale tipo di musica ti piace? *kwa*·le *tee*·po dee *moo*·zee·ka tee *pya*·che
... music	musica ... *moo*·zee·ka ...

classical	classica	*kla*·see·ka
electronic	elettronica	e·le·*tro*·nee·ka
traditional	tradizionale	tra·dee·tsyo·*na*·le
world	etnica	*et*·nee·ka

Planning to go to a concert? See **buying tickets** (p41), and **going out** (p122).

SOCIAL INTERESTS

Likes & Dislikes

In Italian, to say you like something, use the expression *mi piace* mee *pya*·che (lit: me it-pleases). For plural, use *mi piacciono* mee *pya*·cho·no (lit: me they-please). To say 'no', just add *non* non: *non mi piace* non mee *pya*·che (lit: not me it-pleases).

I like this band.	Mi piace questo gruppo.	mee *pya*·che *kwe*·sto *groo*·po
I like soap operas.	Mi piacciono le telenovelle.	mee *pya*·cho·no le te·le·no·ve·le
I don't like to sing.	Non mi piace cantare.	non mee *pya*·che kan·*ta*·re

Cinema & Theatre

I feel like going to a ...	Ho voglia d'andare a ...	o *vo*·lya dan·*da*·re a ...
ballet	un balletto	oon ba·*le*·to
comedy	una commedia comica	*oo*·na ko·*me*·dya *ko*·mee·ka
film	vedere un film	ve·*de*·re oon feelm
play	teatro	te·*a*·tro

What's showing at the cinema/theatre tonight?	Cosa danno al cinema/teatro stasera? *ko*·za *da*·no al *chee*·ne·ma/te·*a*·tro sta·*se*·ra
Is it in English/Italian?	È in inglese/italiano? e een een·*gle*·ze/ee·ta·*lya*·no
Does it have subtitles?	Ci sono i sottotitoli? chee *so*·no ee so·to·*tee*·to·lee

Have you seen ...?	Hai visto ...?
	ai *vee*·sto ...

Who's in it?	Chi sono i protagonisti?
	kee *so*·no ee
	pro·ta·go·*nee*·stee

Q Did you like (the film)?	Ti è piaciuto (il film)?
	tee e pya·*choo*·to (eel feelm)

A I thought it was excellent.	L'ho trovato/a ottimo/a. m/f
	lo tro·*va*·to/a o·tee·mo/a

A I thought it was long.	L'ho trovato/a lungo/a. m/f
	lo tro·*va*·to/a *loon*·go/a

A I thought it was OK.	L'ho trovato/a passabile. m/f
	lo tro·*va*·to/a pa·*sa*·bee·le

I (don't) like ...	(Non) Mi piacciono ...
	(non) mee pya·cho·no ...

action movies	i film d'azione	ee feelm da·*tsyo*·ne
animated films	i film animati	ee feelm a·nee·*ma*·tee
black comedy	i film tragicomici	ee feelm tra·jee·ko·*mee*·chee
comedies	le commedie comiche	le ko·*me*·dye *ko*·mee·ke
documentaries	i documentari	ee do·koo·men·*ta*·ree
drama	i film drammatici	ee feelm dra·*ma*·tee·chee
horror movies	i film d'orrore	ee feelm do·*ro*·re
period dramas	i drammi d'ambiente	ee *dra*·mee dam·*byen*·te
sci-fi	i film di fantascienza	ee feelm dee fan·ta·*shen*·tsa
short films	i film corti	ee feelm *kor*·tee
thrillers	i gialli	ee *ja*·lee
war movies	i film di guerra	ee feelm dee *gwe*·ra

Feelings & Opinions

KEY PHRASES

Are you ...?	È/Sei ...? pol/inf	e/say ...
	Ha/Hai ...? pol/inf	a/ai ...
I'm (not) ...	(Non) Sono ...	(non) *so*·no ...
	(Non) Ho ...	(non) o ...
What did you think of it?	Che cosa ne pensi?	ke *ko*·za ne *pen*·see
I thought it was OK.	Pensavo che fosse passabile.	pen·*sa*·vo ke *fo*·se pa·*sa*·bee·le
How do people feel about ...?	Cosa pensa la gente di ...?	*ko*·za *pen*·sa la *jen*·te dee ...

Feelings

Feelings are described with nouns or adjectives: nouns use 'have' (eg 'I have hunger') and adjectives use 'be' (as in English).

Q Are you (sad)?	È/Sei (triste)? pol/inf e/say (*tree*·ste)
A I'm (worried).	Sono (preoccupato/a). m/f *so*·no (pre·o·koo·*pa*·to/a)
A I'm not (happy).	Non sono (felice). non *so*·no (fe·*lee*·che)
Q Are you (sleepy)?	Ha/Hai (sonno)? pol/inf a/ai (*so*·no)
A I'm (cold).	Ho (freddo). o (*fre*·do)
A I'm not (hungry).	Non ho (fame). non o (*fa*·me)

I'm a little (sad).	Sono un po' (triste).
	*so·no oon po (tree·*ste)
I'm very (content).	Sono molto (contento/a). m/f
	*so·no mol·*to (kon·*ten·*to/a)
I feel (extremely lucky).	Mi sento
	(fortunatissimo/a). m/f
	mee *sen·*to
	(for·too·na·*tee·*see·mo/a)

If you're not feeling well, see **health** (p150).

Opinions

Q	**Did you like it?**	Ti è piaciuto/a? m/f
		tee e pya·*choo·*to/a
Q	**What did you think of it?**	Che cosa ne pensi?
		ke *ko·*za ne *pen·*see
A	**I thought it was ...**	Pensavo che fosse ...
		pen·*sa·*vo ke *fo·*se ...
A	**It's ...**	È ...
		e .

boring	noioso/a m/f	no·*yo·*zo/a
great	ottimo/a m/f	o·*tee·*mo/a
interesting	interessante	een·te·re·*san·*te
OK	passabile	pa·*sa·*bee·le
weird	strano/a m/f	*stra·*no/a

Politics & Social Issues

Italians don't shy away from discussing political and social issues and might be interested in knowing your opinion on all kinds of topics. Even *il campionato* eel kam·pyo·*na·*to (football/soccer) takes on the dimensions of a serious political issue.

Q Who do you vote for?	Per chi vota Lei? pol per kee *vo*·ta lay Per chi voti? inf per kee *vo*·tee

A I support the ... party.	Sono per il partito ... *so*·no per eel par·*tee*·to ...

communist	comunista	ko·moo·*nee*·sta
conservative	conservatore	kon·ser·va·*to*·re
green	verde	*ver*·de
labour	laburista	la·boo·*ree*·sta
liberal	liberale	lee·be·*ra*·le
socialist	socialista	so·cha·*lee*·sta

Are you against ... ?	È/Sei contro ...? pol/inf e/say *kon*·tro ..

Are you in favour of ...?	È/Sei a favore di ...? pol/inf e/say a fa·*vo*·re dee ...

Q Do you agree with it?	È/Sei d'accordo con ...? pol/inf e/say da·*kor*·do kon ...

A I (don't) agree with ...	(Non) Sono d'accordo con ... (non) *so*·no da·*kor*·do kon ...

How do people feel about (the) ...?	Cosa pensa la gente di ...? *ko*·za *pen*·sa la *jen*·te dee ...

economy	economia	e·ko·no·*mee*·a
health care	servizi	ser·*vee*·tsee
	sanitari	sa·nee·*ta*·ree
immigration	immigrazione	ee·mee·gra·*tsyo*·ne
organised crime	criminalità organizzata	kree·mee·na·lee·*ta* or·ga·nee·*dza*·ta
war in ...	guerra in ...	*gwe*·ra een ...

The Environment

Is there a/an (environmental) problem here?	C'è un problema (ambientale) qui? che oon pro·*ble*·ma (am·byen·*ta*·le) kwe
Where can I recycle this?	Dove lo posso riciclare? *do*·ve lo *po*·so ree·chee·*kla*·re
Is this a protected forest?	È una foresta protetta questa? e *oo*·na fo·*res*·ta pro·*te*·ta *kwe*·sta
Is this a protected park?	È un parco protetto questo? e oon *par*·ko pro·*te*·to *kwe*·sto
Is this a protected species?	È una specie protetta questa? e *oo*·na *spe*·che pro·*te*·ta *kwe*·sta
climate change	cambiamento m del clima kam·bya·*men*·to del *klee*·ma
pollution	inquinamento m een·kwee·na·*men*·to
recycling programme	programma m di riciclaggio pro·*gra*·ma dee ree·chee·*kla*·jo
the environment	ambiente m am·*byen*·te

Going Out

KEY PHRASES

What's on tonight?	Che c'è in programma stasera?	ke che een pro·*gra*·ma sta·*se*·ra
Where are the clubs?	Dove sono dei clubs?	*do*·ve *so*·no day kloobs
Would you like to go for a coffee?	Vuoi/Volete andare a prendere un caffè? sg/pl	vwoy/vo·*le*·te an·*da*·re a *pren*·de·re oon ka·*fe*
What time shall we meet?	A che ora ci vediamo?	a ke *o*·ra chee ve·*dya*·mo
Where will we meet?	Dove ci vediamo?	*do*·ve chee ve·*dya*·mo

Where to Go

What's there to do in the evenings?	Cosa si fa di sera? *ko*·za see fa dee *se*·ra
What's on ...?	Che c'è in programma ...? ke che een pro·*gra*·ma ...

locally	in zona	een *dzo*·na
this weekend	questo finesettimana	*kwe*·sto fee·ne·se·tee·*ma*·na
today	oggi	*o*·jee
tonight	stasera	sta·*se*·ra

Where are the ...?	Dove sono ...?	*do·ve so·no ...*

bars	dei locali	day lo·*ka*·lee
cafes	dei bar	day bar
clubs	dei clubs	day kloobs
gay venues	dei locali gay	day lo·*ka*·lee ge
places to eat	posti in	*pos*·tee *een*
	cui mangiare	koo·ee man·*ja*·re

Is there a local entertainment guide?	C'è una guida agli spettacoli in questa città?	che *oo*·na *gwee*·da *a*·lyee spe·*ta*·ko·lee een *kwe*·sta *chee·ta*
What's the cover charge?	Quant'è l'ingresso?	kwan·*te* leen·*gre*·so
I feel like going to a/the ...	Ho voglia d'andare ...	o *vo*·lya dan·*da*·re ...

bar	a un locale	a oon lo·*ka*·le
coffee bar	a un caffè	a oon ka·*fe*
concert	a un concerto	a oon kon·*cher*·to
movies	al cinema	al *chee*·nee·ma
nightclub	in un locale notturno	een oon lo·*ka*·le no·*toor*·no
party	a una festa	a *oo*·na *fes*·ta
restaurant	in un ristorante	een oon rees·to·*ran*·te
theatre	al teatro	al te·*a*·tro

For more on bars, drinks and partying, see **eating out** (p173).

Invitations

What are you doing right now?	Cosa fai/fate proprio adesso? sg/pl *ko·*za fai/*fa·*te *pro·*pryo a·*de·*so
What are you doing this evening?	Cosa fai/fate stasera? sg/pl *ko·*za fai/*fa·*te sta·*se·*ra
What are you doing this weekend?	Cosa fai/fate questo fine settimana? sg/pl *ko·*za fai/*fa·*te *kwe·*sto *fee·*ne se·tee·*ma·*na
Do you know a good restaurant?	Conosci/Conoscete un buon ristorante? sg/pl ko·*no·*shee/ko·*no·*she·te oon bwon rees·to·*ran·*te

Facciamo una festa.
fa·*chya·*mo *oo·*na *fes·*ta

We're having a party.

> **CULTURE TIP**
>
> **Night Spots**
>
> **bar** m bar – like a snack bar which also sells hot drinks and alcohol
>
> **birreria** f bee·re·*ree*·a – has a pub-like atmosphere but specialises in beer
>
> **discoteca** m dees·ko·*te*·ka – the most commonly frequented night spot for the under-30 age group
>
> **locale** m **notturno** lo·*ka*·le no·*toor*·no – generic term for every type of night spot
>
> **nite** m nait – a more elegant nightclub
>
> **osteria** f os·te·*ree*·a – a sit-down eating place where people have wine with their meal

Would you like to go (for a) ...?	Vuoi/Volete andare a ...? sg/pl	
	vwoy/vo·*le*·te an·*da*·re a ...	
I feel like going (for a) ...	Ho voglia d'andare a ...	
	o *vo*·lya dan·*da*·re a ...	

coffee	prendere un caffè	*pren·de·re oon ka·fe*
dancing	ballare	ba·*la*·re
drink	bere qualcosa	*be*·re kwal·*ko*·za
meal	mangiare qualcosa	man·*ja*·re kwal·*ko*·za
walk	fare una passeggiata	*fa*·re oo·na pa·se·*ja*·ta

My round.	Offro io.
	o·fro ee·o
Do you want to come to a (jazz) concert with me?	Vuoi/Volete venire a un concerto (di jazz)? sg/pl
	vwoy/vo·*le*·te ve·*nee*·re a oon kon·*cher*·to (dee jaz)

| We're having a party. | Facciamo una festa.
fa·*chya*·mo *oo*·na *fes*·ta |
| You should come. | Dovresti/Dovreste
venire. sg/pl
dov·*res*·tee/dov·*res*·te
ve·*nee*·re |

Responding to Invitations

Yes, I'd love to.	Sì, mi piacerebbe. see mee pya·che·*re*·be
Where shall we go?	Dove andiamo? *do*·ve an·*dya*·mo
No, I'm afraid I can't.	No, temo di no. no *te*·mo dee no
What about tomorrow?	Domani che ne dici/ dite? sg/pl do·*ma*·nee ke ne *dee*·chee/ *dee*·te

Arranging to Meet

Q What time shall we meet?	A che ora ci vediamo? a ke *o*·ra chee ve·*dya*·mo
A Let's meet at (eight) o'clock.	Incontriamoci alle (otto). een·kon·*trya*·mo·chee *a*·le (*o*·to)
Q Where will we meet?	Dove ci vediamo? *do*·ve chee ve·*dya*·mo
A Let's meet at the entrance.	Incontriamoci all'entrata. een·kon·*trya*·mo·chee a·len·*tra*·ta

I'll pick you up.	Ti/Vi vengo a prendere. sg/pl tee/vee *ven*·go a *pren*·de·re
If I'm not there by (nine), don't wait for me.	Se non ci sono entro le (nove), non aspettarmi. se non chee *so*·no *en*·tro le (*no*·ve) non as·pe·*tar*·mee
I'll see you then.	Ci vediamo allora. chee ve·*dya*·mo a·*lo*·ra
I'm looking forward to it.	Non vedo l'ora. non *ve*·do *lo*·ra
Sorry I'm late.	Scusa, sono in ritardo. *skoo*·za *so*·no een ree·*tar*·do

Drugs

I don't take drugs.	Non mi drogo. non mee *dro*·go
I have ... occasionally.	Prendo ... ogni tanto. *pren*·do ... o·nyee *tan*·to
Do you want to have a smoke?	Lo vuoi uno spinello? lo vwoy oo·no spee·*ne*·lo
Do you have a light?	Hai d'accendere? ai da·*chen*·de·re

If the police are talking to you about drugs, see **police** (p148), for useful phrases.

SOCIAL ROMANCE

Romance

KEY PHRASES

Would you like to do something?	Vuoi fare qualcosa?	vwoy *fa*·re kwal·*ko*·za
I love you.	Ti amo.	tee *a*·mo
Leave me alone!	Lasciami in pace!	*la*·sha·mee een *pa*·che

Asking Someone Out

Q	Would you like to do something (tonight)?	Vuoi fare qualcosa (stasera)? vwoy *fa*·re kwal·*ko*·za (sta·*se*·ra)
A	Yes, I'd love to.	Sì, mi piacerebbe molto. see mee pya·che·*re*·be *mol*·to
A	No, I'm afraid I can't.	No, temo di no. no *te*·mo dee no

Pick-Up Lines

Would you like a drink?	Prendi qualcosa da bere? *pren*·dee kwal·*ko*·za da *be*·re
Do you have a light?	Hai d'accendere? ai da·*chen*·de·re
Can I dance with you?	Posso ballare con te? *po*·so ba·*la*·re kon te

Shall we get some fresh air?	Andiamo a prendere un po' d'aria fresca? an·*dya*·mo a *pren*·de·re oon po *da*·rya *fres*·ka
Can I sit here?	Posso sedermi qui? *po*·so se·*der*·mee kwee

Rejections

I'm here with my boyfriend.	Sono qui con il mio ragazzo. *so*·no kwee kon eel *mee*·o ra·*ga*·tso
I'm here with my girlfriend.	Sono qui con la mia ragazza. *so*·no kwee kon la *mee*·a ra·*ga*·tsa
Excuse me, I have to go now.	Scusa, adesso devo andare. *skoo*·za a·*de*·so *de*·vo an·*da*·re
I'm sorry, but I don't feel like it.	Mi dispiace ma non ne ho voglia. mee dees·*pya*·che ma non ne o *vo*·lya
I'm not interested.	Non mi interessa. non mee een·te·*re*·sa
Leave me alone!	Lasciami in pace! *la*·sha·mee een *pa*·che
Don't touch me!	Non mi toccare! non mee to·*ka*·re
Let me through!	Lasciami passare! *la*·sha·mee pa·*sa*·re

> **LANGUAGE TIP** **Masculine & Feminine**
> Throughout this book we have used the abbreviations m and f to indicate whether a word is masculine or feminine. Where a word has both a masculine and a feminine form, the feminine ending is added after a slash, eg *bello/a* m/f *be*·lo/a (beautiful). See also **gender** in the **grammar** chapter (p19).

Icebreakers

Do you like ...?	Ti piace....?
	tee *pya*·che
I (don't) like ...	(Non) Mi piace...
	(non) mee *pya*·che

art	l'arte	*lar*·te
cooking	cucinare	koo·chee·*na*·re
movies	i film	ee feelm
nightclubs	le discoteche	le dees·ko·*te*·ke
reading	leggere	*le*·je·re
shopping	lo shopping	lo *sho*·ping
sport	lo sport	lo sport
travelling	viaggiare	vee·a·*ja*·re

Do you like to ...?	Ti piace ...?
	tee *pya*·che ...

dance	ballare	ba·*la*·re
go to concerts	andare ai concerti	an·*da*·re ai kon·*cher*·tee
listen to music	ascoltare la musica	as·kol·*ta*·re la *moo*·zee·ka

Getting Closer

You're very nice.	Sei molto simpatico/a. m/f say mol·to seem·pa·tee·ko/a
You're great.	Sei fantastico/a. m/f say fan·tas·tee·ko/a
Can I kiss you?	Ti posso baciare? tee po·so ba·cha·re
Do you want to come inside for a while?	Vuoi entrare per un po'? vwoy en·tra·re per oon po

Sex

I want to make love to you.	Voglio fare l'amore con te. vo·lyo fa·re la·mo·re kon te
Do you have a condom?	Hai un preservativo? ai oon pre·ser·va·tee·vo
I won't do it without protection.	Non lo farò senza protezione. non lo fa·ro sen·tsa pro·te·tsyo·ne

Love

I'm in love with you.	Sono innamorato/a di te. m/f so·no ee·na·mo·ra·to/a dee te
Q **Do you love me?**	Mi ami? mee a·mee
A **I love you.**	Ti amo. tee a·mo

LANGUAGE TIP — **Double Entendre**

Be mindful of the word *uccello* oo·che·lo which can mean either 'bird' or 'dick'.

SOCIAL ROMANCE

🔊 LISTEN FOR

amore mio	a·*mo*·re *mee*·o	my love
caro/a mio/a m/f	*ka*·ro/a *mee*·o/a	my darling
gioia mia	*jo*·ya *mee*·a	my joy
tesoro mio	te·*zo*·ro *mee*·o	my treasure

I think we're good together.	Penso che stiamo bene insieme. *pen*·so ke *stya*·mo *be*·ne een·*sye*·me

Problems

Are you seeing someone else?	Frequenti qualcun'altro/a? m/f fre·*kwen*·tee kwal·koo·*nal*·tro/a
He's just a friend.	È solo un amico. e *so*·lo oo·na·*mee*·ko
She's just a friend.	È solo un'amica. e *so*·lo oo·na·*mee*·ka
I don't think it's working out.	Non credo che stia funzionando fra noi due. non *kre*·do ke *stee*·a foon·tsyo·*nan*·do fra noy *doo*·e
We'll work it out.	Troveremo una soluzione. tro·ve·*re*·mo oo·na so·loo·*tsyo*·ne
I never want to see you again.	Non voglio vederti mai più. non *vo*·lyo ve·*der*·tee mai pyoo
I want to stay friends.	Voglio che restiamo amici. *vo*·lyo ke res·*tya*·mo a·*mee*·chee

Beliefs & Culture

KEY PHRASES

What's your religion?	Di che religione è Lei? pol	dee ke re·lee·*jo*·ne e lay
	Di che religione sei tu? Inf	dee ke re·lee·*jo*·ne say too
I'm (not) ...	(Non) Sono ...	(non) *so*·no ...
I'm sorry, it's against my beliefs.	Mi dispiace, non è permesso dalla mia fede.	mee dees·*pya*·che non e per·*me*·so *da*·la *mee*·a *fe*·de

Religion

Q **What's your religion?**
Di che religione è Lei? pol
dee ke re·lee·*jo*·ne e lay
Di che religione sei tu? inf
dee ke re·lee·*jo*·ne say too

A **I (don't) believe in God.**
(Non) Credo in Dio.
(non) *kre*·do een *dee*·o

A **I'm (not) ...**
(Non) Sono ...
(non) *so*·no ...

agnostic	agnostico/a m/f	a·*nyos*·lee·ko/a
atheist	ateo/a m/f	a·*te*·o/a
practising	praticante	pra·tee·*kan*·te
religious	religioso/a m/f	re·lee·*jo*·zo/a

Where can I pray?
Dove posso pregare?
do·ve *po*·so pre·*ga*·re

I'd like to go to (the) ...	Vorrei andare ...
	vo·*ray* an·*da*·re ...

church	alla chiesa	a·la *kye*·za
mosque	alla moschea	a·la mos·*ke*·a
synagogue	alla sinagoga	a·la see·na·*go*·ga
temple	al tempio	a·la *tem*·pyo

For religions, see the **dictionary**.

Cultural Differences

Is this a local custom?	È una tradizione locale?
	e *oo*·na tra·dee·*tsyo*·ne lo·*ka*·le
I'm not used to this.	Non ci sono abituato/a. **m/f**
	non chee *so*·no a·bee·*twa*·to/a
I'll try it.	Lo proverò.
	lo pro·ve·*ro*
I didn't mean to do/say anything wrong.	Non volevo dire/fare qualcosa di sbagliato.
	non vo·*le*·vo *dee*·re/*fa*·re kwal·*ko*·za dee sba·*lya*·to
I'm sorry, it's against my beliefs.	Mi dispiace, non è permesso dalla mia fede.
	mee dees·*pya*·che non e per·*me*·so *da*·la *mee*·a *fe*·de
I'm sorry, it's against my culture.	Mi dispiace, non è permesso dalla mia cultura.
	mee dees·*pya*·che non e per·*me*·so *da*·la *mee*·a kool·*too*·ra

Sports

KEY PHRASES

Which sport do you play?	Quale sport pratichi?	*kwa*·le sport *pra*·tee·kee
Who's your favourite team?	Qual'è la tua squadra preferita?	kwa·*le* la *too*·a *skwa*·dra pre·fe·*ree*·ta
What's the score?	Qual'è il punteggio?	kwa·*le* eel poon·*te*·jo

Sporting Interests

Q Do you like (sport)?	Ti piace (lo sport)? tee *pya*·che (lo sport)
A Yes, very much.	Sì, moltissimo. see mol·*tee*·see·mo
A Not really.	Non molto. non *mol*·to
A I like watching it.	Mi piace assistere. mee *pya*·che a·*see*·ste·re
A I follow (cycling).	Seguo (il ciclismo). *se*·gwo (eel cheek·*leez*·mo)
Q Which sport do you play?	Quale sport pratichi? *kwa*·le sport *pra*·tee·kee
A I play (football/soccer).	Pratico (il calcio). *pra*·tee·ko (eel *kal*·cho)

For more sports, see the **dictionary**.

Who's your favourite sportsman?	Chi è il tuo sportivo preferito? kee e eel *too*·o spor·*tee*·vo pre·fe·*ree*·to
Who's your favourite sportswoman?	Chi è la tua sportiva preferita? kee e la *too*·a spor·*tee*·va pre·fe·*ree*·ta
Who's your favourite team?	Qual'è la tua squadra preferita? kwa·*le* la *too*·a *skwa*·dra pre·fe·*ree*·ta

Going to a Game

Would you like to go to a game?	Ti piacerebbe andare ad una partita? tee pya·che·*re*·be an·*da*·re a·*doo*·na par·*tee*·ta
Who are you supporting?	Per chi fai il tifo? per kee fai eel *tee*·fo
Who's playing?	Chi gioca? kee *jo*·ka
Who's winning?	Chi vince? kee *veen*·che
How much time is left?	Quanto tempo manca? *kwan*·to *tem*·po *man*·ka
Q **What's the score?**	Qual'è il punteggio? kwa·*le* eel poon·*te*·jo
A **It's a draw.**	Hanno pareggiato. *a*·no pa·re·*ja*·to
That was a bad/great game!	Che partita brutta/fantastica! ke par·*tee*·ta *broo*·ta/fan·*tas*·tee·ka

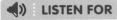
🔊 LISTEN FOR

Che passaggio!	ke pa·*sa*·jo	What a pass!
Che calcio!	ke *kal*·cho	What a kick!
Che colpo!	ke *kol*·po	What a hit!

SOCIAL

SPORTS

Playing Sport

Q Do you want to play?	Vuoi giocare? vwoy jo·*ka*·re
A Yes, that'd be great.	Sì, sarebbe bello. see sa·*re*·be *be*·lo
A I'm sorry, I can't.	Mi dispiace, non posso. mee dees·*pya*·che non *po*·so
Can I join in?	Posso giocare anch'io? *po*·so jo·*ka*·re an·*kee*·o
Where's the nearest gym?	Dov'è la palestra più vicina? do·*ve* la pa·*le*·stra pyoo vee·*chee*·na
Where's the nearest swimming pool?	Dov'è la piscina più vicina? do·*ve* la pee·*shee*·na pyoo vee·*chee*·na
Where's the nearest tennis court?	Dov'è il campo da tennis più vicino? do·ve eel *kam*·po da te·nees pyoo vee·*chee*·no
What's the charge per ...?	Qual è il prezzo richiesto ...? kwa·*le* eel *pre*·tso ree·*kye*·sto ...

day	per la giornata	per la jor·*na*·ta
game	per una partita	per oo·na par·*tee*·ta
hour	all'ora	a·*lo*·ra
visit	a visita	a vee·see·ta

🔊 LISTEN FOR

Passala a me!	*pa·sa·la a me*	Kick/Pass it to me!
Punto a me/te.	*poon·to a me/te*	My/Your point.
Era fuori.	*e·ra fwo·ree*	That was out.
Giochi bene.	*jo·kee be·ne*	You're a good player.
Imbroglione/a! m/f	*eem·bro·lyo·ne/a*	Cheat!
Grazie della partita.	*gra·tsye de·la par·tee·ta*	Thanks for the game.

Can I hire a court?	Posso noleggiare un campo? *po·so no·le·ja·re oon kam·po*
Can I hire a ball?	Posso noleggiare una palla? *po·so no·le·ja·re oo·na pa·la*
Can I hire a racquet?	Posso noleggiare una racchetta? *po·so no·le·ja·re oo·na ra·ke·ta*
Do I have to be a member to attend?	È necessario essere soci? *e ne·che·sa·ryo e·se·re so·chee*
Is there a women-only session?	Ci sono i corsi per sole donne? *chee so·no ee kor·see per so·le do·ne*
Where are the changing rooms?	Dove sono gli spogliatoi? *do·ve so·no lyee spo·lya·to·ee*

Football/Soccer

Who plays for (Sampdoria)?	Chi gioca per (la Sampdoria)? *kee jo·ka per (la samp·do·ree·a)*

🔊 LISTEN FOR

allenatore/ **allenatrice** m/f	a·le·na·*to*·re/ a·le·na·*tree*·che	coach
angolo m	*an*·go·lo	corner
cannoniere m	ka·no·*nye*·re	goal-scorer
calciatore/ **calciatrice** m/f	kal·cha·*to*·re/ kal·cha·*tree*·che	football/soccer player
cartellino m **giallo/rosso**	kar·te·*lee*·no *ja*·lo/*ro*·so	yellow/red card
fallo m	*fa*·lo	foul
fuorigioco m	fwo·ree·*jo*·ko	offside
giocatore/ **giocatrice** m/f	jo·ka·*to*·re/ jo·ka·*tree*·che	player
pallone m	pa·*lo*·ne	ball
porta f	*por*·la	goal (place)
portiere m&f	por·*tye*·re	goalkeeper
rigore m	ree·*go*·re	penalty (kick)
serie f	*se*·rye	league
tifosi m pl	tee·*fo*·zoo	fans/supporters

SOCIAL SPORTS

He's a great (player).	È un bravo (giocatore). e oon *bra*·vo (jo·ka·*to*·re)
Which team is at the top of the league?	Quale squadra è in testa alla classifica? *kwa*·le *skwa*·dra e een *tes*·ta a·la kla·*see* fee·ka
What a terrible team!	Che squadra schifosa! ke *skwa*·dra skee·*fo*·za
Come on boys!	Forza ragazzi! *for*·tsa ra·*ga*·tsee

Outdoors

KEY PHRASES

Where can I buy supplies?	Dove posso comprare delle provviste?	do·ve po·so kom·pra·re de·le pro·vee·ste
Do we need a guide?	Occorre una guida?	o·ko·re oo·na gwee·da
Is it safe?	È sicuro?	e see·koo·ro
I'm lost.	Mi sono perso/a. m/f	mee so·no per·so/a
What's the weather like?	Che tempo fa?	ke tem·po fa

Hiking

Where can I ...?		Dove posso ...? do·ve po·so ...
buy supplies	comprare delle provviste	kom·pra·re de·le pro·vee·ste
find out about hiking trails	informarmi sulle piste per l'escursionismo a piedi	een·for·mar·mee soo·le pee·ste per les·koor·syo·neez·mo a pye·dee
get a map	trovare una carta	tro·va·re oo·na kar·ta
hire hiking gear	noleggiare l'attrezzatura per l'escursionismo a piedi	no·le·ja·re la·tre·tsa·too·ra per les·koor·syo·neez·mo a pye·dee

Do we need to take food?	Dobbiamo portare del cibo? do·*bya*·mo por·*ta*·re del *chee*·bo
Do we need to take water?	Dobbiamo portare dell'acqua? do·*bya*·mo por·*ta*·re de·la·kwa
How high is the climb?	Quant'è alta la salita? kwan·*te al*·ta la sa·*lee*·ta
How long is the hike?	Quant'è lunga l'escursione? kwan·*te loon*·ga les·koor·*syo*·ne
How long is the trail?	Quant'è lungo il sentiero? kwan·*te loon*·go eel sen·*tye*·ro
Is the track (well-)marked?	La pista è (ben) segnata? la *pee*·sta e (ben) se·*nya*·ta
Is the track open?	La pista è aperta? la *pee*·sta e a·*per*·ta
Is the track scenic?	La pista è panoramica? la *pee*·sta e pa·no·*ra*·mee·ka
Which is the easiest route?	Qual'è il percorso più facile? kwa·*le* eel per·*kor*·so pyoo *fa*·chee·le
Which is the most interesting route?	Qual'è il percorso più interessante? kwa·*le* eel per·*kor*·so pyoo een·te·re·*san*·te
Where's the nearest village?	Dov'è il villaggio più vicino? do·*ve* eel vee·*la*·jo pyoo vee·*chee*·no
Do we need a guide?	Occorre una guida? o·*ko*·re *oo*·na *gwee*·da
I'm lost.	Mi sono perso/a. m/f mee *so*·no *per*·so/a

Are there guided treks?	Ci sono delle escursioni guidate? chee *so*·no *de*·le es·koor·*syo*·nee gwee·*da*·te
Is it safe?	È sicuro? e see·*koo*·ro
Is there a hut there?	C'è un rifugio là? che oon re·*foo*·jo la
When does it get dark?	Quando fa buio? *kwan*·do fa *boo*·yo
Does this path go to (Ginostra)?	Questo sentiero va verso (Ginostra)? *kwe*·sto sen·*tye*·ro va *ver*·so (jee·*nos*·tra)
Can we go through here?	Possiamo passare da qui? po·*sya*·mo pa·*sa*·re da kwee
Is the water OK to drink?	Si può bere l'acqua? see pwo *be*·re *la*·kwa

At the Beach

Where's the best beach?	Dov'è la spiaggia migliore? do·*ve* la *spya*·ja mee·*lyo*·re
Where's the nearest beach?	Dov'è la spiaggia più vicina? do·*ve* la *spya*·ja pyoo vee·*chee*·na
Is it safe to dive here?	Si può fare i tuffi senza pericolo? see pwo *fa*·re ee *too*·fee *sen*·tsa pe·*ree*·ko·lo
Is it safe to swim here?	Si può nuotare senza pericolo? see pwo nwo·*ta*·re *sen*·tsa pe·*ree*·ko·lo

🔍 LOOK FOR

Vietato Nuotare	vye·*ta*·to noo·o·*ta*·re	No Swimming

What time is high tide?	A che ora è l'alta marea? a ke o·ra e *lal*·ta ma·*re*·a
What time is low tide?	A che ora è la bassa marea? a ke o·ra e la *ba*·sa ma·*re*·a
How much for a deckchair?	Quanto costa una sedia a sdraio? *kwan*·to *ko*·sta oo·na *se*·dya a *zdra*·yo
How much for an umbrella?	Quanto costa un ombrello? *kwan*·to *ko*·sta oo·nom·*bre*·lo

Weather

🇶 **What's the weather like?**	Che tempo fa? ke *tem*·po fa
🇦 It's cloudy.	È nuvoloso. e noo·vo·*lo*·zo
🇦 It's windy.	Tira vento. tee·ra *ven*·to
🇦 It's cold.	Fa freddo. fa *fre*·do
🇦 It's hot.	Fa caldo. fa *kal*·do
🇦 It's raining.	Piove. *pyo*·ve
🇦 It's snowing.	Nevica. ne·*vee*·ka

SOCIAL OUTDOORS

| What's the weather forecast? | Cosa dicono le previsioni del tempo? ko·za *dee*·ko·no le pre·vee·*zyo*·nee del *tem*·po |

Flora & Fauna

| What (kind of) ... is that? | Che (tipo di) ... è quello? ke (*tee*·po dee) ... e *kwe*·lo |

animal	animale	a·nee·*ma*·le
bird	uccello	oo·*che*·lo
plant	pianta	*pyan*·ta
tree	albero	*al*·be·ro

| Is it ...? | È ...? e ... |

common	comune	ko·*moo*·ne
dangerous	pericoloso/a m/f	pe·ree·ko·*lo*·zo/a
poisonous	velenoso/a m/f	ve·le·*no*·zo/a
protected	protetto/a m/f	pro·*te*·to/a

For geographical and agricultural terms, and names of animals and plants, see the **dictionary**.

Safe Travel

Emergencies

KEY PHRASES

Help!	Aiuto!	a·*yoo*·to
There's been an accident.	C'è stato un incidente.	che *sta*·to oon een·chee·*den*·te
It's an emergency!	È un'emergenza!	e oo·ne·mer·*jen*·tsa

Help!	Aiuto! a·*yoo*·to	
Stop!	Fermi! *fer*·mee	
Go away!	Vai via! vai *vee*·a	
Thief!	Ladro! *la*·dro	
Fire!	Al fuoco! al *fwo*·ko	
Watch out!	Attenzione! a·ten·*tsyo*·ne	
Call the police!	Chiami la polizia! *kya*·mee la po·lee·*tsee*·a	
Call a doctor!	Chiami un medico! *kya*·mee oon *me*·dee·ko	
Call an ambulance!	Chiami un'ambulanza! *kya*·mee o·nam·boo·*lan*·tsa	
It's an emergency!	È un'emergenza! e oo·ne·mer·*jen*·tsa	

🔊 LISTEN FOR

Cristo!	*kree*·sto	Christ!
Dio!	*dee*·o	God!
Gesù!	je·*soo*	Jesus!
Madonna!	ma·*do*·na	Goodness!
Maledizione!	ma·le·dee·*tsyo*·ne	Damn!
Merda!	*mer*·da	Shit!

There's been an accident.	C'è stato un incidente. che *sta*·to oon een·chee·*den*·te
Can you help me, please?	Mi può aiutare, per favore? mee pwo a·yoo·*ta*·re per fa·*vo*·re
I have to use the telephone.	Devo fare una telefonata. *de*·vo *fa*·re oo·na te·le·fo·*na*·ta
I'm lost.	Mi sono perso/a. m/f mee *so*·no *per*·so/a
Do you have a first-aid kit?	Avete una cassetta di pronto soccorso? a·*ve*·te oo·na ka·*se*·ta dee *pron*·to so·*kor*·so
Where are the toilets?	Dove sono i gabinetti? *do*·ve so·no ee ga·bee·*ne*·te toc

Police

KEY PHRASES

Where's the police station?	Dov'è il posto di polizia?	do·*ve* eel *pos*·to dee po·lee·*tsee*·a
I want to contact my embassy.	Vorrei contattare la mia ambasciala.	vo·*ray* kon·ta·*ta*·re la *mee*·a am·ba·*sha*·ta
My bag was stolen.	Mi hanno rubato la mia borsa.	mee *a*·no roo·*ba*·to la *mee*·a bor·sa

Where's the police station?	Dov'è il posto di polizia? do·*ve* eel *pos*·to dee po·lee·*tsee*·a
I want to report an offence.	Voglio fare una denuncia. *vo*·lyo *fa*·re oo·na de·*noon*·cha
I have insurance.	Ho l'assicurazione. o la·see·koo·ra·*tsyo*·ne
(My bag) was stolen.	Mi hanno rubato (la mia borsa). mee *a*·no roo·*ba*·to (la *mee*·a *bor*·sa)
I've lost (my wallet).	Ho perso (il mio portafoglio). o *per*·so (eel *mee*·o por·ta·*fo*·lyo)
I've been raped.	Sono stato/a violentato/a. m/f *so*·no *sta*·to/a vyo·len·*ta*·to/a

I want to contact my embassy.	Vorrei contattare la mia ambasciata. vo·*ray* kon·ta·*ta*·re la *mee*·a am·ba·*sha*·ta
Can I have a lawyer (who speaks English)?	Posso avere un avvocato (che parli inglese)? *po*·so a·*ve*·re oo·na·vo·*ka*·to (ke *par*·lee een·*gle*·ze)
Can I have a copy, please?	Potrei avere una copia, per favore? po·*tray* a·*ve*·re oo·na *ko*·pya per fa·*vo*·re
I have a prescription for this drug.	Ho una ricetta per questa medicina. o oo·na re·*che*·ta per *kwe*·sta me·dee·*chee*·na
What am I accused of?	Di che cosa sono stato/a accusato/a? **m/f** dee ke *ko*·za *so*·no *sta*·to/a a·koo·*za*·to/a
I didn't realise I was doing anything wrong.	Non sapevo che facessi qualcosa di male. non sa·*pe*·vo ke fa·*che*·see kwal·*ko*·za dee *ma*·le

---

CULTURE TIP   **Cop Shops**

In Italy, both the *polizia* po·lee·*tsee*·a (civilian police) and the *carabinieri* ka·ra·bee·*nye*·ree (administered by the Ministry of Defence) investigate crimes, but the *posto di polizia* *pos*·to dee po·lee·*tsee*·a (civilian police station) or the *questura* kwes·*too*·ra (police headquarters) is where to go to report a theft. Nevertheless, if you happen to be closer to the *carabinieri*, they'll redirect you from their *caserma* ka·*ser*·ma (barracks) if necessary.

Health

KEY PHRASES

Where's the nearest hospital?	Dov'è l'ospedale più vicino?	do·ve los·pe·da·le pyoo vee·chee·no
I'm sick.	Mi sento male.	mee sen·to ma·le
I need a doctor.	Ho bisogno di un medico.	o bee·zo·nyo dee oon me·dee·ko
I'm on medication for ...	Prendo la medicina per ...	pren·do la me·dee·chee·na per ...
I'm allergic to ...	Sono allergico/a ... m/f	so·no a·ler·jee·ko/a ...

Where's the nearest ...?　　Dov'è ... più vicino/a? m/f
do·ve ... pyoo vee·chee·no/a

(night) chemist	la farmacia f (di turno)	la far·ma·chee·a (dee toor·no)
dentist	il/la dentista m/f	eel/la den·tee·sta
doctor	il medico m	eel me·dee·ko
hospital	l'ospedale m	los·pe·da·le
optometrist	l'ottico m	lo·tee·ko

I need a doctor (who speaks English).	Ho bisogno di un medico (che parli inglese). o bee·zo·nyo dee oon me·dee·ko (ke par·lee een·gle·ze)
Could I see a female doctor?	Posso vedere una dottoressa? po·so ve·de·re oo·na do·to·re·sa

🔊 LISTEN FOR

Dove Le fa male?	do·ve le fa *ma*·le	Where does it hurt?
Ha la febbre?	a la *fe*·bre	Do you have a temperature?
Da quanto (tempo) è che si sente così?	da *kwan*·to (*tem*·po) e ke see *sen*·te ko·*zee*	How long have you been like this?
Si è mai sentito/a così prima? m/f	see e mai sen·*tee*·to/a ko·*zee* *pree*·ma	Have you had this before?

Can the doctor come here?	Può venire qui il medico? pwo ve·*nee*·re kwee eel *me*·dee·ko
I've been vaccinated for hepatitis A/B/C.	Sono stato/a vaccinato/a per l'epatite A/B/C. m/f *so*·no *sta*·to/a va·chee·*na*·to/a per le·pa·*tee*·te a/bee/chee
I've been vaccinated for tetanus.	Sono stato/a vaccinato/a per il tetano. m/f *so*·no *sta*·to/a va·chee·*na*·to/a per eel *te*·ta·no
I've been vaccinated for typhoid.	Sono stato/a vaccinato/a per il tifo. m/f *so*·no *sta*·to/a va·chee·*na*·to/a per eel *tee*·fo
I need new contact lenses.	Ho bisogno di nuove lenti a contatto. o bee·*zo*·nyo dee *nwo*·ve *len*·tee a kon·*ta*·to

I need new glasses.	Ho bisogno di nuovi occhiali. o bee·zo·nyo dee *nwo*·vee o·*kya*·lee
I've run out of my medication.	Ho finito la mia medicina. o fee·*nee*·to la *mee*·a me·dee·*chee*·na
Can I have a receipt for my insurance?	Potrebbe darmi una ricevuta per l'assicurazione? po·*tre*·be *dar*·mee oo·na ree·che·*voo*·ta per la·see·koo·ra·*tsyo*·ne

Symptoms & Conditions

I'm sick.	Mi sento male. mee *sen*·to *ma*·le
It hurts here.	Mi fa male qui. mee fa *ma*·le kwee
I've been injured.	Sono stato/a ferito/a. m/f *so*·no *sta*·to/a fe·*ree*·to/a
I've been vomiting.	Ho vomitato alcune volte. o vo·mee·*ta*·to al·*koo*·ne *vol*·te
I can't sleep.	Non riesco a dormire. non *ryes*·ko a dor·*mee*·re

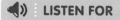

LISTEN FOR

È allergico/a a qualcosa? m/f	e a·*ler*·jee·ko/a a kwal·*ko*·za	Are you allergic to anything?
Sta prendendo medicine?	sta pren·*den*·do me·dee·*chee*·ne	Are you on medication?
Beve?	*be*·ve	Do you drink?
Fuma?	*foo*·ma	Do you smoke?
Si droga?	see *dro*·ga	Do you take drugs?

I have an infection.	Ho un'infezione.	o oon een·fe·*tsyo*·ne
I have a rash.	Ho uno sfogo.	o *oo*·no *sfo*·go
I feel weak.	Mi sento debole.	mee *sen*·to *de*·bo·le
I feel ...	Ho ...	o ...

dizzy	il capogiro	eel ka·po·*gee*·ro
hot and cold	vampate di calore	vam·*pa*·te dee ka·*lo*·re
nauseous	la nausea	la *now*·ze·a
shivery	i brividi	ee *bree*·vee·dee

I have a ...	Ho ...	o ...

cold	un raffreddore	oon ra·fre·*do*·re
fever	la febbre	la *fe*·bre
headache	mal di testa	mal dee *tes*·ta
heart condition	un problema cardiaco	oon pro·*ble*·ma kar·*dee*·a·ko
migraine	un'emicrania	oo·ne·mee·*kra*·nya

I'm asthmatic.	Sono asmatico/a. m/f *so*·no az·*ma*·tee·ko/a
I'm diabetic.	Sono diabetico/a. m/f *so*·no dee·a·*be*·tee·ko/a
I'm epileptic.	Sono epilettico/a. m/f *so*·no e·pee·*le*·tee·ko/a
I've (recently) had ...	Ho avuto ... (di recente). o a·*voo*·to ... (dee re·*chen*·te)

I'm on medication for ...	Prendo la medicina per ... *pren·do la me·dee·chee·na per ..*
I've noticed a lump/ swelling here	Ho notato un nodulo/gonfiore qui. *o no·ta·to oon no·doo·lo/ gon·fyo·re kwee*

For more symptoms and conditions, see the **dictionary**.

Women's Health

I'm pregnant.	Sono incinta. *so·no een·cheen·ta*
I need a pregnancy test.	Ho bisogno di un test di gravidanza. *o bee·zo·nyo dee oon test dee gra·vee·dan·tsa*

🔊 LISTEN FOR

Prende contraccettivi?	*pren·de kon·tra·che·tee·vee*	Are you using contraception?
Ha avuto rapporti non protetti?	*a a·voo·to ra·por·tee non pro·te·tee*	Have you had unprotected sex?
Ha le mestruazioni?	*a le mes·troo·a·tsyo·nee*	Are you menstruating?
È incinta?	*e een·cheen·ta*	Are you pregnant?
Quand'è l'ultima volta che Le sono venute le mestruazioni?	*kwan·de lool·tee·ma vol·ta ke le so·no ve·noo·te le mes·troo·a·tsyo·nee*	When did you last have your period?
È incinta.	*e een·cheen·ta*	You're pregnant.

I'm on the Pill.	Prendo la pillola *pren*·do la *pee*·lo·la.
I have period pain.	Ho dolori mestruali. o do·*lo*·ree mes·*trwa*·lee
I haven't had my period for (two) weeks.	Sono (due) settimane che non mi vengono le mestruazioni. *so*·no (*doo*·e) se·tee·*ma*·ne ke non mee *ven*·go·no le mes·troo·a·*tsyo*·nee
I need contraception.	Ho bisogno di contraccettivi. o bee·*zo*·nyo dee kon·tra·che·*tee*·vee
I need the morning-after pill.	Ho bisogno della pillola del mattino dopo. o bee·*zo*·nyo *de*·la *pee*·lo·la del ma·*tee*·no *do*·po

Allergies

I have a skin allergy.	Ho un'allergia alla pelle. o oo·na·ler·*jee*·a *a*·la *pe*·le
I'm allergic to ...	Sono allergico/a ... **m/f** *so*·no a·*ler*·jee·ko/a ...

antibiotics	agli antibiotici	*a*·lyee an·tee·bee·o·*tee*·chee
anti-inflam matories	agli antinfiammatori	*a*·lyee an·teen·fya·ma·*to*·ree
bees	alle api	*a*·le *a*·pee
sulphur-based drugs	agli medicinali a base di zolfo	*a*·lyee me·dee·chee·*na*·lee a *ba*·ze dee *dzol*·fo

For food-related allergies, see **vegetarian & special meals** (p181).

Parts of the Body

My (stomach) hurts.	Mi fa male (lo stomaco). mee fa *ma*·le (lo *sto*·ma·ko)
I can't move (my ankle).	Non riesco a muovere (la caviglia). non *ryes*·ko a *mwo*·ve·re (la ka·*vee*·lya)
I have a cramp (in my foot).	Ho crampi (al piede). o *kram*·pee (al *pye*·de)
(My throat) is swollen.	(La gola) è gonfia. (la *go*·la) e *gon*·fya

Chemist

I need something for (diarrhoea).	Ho bisogno di qualcosa per (la diarrea). o bee·*zo*·nyo dee kwal·*ko*·za per (la dee·a·*re*·a)
Do I need a prescription for (antihistamines)?	C'è bisogno di una ricetta per (gli antistaminici)? che bee·*zo*·nyo dee *oo*·na re·*che*·ta per (lyee an·tee·sta·*mee*·nee·chee)

 LISTEN FOR

Questo l'ha mai preso?	*kwe*·sto la mai *pre*·so	Have you taken this before?
Deve completare il ciclo.	*de*·ve kom·ple·*ta*·re eel *cheek*·lo	You must complete the course.
Due volte al giorno (con i pasti).	*doo*·e *vol*·te al *jor*·no (kon ee *pas*·tee)	Twice a day (with food).

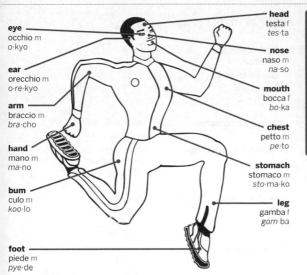

eye
occhio m
o·kyo

ear
orecchio m
o·re·kyo

arm
braccio m
bra·cho

hand
mano m
ma·no

bum
culo m
koo·lo

foot
piede m
pye·de

head
testa f
tes·ta

nose
naso m
na·so

mouth
bocca f
bo·ka

chest
petto m
pe·to

stomach
stomaco m
sto·ma·ko

leg
gamba f
gam·ba

SAFE TRAVEL   HEALTH

| **How many times a day?** | Quante volte al giorno?
kwan·te vol·te al jor·no |
| **Will it make me drowsy?** | Mi farà dormire?
mee fa·ra dor·mee·re |

For pharmaceutical items, see the **dictionary**.

Dentist

| **I have a broken tooth.** | Ho un dente rotto.
o oon den·te ro·to |
| **I have a cavity.** | Ho una cavità.
o oo·na ka·vee·ta |

🔊 LISTEN FOR

Apra bene la bocca.	*a*·pra *be*·ne la *bo*·ka	Open wide.
Morda questo.	*mor*·da *kwe*·sto	Bite down on this.
Sciacqui!	*sha*·kwee	Rinse!

I have a toothache.	Ho mal di denti. o mal dee *den*·tee
I need an anaesthetic.	Ho bisogno di un anestetico. o bee·*zo*·nyo dee oo·na·nes·*te*·tee·ko
I need a filling.	Ho bisogno di un'otturazione. o bee·*zo*·nyo dee oo·no·too·ra·*tsyo*·ne
I need a crown.	Ho bisogno di una corona. o bee·*zo*·nyo dee oo·na ko·*ro*·na
I've lost a filling.	Ho perso un'otturazione. o *per*·so oo·no·too·ra·*tsyo*·ne
My dentures are broken.	La mia dentiera è rotta. la *mee*·a den·*tye*·ra e *ro*·ta
My gums hurt.	Mi fanno male le gengive. mee *fa*·no *ma*·le le jen·*jee*·ve
My orthodontic braces broke.	Mi si è rotto l'apparecchio. mee see e *ro*·to la·pa·*re*·kyo
My orthodontic braces fell off.	Mi è caduto l'apparecchio. mee e ka·*doo*·to la·pa·*re*·kyo
I don't want it extracted.	Non voglio che mi venga tolto. non *vo*·lyo ke mee *ven*·ga *tol*·to

Food

Eating Out

KEY PHRASES

Can you recommend a restaurant?	Potrebbe consigliare un ristorante?	po·*tre*·be kon·see·*lya*·re oon rees·to·*ran*·te
A table for two people, please.	Un tavolo per due persone, per favore.	oon *ta*·vo·lo per *doo*·e per·*so*·ne per fa·*vo*·re
Can I see the menu, please?	Vorrei il menù, per favore.	vo·*ray* eel me·*noo* per fa·*vo*·re
I'd like a beer, please.	Vorrei una birra, per favore.	vo·*ray* oo·na *bee*·ra per fa·*vo*·re
Please bring the bill.	Mi porta il conto, per favore?	mee *por*·ta eel *kon*·to per fa·*vo*·re

Basics

breakfast	prima colazione f *pree*·ma ko·la·*tsyo*·ne
lunch	pranzo m *pran*·dzo
dinner	cena f *che*·na
afternoon snack	merenda f me·*ren*·da
snack	spuntino m spoon·*tee*·no

CULTURE TIP **Eateries**

bar/caffè m bar/ka·*fe* – serves drinks and offers light meals, eg bread rolls and snacks

osteria/trattoria f os·te·*ree*·a/tra·to·*ree*·a – provides simple food and some local specialities

paninoteca f pa·nee·no·*te*·ka – serves delicious sandwiches made with cheese and cold meats

pizzeria f pee·tse·*ree*·a – specialises in pizza and *calzoni* kal·*tso*·nee (a folded pizza dish), usually prepared in a wood-fired oven

ristorante m ree·sto·*ran*·te – a more sophisticated eatery, with a higher standard of service, a more expensive menu and a decent wine list

tavola f **calda** *ta*·vo·la *kal*·da – a buffet offering local specialities, pizza, roasted meats and salads

FOOD EATING OUT

set menu	menu m turistico me·*noo* too·*ree*·stee·ko
daily special	piatto m del giorno *nya*·to del *jor*·no
eat	mangiare man·*ja*·re
drink	bere *be*·re
Enjoy the meal!	Buon appetito! bwon a·pe·*tee*·to

Finding a Place to Eat

Can you recommend a cafe?	Potrebbe consigliare un bar? po·*tre*·be kon·see·*lya*·re oon bar

Can you recommend a restaurant?	Potrebbe consigliare un ristorante?
	po·*tre*·be kon·see·*lya*·re oon rees·to·*ran*·te

Where would you go for (a) ...?	Dove andrebbe per ...?
	do·ve an·*dre*·be per ...

business lunch	un pranzo d'affari	oon *pran*·dzo da·*fa*·ree
celebration	una celebrazione	*oo*·na che·le·bra·*tsyo*·ne
cheap meal	un pasto economico	oon *pas*·to e·ko·*no*·mee·ko
local specialities	le specialità locali	le spe·cha·lee·*ta* lo·*ka*·lee

I'd like to reserve a table for (eight) o'clock.	Vorrei prenotare un tavolo per le (otto).
	vo·*ray* pre·no·*ta*·re oon *ta*·vo·lo per le (*o*·to)

I'd like to reserve a table for (two) people.	Vorrei prenotare un tavolo per (due) persone.
	vo·*ray* pre·no·*ta*·re oon *ta*·vo·lo per (*doo*·e) per·*so*·ne

✂ **For two, please.**	Per due, per favore.	per *doo*·e per fa·*vo*·re

Are you still serving food?	Servite ancora da mangiare?
	ser·*vee*·te an·*ko*·ra da man·*ja*·re

How long is the wait?	Quanto si deve aspettare?
	kwan·to see *de*·ve as·pe·*ta*·re

◀)) **LISTEN FOR**

È al completo.	e al kom·*ple*·to	We're fully booked.
Non abbiamo tavoli.	non a·*bya*·mo *ta*·vo·lee	We have no tables.
Siamo chiusi.	*sya*·mo *kyoo*·zee	We're closed.

FOOD EATING OUT

At the Restaurant

I'd like ..., please.	Vorrei ..., per favore.	vo·*ray* ... per fa·*vo*·re
a table for (four)	un tavolo per (quattro)	oon *ta*·vo·lo per (*kwa*·tro)
the drink list	la lista delle bevande	la *lee*·sta *de*·le be·*van*·de
the menu	il menù	eel me·*noo*

✂	**Menu, please.**	Il menù, per favore.	eel me·*noo* per fa·*vo*·re

Do you have a menu in English?	Avete un menù in inglese? a·*ve*·te oon me·*noo* een een·*gle*·ze
Do you have children's meals?	Avete pasti per bambini? a·*ve*·te *pas*·tee per bam·*bee*·nee

We're just having drinks.	Prendiamo solo da bere.	
	pren·*dya*·mo *so*·lo da *be*·re	

| ✂ **Just drinks.** | Solo da bere, grazie. | *so*·lo da *be*·re *gra*·tsye |

What would you recommend?	Cosa mi consiglia?
	ko·za mee kon·*see*·lya

I'll have what they're having.	Vorrei quello che stanno mangiando loro.
	vo·*ray* kwe·lo ke *sta*·no man·*jan*·do *lo*·ro

I'd like a local speciality.	Vorrei una specialità di questa regione.
	vo·*ray* oo·na spe·cha·lee·*ta* dee *kwe*·sta re·*jo*·ne

What's in that dish?	Quali ingredienti ci sono in questo piatto?
	kwa·li een·gre·*dyen*·tee chee *so*·no een *kwe*·sto *pya*·to

Does it take long to prepare?	Ci vuole molto per prepararlo?
	chee *vwo*·le *mol*·to per pre·pa·*rar*·lo

🔊 LISTEN FOR

Dove vuole sedersi?	*do*·ve *vwo*·le se·*der*·see	Where would you like to sit?
Cosa Le porto?	*ko*·za le *por*·to	What can I get for you?
Come la vuole cotta?	*ko*·me la *vwo*·le *ko*·ta	How would you like that cooked?
Ecco!	*e*·ko	Here you go!

Eating Out

Can I see the menu, please?

Posso vedere il menù, per favore?
po·so ve·de·re eel me·noo per fa·vo·re

What would you recommend for ...?

Cosa mi consiglia ...?
ko·za mee kon·see·lya ...

the main course
per il secondo piatto
per eel se·kon·do pya·to

dessert
per dolci
per dol·chee

drinks
da bere
da be·re

Can you bring me some ..., please?

Mi porta ..., per favore?
mee por·ta ... per fa·vo·re

I'd like the bill, please.

Vorrei il conto, per favore.
vo·ray eel kon·to per fa·vo·re

FOOD EATING OUT

Requests

Please bring a glass.	Mi porta un bicchiere, per favore?	mee *por*·ta oon bee·*kye*·re per fa·*vo*·re
Is there (any Parmesan cheese)?	C'è (del parmigiano)?	che (del par·mee·*ja*·no)
I'd like it ...	Lo/La vorrei ... m/f	lo/la vo·*ray* ...
I don't want it ...	Non lo/la voglio ... m/f	non lo/la *vo*·lyo ...

boiled	bollito/a m/f	bo·*lee*·to/a
broiled	cotto/a m/f a fuoco vivo	*ko*·to/a a *fwo*·ko *vee*·vo
deep-fried	fritto/a m/f in abbondante olio	*free*·to/a een a·bon·*dan*·te o·lyo
fried	fritto/a m/f	*free*·to/a
grilled	(cotto/a) m/f ai ferri	(*ko*·to/a) ai *fe*·ree
medium	non troppo cotto/a m/f	non *tro*·po *ko*·to/a
rare	al sangue	al *san*·gwe
re-heated	riscaldato/a m/f	rees·kal·*da*·to/a
steamed	cotto/a m/f a vapore	*ko*·to/a a va·*po*·re
well-done	ben cotto/a m/f	ben *ko*·to/a
with the dressing on the side	con il condimento a parte	kon eel kon·dee·*men*·to a *par*·te

For other specific meal requests, see **vegetarian & special meals** (p181).

LOOK FOR

Antipasti	an·tee·*pas*·tee	Appetisers
Zuppe	*tsoo*·pe	Soups
Primi (Piatti)	*pree*·mee (*pya*·tee)	Entrees
Insalate	een·sa·*la*·te	Salads
Contorni	kon·*tor*·nee	Side Dishes
Pasti Leggeri	*pas*·tee le·*je*·ree	Light Meals
Secondi (Piatti)	se·*kon*·dee (*pya*·tee)	Main Courses
Dolci	*dol*·chee	Desserts
Bevande	be·*van*·de	Drinks
Aperitivi	a·pe·ree·*tee*·vee	Aperitifs
Bibite	*bee*·bee·te	Soft Drinks
Liquori	lee·*kwo*·ree	Spirits
Birre	*bee*·re	Beers
Vini della Casa	*vee*·nee *de*·la *ka*·za	House Wines
Vini Locali	*vee*·nee lo·*ka*·lee	Local Wines
Vini Frizzanti	*vee*·nee free·*tsan*·tee	Sparkling Wines
Vini Bianchi	*vee*·nee *byan*·kee	White Wines
Vini Rossi	*vee*·nee ro·see	Red Wines
Vini Rosati	*vee*·nee ro·*za*·tee	Roses
Vini da Dessert	*vee*·nee da de·*sert*	Dessert Wines
Digestivi	dee·jes·*tee*·vee	Digestifs

For more words you might see on a menu, see the **menu decoder** (p184), and the **dictionary**.

FOOD EATING OUT

FOOD EATING OUT

Donne	*do*·ne	Women
Gabinetti	ga·bee·*ne*·tee	Toilets
Prenotato	pre·no·*ta*·to	Booked
Riservato	ree·ser·*va*·to	Reserved
Uomini	*wo*·mee·nee	Men

Compliments & Complaints

I didn't order this.	Questo non l'ho ordinato. *kwe*·sto non lo or·dee·*na*·to
That was delicious!	Era squisito! *e*·ra skwee·*zee*·to
My compliments to the chef.	Complimenti al cuoco! kom·plee·*men*·tee al *kwo*·ko
I'm full.	Sono sazio/a. **m/f** *so*·no *sa*·tsyo/a
I love this dish.	Vado matto/a per questo piatto. **m/f** *va*·do *ma*·to/a per *kwe*·sto *pya*·to
I love the local cuisine.	Vado matto/a per la cucina locale. **m/f** *va*·do *ma*·to/a per la koo·*chee*·na lo·*ka*·le
This is ...	Questo/a è ... **m/f** *kwe*·sto/a e ...

cold	freddo/a **m/f**	*fre*·do/a
(too) hot	(troppo) caldo/a **m/f**	(*tro*·po) *kal*·do/a
spicy	piccante	pee·*kan*·te
superb	delizioso/a **m/f**	de·lee·*tsyo*·zo/a

Paying the Bill

Is the cover charge included in the bill?	Il coperto è compreso nel conto? eel ko·*per*·to e kom·*pre*·zo nel *kon*·to
Is the service included in the bill?	Il servizio è compreso nel conto? eel ser·*vee*·tsyo e kom·*pre*·zo nel *kon*·to
Please bring the bill.	Mi porta il conto, per favore? mee *por*·ta eel *kon*·to per fa·*vo*·re

✂ | **Bill, please.** | Il conto, per favore. | eel *kon*·to per fa·*vo*·re

There's a mistake in the bill.	C'è un errore nel conto. che oo·ne·*ro*·re nel *kon*·to

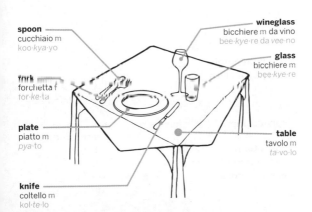

spoon
cucchiaio m
koo·*kya*·yo

wineglass
bicchiere m da vino
bee·*kye*·re da *vee*·no

glass
bicchiere m
bee·*kye*·re

fork
forchetta f
tor·*ke*·la

plate
piatto m
pya·to

table
tavolo m
ta·vo·lo

knife
coltello m
kol·*te*·lo

FOOD EATING OUT

FOOD EATING OUT

 LOOK FOR

Pasta comes in all shapes and sizes from the standard *spaghetti* spa·*ge*·tee to potato *gnocchi* nyo·kee and bow-shaped *farfalle* far·*fa*·le. Note that *alla/al* a·la/al means 'in the style of'.

aglio e olio	*a*·lyo e o·lyo	oil, garlic and sometimes chilli
al ragù	al ra·*goo*	meat, vegetables, lemon peel and nutmeg
all'amatriciana	a·la·ma·tree·*cha*·na	pig's cheek, lard, white wine, tomato, chilli and sheep's cheese
alla carbonara	a·la kar·bo·*na*·ra	bacon, butter, eggs and sheep's cheese
alla partenopea	a·la par·te·no·*pe*·a	mozzarella, olives, tomato, bread crust, capers, anchovies, basil, oil, chilli and salt
alla pescatora	a·la pes·ka·*to*·ra	fish, tomato and sweet herbs
alla pommarola	a·la po·ma·*ro*·la	tomato
alla puttanesca	a·la poo·ta·*nes*·ka	garlic, anchovies, black olives, capers, tomato, oil and chilli
cacio e pepe	*ka*·cho e *pe*·pe	black pepper and sheep's cheese
con il tonno	kon eel *to*·no	with tuna
con le vongole	kon le *von*·go·le	with clams
con tartufo di Norcia	kon tar·*too*·fo dee *nor*·cha	with Norcia truffles

Nonalcoholic Drinks

almond milk	orzata f or·*dza*·ta
bitter cola	chinotto m kee·*no*·to
fruit juice (bottled)	succo m di frutta *soo*·ko dee *froo*·ta
fruit juice (fresh)	spremuta f spre·*moo*·ta
lemonade	limonata f lee·mo·*na*·ta
orangeade	aranciata f a·ran·*cha*·ta
soft drink	bibita f *bee*·bee·ta
(cup of) tea/coffee	(un) tè/caffè (oon) te/ka·*fe*
with milk	con latte kon *la*·te
without sugar	senza zucchero *sen*·tsa *tsoo*·ke·ro
... water	acqua ... *a*·kwa ...

boiled	bollita	bo·*lee*·ta
mineral	minerale	mee·ne·*ra*·le
sparkling	frizzante	free·*tsan*·te
still	naturale	na·too·*ra*·le

🔍 LOOK FOR

Italians often drink their coffee standing up at the bar. Simply ask for a *caffè* ka·*fe* and you'll get an *espresso* es·*pre*·so, but don't order a *latte la*·te unless you want a glass of milk. Make sure you don't ask for coffee with milk in the afternoon.

caffè m **alla valdostana**	ka·*fe a*·la val·dos·*ta*·na	with grappa, lemon peel and spices
caffè m **americano**	ka·*fe* a·me·ree·*ka*·no	long and black
caffè m **corretto**	ka·*fe* ko·*re*·to	with a dash of liqueur
caffè m **doppio**	ka·*fe do*·pyo	long, strong and black
caffè m **macchiato**	ka·*fe* ma·*kya*·to	strong coffee with a drop of milk
caffè m **ristretto**	ka·*fe* ree·*stre*·to	superstrong black coffee
caffellatte m	ka·fe·*la*·te	coffee with milk
cappuccino m	ka·poo·*chee*·no	coffee with milk, served with a lot of froth and sprinkled with cocoa
espresso m	es·*pre*·so	short black coffee
ristretto m	ree·*stre*·to	very short black coffee

Alcoholic Drinks

draught beer	birra f a la spina *bee*·ra a la *spee*·na
a shot of ...	un sorso di ... oon *sor*·so dee ...

a bottle of ... wine	una bottiglia di vino ... *oo*·na bo·*tee*·lya dee *vee*·no ...

a glass of ... wine	un bicchiere di vino ... oon bee·*kye*·re dee *vee*·no ...

dessert	da dessert	da de·*sert*
red	rosso	*ro*·so
rose	rosato	ro·*za*·to
sparkling	spumante	spoo·*man*·te
white	bianco	*byan*·ko

a ... of beer	... di birra ... dee *bee*·ra

bottle	una bottiglia	*oo*·na bo·*tee*·lya
glass	un bicchiere	oon bee·*kye*·re
jug	una caraffa	*oo*·na ka·*ra*·fa
pint	una pinta	*oo*·na *peen*·ta

In the Bar

I'll have (a glass of red wine).	Prendo (un bicchiere di vino rosso). *pren*·do (oon bee·*kye*·re dee *vee*·no *ro*·so)
I'd like a beer, please.	Vorrei una birra, per favore. vo·*ray oo*·na *bee*·ra per fa·*vo*·re
Same again, please.	Un altro, per favore. oon *al*·tro per fa·*vo*·re
No ice, thanks.	Senza ghiaccio, grazie. *sen*·tsa *gya*·cho *gra*·tsye
Straight, please.	Liscio, per favore. *lee*·sho per fa·*vo*·re

LANGUAGE TIP

Tongue Twisters
The sing-song music of the Italian language lends itself beautifully to tongue twisters or *scioglilingue* sho·lyee·*leen*·gwe. Try to impress Italian acquaintances by casually slipping out one of these:

O schiavo con lo schiaccianoci che cosa schiacci? Schiaccio sei noci del vecchio noce con lo schiaccianoci.

o *skya*·vo kon lo skya·cha·*no*·chee ke *ko*·za *skya*·chee *skya*·cho say *no*·chee del *ve*·kyo *no*·che kon lo skya·cha·*no*·chee

Oh, slave with the nutcracker what are you cracking? I am cracking six nuts from the old walnut tree with the nutcracker.

Orrore, orrore, un ramarro verde su un muro marrone!

o·*ro*·re o·*ro*·re oon ra·*ma*·ro *ver*·de soo oon *moo*·ro ma·*ro*·ne

Horror, horror, a green lizard on a brown wall!

Trentatre Trentini entrarono a Trento, tutti e trentatre trotterelando.

tren·ta·*tre* tren·*tee*·nee en·*tra*·ro·na a *tren*·to *too*·tee e tren·ta·*tre* tro·te·re·*lan*·do

Thirty-three Trentonians came into Trento, all thirty-three trotting.

I'll buy you a drink.	Ti offro da bere. tee *of*·ro da *be*·re
What would you like?	Cosa prendi? *ko*·za *pren*·dee
It's my round.	Offro io. *of*·ro *ee*·o

You can get the next one.	La prossima la paghi tu. la *pro*·see·ma la *pa*·gee too
How much alcohol does this contain?	Quanto alcool contiene? *kwan*·to *al*·kol kon·*tye*·ne
Do you serve meals here?	Servite da mangiare qui? ser·*vee*·te da man·*ja*·re kwee

Drinking Up

Cheers!	Salute! sa·*loo*·te
Thanks, but I don't feel like it.	Grazie, ma non mi va. *gra*·tsye ma non mee va
No thanks, I'm driving.	No, grazie, devo guidare. no *gra*·tsye *de*·vo gwee·*da*·re
I don't drink alcohol.	Non bevo non *be*·vo
This is hitting the spot.	Ci voleva proprio! chee vo·*le*·va *pro*·pryo
I'm feeling drunk.	Mi sento un po' ubriaco/a. m/f mee *sen*·to oon po oo·*bree*·a·ko/a
I think I've had one too many.	Penso d'aver bevuto troppo. *pen*·so da·*ver* be·*voo*·to *tro*·po
Can you call a taxi for me?	Mi puoi chiamare un tassì? mee pwoy kya·*ma*·re oon ta·*see*
I don't think you should drive.	È meglio che non guidi. e *me*·lyo ke non *gwee*·dee

Self-Catering

KEY PHRASES

What's the local speciality?	Qual'è la specialità di questa regione?	kwa·*le* la spe·cha·lee·*ta* dee *kwe*·sta re·*jo*·ne
Where can I find the ... section?	Dove posso trovare il reparto ...?	*do*·ve *po*·so tro·*va*·re eel re·*par*·to ...
I'd like ...	Vorrei ...	vo·*ray* ...

Buying Food

What's the local speciality?	Qual'è la specialità di questa regione? kwa·*le* la spe·cha·lee·*ta* dee *kwe*·sta re·*jo*·ne
Can I taste it?	Lo/La posso assaggiare? **m/f** lo/la *po*·so a·sa·*ja*·re

 LISTEN FOR

Cosa desidera?	*ko*·za de·*see*·de·ra	What would you like?
E poi?	e poy	Anything else?
È (una gorgonzola).	e (*oo*·na gor·gon·*dzo*·la)	That's (a gorgonzola).
Non ne ho.	non ne ho	I don't have any.
Sono (cinque euro).	*so*·no (*cheen*·kwe e·*oo*·ro)	That's (five euros).

How much is (a kilo of cheese)?	Quanto costa (un chilo di formaggio)? *kwan·*to *kos·*ta (oon *kee·*lo dee for·*ma·*jo)
Do you have anything cheaper?	Avete qualcosa di meno costoso? a·*ve·*te kwal·*ko·*za dee *me·*no kos·*to·*zo
Do you have other kinds?	Avete altri tipi? a·*ve·*te *al·*tree *tee·*pee
Can I have a bag, please?	Posso avere un sacchetto, per favore? *po·*so a·*ve·*re oon sa·*ke·*to per fa·*vo·*re
I'd like ...	Vorrei ... vo·*ray* ...

100 grams	un etto	*oo·*ne·to
200 grams	due etti	*doo·*e e·tee
a kilo	un chilo	oon *kee·*lo
(two) kilos	(due) chili	(*doo·*e) *kee·*lee
a bottle	una bottiglia	*oo·*na bo·*tee·*lya
a dozen	una dozzina	*oo·*na do·*dzee·*na
a jar	un barattolo	oon ba·*ra·*to·lo
a packet	un sacchetto	oon sa·*ke·*to
a piece	un pezzo	oon *pe·*tso
(three) pieces	(tre) pezzi	(tre) *pe·*tsee
a slice	una fetta	*oo·*na *fe·*ta
(six) slices	(sei) fette	(say) *fe·*te
a tin	una scatola	*oo·*na *ska·*to·la
some ...	alcuni/e ... m/f	al·*koo·*nee/ al·*koo·*ne ...
that one	quello/a m/f	*kwe·*lo/a
this one	questo/a m/f	*kwe·*sto/a

FOOD SELF-CATERING

FOOD | **SELF-CATERING**

 **LOOK FOR**

alimentari m	a·lee·men·*ta*·ree	grocery store
caseificio m	ka·ze·ee·*fee*·cho	creamery
enoteca f	e·no·*te*·ka	wine shop
formaggeria f	for·ma·je·*ree*·a	cheese shop (also sells other dairy products)
macelleria f	ma·che·le·*ree*·a	butcher
mercato m	mer·*ka*·to	market
pasticceria f	pas·tee·che·*ree*·a	cake shop
pastificio m	pas·tee·*fee*·cho	specialist pasta shop
pescheria f	pes·ke·*ree*·a	fish shop
polleria f	po·le·*ree*·a	poultry shop
salumeria f	sa·loo·me·*ree*·a	delicatessen
tabacchi m	ta·*ba*·kee	tobacconist
torrefazione f	to·re·fa·*tsyo*·ne	coffee roasting house

Enough.	Basta, grazie. *bas*·ta *gra*·tsye
A bit more.	Un po' di più. oon po dee pyoo
Less.	(Di) Meno. (dee) *me*·no

For food items, see the **menu decoder** (p184), and the **dictionary**.

| **Where can I find the ... section?** | Dove posso trovare il reparto ...? |
| | do·ve po·so tro·va·re eel re·par·to ... |

dairy	dei latticini	day la·tee·*chee*·nee
frozen goods	dei surgelati	day soor·je·*la*·tee
fruit and vegetable	della frutta e verdura	*de*·la *froo*·ta e ver·*doo*·ra
health-food	dei cibi macrobiotici	day *chee*·bee ma·kro·bee·o·tee·chee
meat	della carne	*de*·la *kar*·ne
poultry	del pollame	del po·*la*·me

Lo/La posso assaggiare? m/f
lo/la *po*·so a·sa·*ja*·re
Can I taste it?

Cooking

Could I please borrow (a corkscrew)?	Posso prendere in prestito (un cavatappi), per favore? *po·so pren·de·re een pres·tee·to (oon ka·va·ta·pee) per fa·vo·re*
Where's (a saucepan)?	Dov'è (un tegame)? *do·ve (oon te·ga·me)*
cooked	cotto/a m/f *ko·to/a*
dried	secco/a m/f *se·ko/a*
fresh	fresco/a m/f *fres·ko/a*
frozen	congelato/a m/f *kon·je·la·to/a*
raw	crudo/a m/f *kroo·do/a*
smoked	affumicato/a m/f *a·foo·mee·ka·to/a*

For more cooking implements, see the **dictionary**.

Vegetarian & Special Meals

KEY PHRASES

Do you have vegetarian food?	Avete piatti vegetariani?	a·ve·te pya·tee ve·je·ta·rya·nee
Could you prepare a meal without ...?	Potreste preparare un pasto senza ...?	po·tres·te pre·pa·ra·re oon pas·to sen·tsa ...
I'm allergic to ...	Sono allergico/a a ... m/f	so·no a·ler·jee·ko/a a ...

Special Diets & Allergies

Is there a vegetarian restaurant near here?	C'è un ristorante vegetariano qui vicino? che oon rees·to·ran·te ve·je·ta·rya·no kwe vee·chee·no
Is there a halal restaurant near here?	C'è un ristorante halal qui vicino? che oon rees·to·ran·te a·lal kwee vee·chee·no
Is there a kosher restaurant near here?	C'è un ristorante kasher qui vicino? che oon rees·to·ran·te ka·sher kwee vee·chee·no
I'm vegan.	Sono vegetaliano/a. m/f so·no ve·je·ta·lya·no/a

I'm on a special diet.	Seguo una dieta speciale.
	se·gwo oo·na dye·ta spe·cha·le

I don't eat (fish).	Non mangio (pesce).
	non man·jo (pe·she)

I'm allergic to ...	Sono allergico/a ... m/f
	so·no a·ler·jee·ko/a ...

dairy produce	ai latticini	ai la·tee·chee·nee
eggs	alle uova	a·le wo·va
fish	al pesce	al pe·she
gelatin	alla gelatina	a·la je·la·tee·na
gluten	al glutine	al gloo·tee·ne
honey	al miele	al mye·le
nuts	alle noci	a·le no·chee
peanuts	alle arachidi	a·le a·ra·kee·dee
seafood	ai frutti di mare	ai froo·tee dee ma·re
shellfish	ai crostacei	ai kros·ta·che·ee

Ordering Food

Do you have (vegetarian) food?	Avete piatti (vegetariani)?
	a·ve·te pya·tee (ve·je·ta·rya·nee)

 LISTEN FOR

Controllo con il cuoco.	kon·tro·lo kon eel kwo·ko	I'll check with the cook.
Può mangiare ...?	pwo man·ja·re ...	Can you eat ...?
Tutto contiene (la carne).	too·to kon·tye·ne (la kar·ne)	It all has (meat) in it.

Is it cooked with (oil)?	È cotto con (olio)?
	e ko·to kon (o·lyo)

Is this ...?	È ...?
	e ...

cholesterol-free	senza colesterolo	sen·tsa ko·le·ste·ro·lo
decaffeinated	decaffeinato/a m/f	de·ka·fey·na·to/a
free of animal produce	senza prodotti animali	sen·tsa pro·do·tee a·nee·ma·lee
free-range	ruspante	roos·pan·te
genetically modified	geneticamente modificato/a m/f	je·ne·tee·ka·men·te mo·dee·fee·ka·to/a
gluten-free	senza glutine	sen·tsa gloo·tee·ne
organic	biologico/a m/f	bee·o·lo·jee·ko/a
salt-free	senza sale	sen·tsa sa·le

Could you prepare a meal without ...?	Potreste preparare un pasto senza ...?
	po·tres·te pre·pa·ra·re oon pas·to sen·tsa ...

butter	burro	boo·ro
eggs	uova	wo·va
meat/fish stock	brodo di carne/pesce	bro·do dee kar·ne/pe·she
poultry	pollame	po·la·me
red meat	carne rossa	kar·ne ro·sa

A

Menu
~ DECODER ~
Il Lessico Culinario

This miniguide to Italian cuisine is designed to help you navigate menus. Italian nouns, and adjectives affected by gender, have their gender indicated by ⓜ and/or ⓕ. If it's a plural noun, you'll also see pl.

MENU DECODER

~ A ~

abbacchio ⓜ a·*ba*·kyo young lamb
— alla cacciatora a·la ka·cha·*to*·ra lamb casserole with spices, white wine & anchovies
— a scottadito a·sko·ta·*dee*·to lamb cutlets fried in oil
acciughe ⓕ pl a·*choo*·ge anchovies (often preserved in salt)
aceto ⓜ a·*che*·to vinegar
acqua ⓕ *a*·kwa water
— bollita bo·*lee*·ta boiled water
— calda *kal*·da hot water
— del rubinetto del roo·bee·*ne*·to tap water
— minerale mee·ne·*ra*·le mineral water
— non gassata non ga·*sa*·ta still water
acquacotta ⓕ a·kwa·*ko*·ta soup prepared with tomato, peppers, celery, eggs, artichokes or mushrooms
acquapazza ⓕ a·kwa·*pa*·tsa 'crazy water' – a type of fish soup
aglio ⓜ *a*·lyo garlic
— e olio e o·lyo garlic & olive oil pasta sauce

agnello ⓜ a·*nye*·lo lamb
— ai funghi ai *foon*·gee with mushrooms
— al forno al *for*·no with garlic & sometimes potatoes
— da latte da *la*·te very young milk-fed lamb
agnolini ⓜ pl a·nyo·*lee*·nee round pasta stuffed with stewed beef, eggs, cheese & other ingredients
agnolotti ⓜ pl **ripieni** a·nyo·*lo*·tee ree·*pye*·nee pasta stuffed with meat, herbs, eggs & parmesan
agro, all' *ag*·ro, al with oil & lemon dressing
albicocca ⓕ al·bee·*ko*·ka apricot
alborella ⓕ al·bo·*re*·la common freshwater fish
alici ⓕ pl a·*lee*·chee anchovies
— a crudo a *kroo*·do raw, marinated in oil & spices
al dente al *den*·te 'to the tooth' – describes cooked pasta & rice that are still slightly hard
all'/alla ... al/*a*·la ... in the style of ...
alloro ⓜ a·*lo*·ro bay leaf
al sangue al *san*·gwe rare (cooked)
amaretti ⓜ pl a·ma·*re*·tee almond biscuits (macaroons)

amatriciana a·ma·tree·*cha*·na spicy sauce with salami, tomato, capsicums & cheese

ananas ⓜ *a*·na·nas pineapple

anatra ⓕ *a*·na·tra duck

— al sale al *sa*·le roast duck cooked in a crust of salt

angiulottus ⓜ an·joo·*lo*·toos stuffed square pasta served with meat sauce or tomato sauce

anguilla ⓕ an·*gwee*·la eel

anice ⓜ *a*·nee·che aniseed

annoglia ⓕ a·*no*·lya dry-cured pork sausage with chilli

anolini ⓜ pl a·no·*lee*·nee stuffed round pasta with braised beef, cheese, parmesan, egg & breadcrumbs

aragosta ⓕ a·ra·*go*·sta lobster • crayfish

arancia ⓕ a·*ran*·cha orange

arancia, all' a·*ran*·cha, al sprinkled or baked with orange juice

arancini ⓜ pl a·ran·*chee*·nee riceballs stuffed with a meat mixture

aranzada ⓕ a·ran·*tsa*·da almond nougat

arborio ⓜ ar·*bo*·ryo short-grain rice used for risotto

aringa ⓕ a·*reen*·ga herring

arista ⓕ a·*ree*·sta loin (generally pork)

— alla fiorentina a·la fyo·ren·*tee*·na baked with spices

aromi ⓜ pl a·*ro*·mee herbs

arrabbiata, all' a·ra·*bya*·ta, al 'angry-style' – with spicy sauce

arrosticini ⓜ a·ros·tee·*chee*·nee skewered & roasted meat (often lamb)

arrosto/a ⓜ/ⓕ a·*ro*·sto/a roasted

— alla griglia a·la *gree*·lya barbecued

artigianale ar·tee·ja·*na*·le home-made

asiago ⓜ a·*zya*·go hard white cheese

asparagi ⓜ pl as·*pa*·ra·jee asparagus

aspro/a ⓜ/ⓕ *as*·pro/a sour

~ B ~

babà ⓜ ba·*ba* dessert containing sultanas

baccalà ⓜ ba·ka·*la* dried salted cod

— alla pizzaiola a·la pee·tsa·*yo*·la with a tomato sauce

— mantecato man·te·*ka*·to mixed to a puree

baci ⓜ pl *ba*·chee 'kisses' – type of chocolate • type of pastry or biscuit

bagnetto verde ba·*nye*·to *ver*·de parsley & garlic sauce

barbabietola ⓕ bar·ba·*bye*·to·la beetroot

basilico ⓜ ba·*zee*·lee·ko basil

batsoà ⓜ bat·so·*a* boned, boiled & fried pig's trotters

battuto ⓜ ba·*too*·to soup or meat seasoning prepared with lard & vegetables

bavetta ⓕ ba·*ve*·ta long, thick pasta

bel paese ⓜ bel pa·*e*·ze soft, creamy cheese

besciamella ⓕ be·sha·*me*·la bechamel sauce

bescó'cc ⓜ bes·*koch* almond biscuits soaked in **grappa**

bianchetti ⓜ pl byan·*ke*·tee whitebait fried in oil

bianco d'uovo byan·ko *dwo*·vo egg white

bigné ⓜ bee·*nye* cream puff

bigoli ⓜ pl *bee*·go·lee thick, wholemeal flour spaghetti

bisció'la ⓕ bee·*sho*·la cake with nuts, dried figs & raisins

biscotti ⓜ pl bee·*ko*·tee biscuits

biscó'cc bees·*koch* see **bescó'cc**

bisi ⓜ pl *bee*·zee peas

bistecca ⓕ bees·*te*·ka steak

— alla fiorentina a·la fyo·ren·*tee*·na tasty, thick loin steak with its bone

bitto ⓜ *bee*·to cow's milk cheese

blanc manger ⓜ blank man·*je* dessert with milk, sugar & vanilla

C

bocconcini ⓜ pl bo·kon·*chee*·nee tiny portions of **mozzarella**

boghe ⓕ pl **in scabescio** *bo*·ge een ska·*be*·sho marinated, floured fish, browned in oil

bollito bo·*lee*·to boiled

bollito (Bú'i) ⓜ bo·*lee*·to (boo·*ee*) mixed boiled meat with various sauces

bomba ⓕ **di riso** bom·ba dee *ree*·zo baked rice with stewed pigeon, eggs, mushrooms, truffles & sausage

bombas ⓕ *bom*·bas stewed veal meatballs

bonèt ⓜ bo·*net* baked pudding of macaroons, cocoa, coffee, **marsala** & rum

bostrengo ⓜ bos·*tren*·go cake prepared with boiled rice, chocolate, sugar, spices & pine nuts

boudin ⓜ boo·*deen* blood sausage

bra ⓜ bra mild cheese

braciola ⓕ bra·*cho*·la chop • cutlet

braciolone ⓜ **napoletano** bra·cho·*lo*·ne na·po·le·*ta*·no steak rolled & filled with bacon, **provolone** & other ingredients

branzi ⓜ pl *bran*·dzee soft table cheese

branzino ⓜ bran·*dzee*·no sea bass

brasato ⓜ bra·*za*·to beef marinated in red wine & spices, then stewed

brioche ⓜ bree·*osh* breakfast pastry

brochat ⓜ bro·*shat* sweet, thick cream made with milk, wine & sugar & eaten with rye bread

brodetto ⓜ **di pesce** bro·*de*·to dee *pe*·she fish soup

brodo ⓜ *bro*·do broth

brôs ⓜ broos creamy paste made by fermenting older cheese with herbs, spices & grappa

bruschetta ⓕ broos·*ke*·ta stale bread sliced, toasted, rubbed with garlic & flavoured with salt, pepper & olive oil

bruscitt ⓜ broo·*sheet* beef pieces cooked with red wine & served with polenta or mashed potatoes

brutti ma buoni ⓜ pl *broo*·tee ma *bwo*·nee 'ugly but good' – hazelnut macaroons

bucatini ⓜ pl boo·ka·*tee*·nee long hollow tubes of pasta

buccellato ⓜ **di Lucca** boo·che·*la*·to dee *loo*·ka traditional ring-shaped cake

budino ⓜ boo·*dee*·no milk-based pudding

bugie ⓕ pl boo·*jee*·e 'lies' – small ribbons of sweet pastry covered with icing sugar

burro ⓜ *boo*·ro butter

burtlèina ⓕ boort·*lay*·na little omelette prepared with water, flour, lard & onion, served with salami

busecca ⓕ boo·*ze*·ka tripe

bussolà ⓜ **vicentino** boo·so·*la* vee·chen·*tee*·no sponge cake-based dessert

~ C ~

caciotta ⓕ ka·*cho*·ta semi-soft mild cheese

cacciucco ⓜ **(alla livornese)** ka·*choo*·ko (a·la lee·vor·*ne*·ze) fish soup with at least five kinds of fish

cacio ⓜ *ka*·cho cheese (in general) • a creamy cheese

caciocavallo ⓜ ka·cho·ka·*va*·lo hard cow's milk cheese from southern Italy

cacioricotta ⓕ ka·cho·ree·*ko*·ta small round cheese made from cow/sheep/goat's milk curd

caciuni ⓜ pl ka·*choo*·nee big ravioli or puff pastry filled with egg yolks, cheeses, sugar & lemon peel

caffè ⓜ ka·*fe* coffee (see also box on p172)

calamari ⓜ pl ka·la·*ma*·ree calamari • squid

C

calhiettes ⓜ **tradizionali** ka-*lyet* tra-dee-tsyo-*na*-lee mixture of raw, grated potatoes, left-over meat, minced lard, onion, flour & eggs mixed & boiled, normally used to prepare dumplings & omelettes

calzone ⓜ kal-*tso*-ne fried or baked flat bread made with two thin sheets of pasta stuffed with any number of ingredients

canederli ⓜ pl ka-*ne*-der-lee big dumplings made with stale bread, speck & other ingredients such as liver, cheese, spinach or dried prunes

cannaroni ⓜ pl ka-na-*ro*-nee large pasta tubes

cannella ① ka-*ne*-la cinnamon

cannelloni ⓜ pl ka-ne-*lo*-nee tubes of pasta stuffed with spinach, minced roast veal, ham, eggs, parmesan & spices

cannoli ⓜ pl **(ripieni)** ka-*no*-lee (ree-*pye*-nee) sweet pastry tubes filled with a mixture of sugar, candied fruit, sweet ricotta & other ingredients

cantarelli ⓜ kan-ta-*re*-lee chanterelle mushrooms

cantucci ⓜ pl kan-*too*-chee crunchy, hard biscuits made with aniseed & almonds

canasante ① pl ka-pa-*san*-te scallops

capocollo ⓜ ka-po-*ko*-lo dry-cured pork sausage washed with red wine

caponata ① ka-po-*na*-ta starter prepared with vegetables cooked in oil & vinegar – served with olives, anchovies & capers

capelli ⓜ pl **d'angelo** ka-*pe*-lee *dan*-je-lo 'angel's hair' – long, thin strands of pasta

cappellacci ⓜ pl **di zucca** ka-pe-*la*-chee dee *tsoo*-ka small pasta, filled with pumpkin & parmesan

cappelletti ⓜ pl ka-pe-*le*-tee similar to **tortellini**, only larger

cappello ⓜ **da prete** ka-*pe*-lo da *pre*-te boiled lower part of the pig's trotter, served with **salsa verde** or mustard

capperi ⓜ pl *ka*-pe-ree capers

cappon ⓜ **magro** ka-*pon* ma-gro salad with vegetables, fish & shellfish, dressed with a rich green sauce

capra ① *ka*-pra goat • goat's cheese

caprese ⓜ ka-*pre*-ze salad with tomato, basil & **mozzarella**

capretto ⓜ ka-*pre*-to kid (goat)

caprino ⓜ ka-*pree*-no tart goat cheese often mixed at the table into a paste

carbonada ① kar-bo-*na*-da diced, salted beef cooked in red wine

carbonara kar-bo-*na*-ra pasta sauce with egg, cheese & pancetta

carciofi ⓜ pl kar-*cho*-fee artichokes

cardoncelli ⓜ pl kar-don-*che*-lee type of mushroom, similar to oyster mushrooms

carnaroli ⓜ pl kar-na-*ro*-lee short-grain rice used for **risotto**

carne ① *kar*-ne meat

— equina e-*kwee*-na horse meat

— suina *swee*-na pork

— trita/tritata *tree*-ta/tree-*ta*-ta mince meat

carota ① ka-*ro*-ta carrot

carpa ① *kar*-pa carp

carpaccio ⓜ kar-pa-*cho* very thin slices of raw meat

carpione ⓜ kar-*pyo*-ne fried fish preserved in a marinade of oil & spices

carta ① **da musica** *kar*-ta da *moo*-zee-ka thin & very crunchy bread

cartoccio ⓜ kar-*to*-cho cooking method – fish, chicken or game are tightly wrapped in tinfoil & baked

cascà ① **di carloforte** kas-*ka* dee kar-lo-*for*-te couscous with vegetables, minced meat & spices

C

câonséi ⓜ pl ka·zon·*say* rectangles of pasta usually stuffed with parmesan, vegetables & sausage

cassata ① ka·*sa*·ta ice cream or sponge cake stuffed with sweet ricotta, vanilla, chocolate, pistachios, candied fruit & liqueur

cassola ① ka·*so*·la fish-soup with tomato sauce & herbs

casoncelli ⓜ pl ka·zon·*che*·lee pasta stuffed with meat & (depending on the region) spinach, eggs, raisins, almond biscuits, breadcrumbs or cheese

castagnaccio ⓜ ka·sta·*nya*·cho cake made with chestnut flour & sprinkled with pine nuts & rosemary

castagne ① pl ka·sta·nye chestnuts

castelmagno ⓜ ka·stel·*ma*·nyo nutty blue cheese

casunzei ① pl ka·zoon·*say* kind of ravioli stuffed with pumpkin or spinach, ham & cinnamon – served with smoked **ricotta**

caulada ① kow·*la*·da cabbage-based soup with meat, mint & garlic

cavallucci ⓜ pl ka·va·*loo*·chee white sweets made with candied orange, nuts & spices

cavatelli ⓜ pl ka·va·*te*·lee small, round home-made pasta – often served with tomato sauce, oil & rocket

cavolo ⓜ *ka*·vo·lo cabbage

cavolfiore ⓜ ka·vol·*fyo*·re cauliflower

cazzimperio ⓜ ka·tseem·*pe*·ree·o fresh & crunchy vegetables dunked into a tasty sauce

cazzmar ⓜ *kats*·mar sliced sausage containing lamb's entrails, liver & giblets

cecenielli ⓜ pl che·che·*nye*·lee very small fish that can be fried or put on pizzas

ceci ⓜ pl *che*·chee chickpeas

cefalo ⓜ *che*·fa·lo mullet

cervello ⓜ cher·*ve*·lo brain

cervo ⓜ *cher*·vo venison

chenella ① ke·*ne*·la meatballs (sometimes fishballs)

chinulille ① pl kee·noo·*lee*·le ravioli stuffed with sugar, ricotta, egg yolks, fried lemon & orange peel

chiodino ⓜ kyo·*dee*·no honey-coloured fungus – mushroom that must be cooked

ciabatta ① cha·*ba*·ta crisp, flat & long bread

cialzons ⓜ pl chal·*tsons* ravioli stuffed with ricotta, spinach, sultanas, chocolate & sometimes chicken & herbs

ciambelle ① pl **al mosto** cham·*be*·le al *mos*·to ring-shaped cakes made with grape must

ciammotta ① cha·*mo*·ta mixed-vegetable fry

cianfotta ① chan·*fo*·ta stew with vegetables, garlic & basil

ciaudedda ① chow·*de*·da vegetable stew with artichokes, onions & potatoes

ciavarro ⓜ cha·*va*·ro spring soup made with cereals & legumes

cibuddau ⓜ chee·boo·*da*·oo onion-based dish

cicala ① chee·*ka*·la crustacean

ciccioli ⓜ pl *chee*·cho·lee tasty pieces of crispy fat

ciceri ⓜ pl **e tria** ① *chee*·che·ree e *tree*·a dish of boiled chickpeas & pasta, served with onions

cicirata ① chee·chee·*ra*·ta small, sweet balls fried & covered with honey

ciliegia ① chee·*lye*·ja cherry

cima ① *chee*·ma breast, normally veal

cime ① pl **di rapa** *chee*·me dee *ra*·pa turnip tops

cioccolato ⓜ cho·ko·*la*·to chocolate

— fondente fon·*den*·te cooking chocolate

cipollata ① chee·po·*la*·ta dish with pork, spare ribs, stale bread & a lot of white onions

cipolle ① pl chee·*po*·le onions

— ripiene ree·*pye*·ne stuffed half onions

— selvatiche sel·*va*·tee·ke wild onions

coccois ⓜ ko·ko·ees flat bread made with salty cheese & crackling

cocomero ⓜ ko·ko·*me*·ro water-melon

coda ① *ko*·da tail • angler fish

cognà ⓜ ko·*nya* apple, pear, fig & grape sauce

coietas ⓜ pl ko·*ye*·tas rouladen made with savoy cabbage & meat sauce

colombo/a ⓜ/① ko·*lom*·bo/a dove • pigeon • type of cake

conchiglie ① pl kon·*kee*·lye pasta shells

condimento ⓜ kon·dee·*men*·to dressing

confetti ⓜ pl kon·*fe*·tee sugar-coated almonds

coniglio ⓜ ko·*nee*·lyo rabbit

conserva ① kon·*ser*·va preserve

— di pomodoro dee po·mo·*do*·ro traditional tomato sauce

cornetto ⓜ kor·*ne*·to breakfast pastry

coscia ① *ko*·sha leg • haunch

costata ① kos·*ta*·ta beef steak (rib)

— alla napoletana a·la na·po·le·*ta*·na ſᴵᴵᴵᴵᴵᴵ ᴵᴵᴵ ᴵᴵᴵᴵᴵᴵᴵᴵ ᴵᴵᴵᴵ ᴵ ᴵᴵᴵᴵᴵᴵᴵ ᴵᴵᴵᴵᴵ & white wine

— di manzo alla pizzaiola dee *man*·dzo a·la pee·tsa·*yo*·la with garlic, oil, tomatoes & oregano

costine ① pl kos·*tee*·ne ribs

— di maiale dee ma·*ya*·le pork spare ribs grilled on stone

costoletta ① kos·to·*le*·ta veal cutlet

cotechinata ① ko·te·kee·*na*·ta roulade of pig rind stuffed with garlic, parsley & lard cooked with tomato sauce

cotechino ⓜ ko·te·*kee*·no boiled pork sausage

— in galera een ga·*le*·ra 'in prison' – meatloaf stuffed with a boiled **cotechino**

cotoletta ① ko·to·*le*·ta (veal) cutlet usually breaded & fried

— alla bolognese a·la bo·lo·*nye*·ze breaded veal cutlet sauteed with butter & baked with cured ham & fresh parmesan

— alla milanese a·la mee·la·*ne*·ze veal loin steak breaded & fried in butter

cotto/a ⓜ/① *ko*·to/a cooked

ben — ben well done

non troppo — non *tro*·po medium rare

poco — *po*·ko rare

cozze ① pl *ko*·tse mussels

crema ① **inglese** *kre*·ma een·*gle*·ze custard

cren ⓜ kren horseradish

crescenza ① kre·*shen*·tsa fresh, soft cheese (see **stracchino**)

crespella ① kres·*pe*·la thin fritter

crespelle ① pl **bagnate** kres·*pe*·le ba·*nya*·te pasta with savoury filling served in chicken stock

crocchette ① pl kro·*ke*·te croquettes of mashed potatoes & various ingredients

crostacei ⓜ pl kro·*sta*·chay crustacean

crostata ① kro·*sta*·ta fruit tart • crust

crostini ⓜ pl kro·*stee*·nee slices of bread toasted with savoury toppings

crostoi ⓜ pl kro·*stoy* little fritters with sweet or savoury fillings

crostoli ⓜ pl *kro*·sto·lee fried sweet pastry with icing sugar • small flat bread

crucetta ① kroo·*che*·ta sweet made with figs stuffed with nuts & arranged as a cross

crudo/a ⓜ/① *kroo*·do/a raw

D

crumiri ⓜ pl *kroo·mee·ree* type of dry biscuits

crusca ⓕ *kroos·ka* bran

culatello ⓜ **(di Busseto)** koo·la·*te*·lo (dee boo·*se*·to) ham made of salted & spiced pig's rump

culingiones ⓜ pl koo·leen·*jo*·nes kind of **ravioli** stuffed with potatoes or chard, sheep's cheese, garlic & mint

cupeta ⓕ koo·*pe*·ta nougat stuffed between two wafers

cuscus ⓜ *koos·*koos couscous

cutturiddi ⓜ pl koo·too·*ree*·dee lamb stew with chilli, tomatoes, small onions & celery

~ D ~

di/d' ... dee·d ... from ...

datteri ⓜ pl *da·*te·ree dates (fruit)

— di mare dee *ma*·re type of mussel

della casa de·la *ka*·za 'of the house' – house speciality

diavola, alla *dya*·vo·la, *a*·la spicy dish

diavolicchio ⓜ dya·vo·*lee*·kyo dynamite chilli

ditali(ni) ⓜ pl dee·*ta*·lee/ dee·ta·*lee*·nee small bits of pasta often used in soups

dolce *dol*·che dessert • sweet • soft

dolcelatte ⓜ dol·che·*la*·te soft mild blue cheese

dolcetti ⓜ pl **di pasta di mandorle** dol·*che*·tee dee *pas*·ta dee *man*·dor·le traditional sweets made with marzipan, sugar & egg whites

~ E ~

erbazzone ⓜ er·ba·*tso*·ne baked pasta stuffed with spinach, lard, spices, parmesan, eggs & parsley

— dolce *dol*·che sweet baked shortcrust pastry filled with boiled & chopped chards mixed with **ricotta**, sugar & almonds

erbe ⓕ pl *er*·be herbs

~ F ~

fagiano ⓜ fa·*ja*·no pheasant

fagioli ⓜ pl fa·*jo*·lee beans (usually dried)

fagiolini ⓜ pl fa·jo·*lee*·nee green beans

false salsicce ⓕ pl *fal*·se sal·*see*·che 'false sausages' – sausages made with lard & potatoes & coloured with beet

farcito/a far·*chee*·to stuffed food

farfalle ⓕ pl far·*fa*·le butterfly-shaped pasta

farina ⓕ fa·*ree*·na flour

farinata ⓕ fa·ree·*na*·ta thin, flat bread made from chickpea flour

farro ⓜ *fa*·ro spelt (an ancient grain)

fasoi ⓜ pl **col muset** fa·*zoy* kol myoo·*zet* dish with dried beans, sausage, pork rind & spices

fatto/a ⓜ/ⓕ *fa*·to/a made

— a mano a *ma*·no made by hand

— in casa een *ka*·za home-made • made on the premises

favata ⓕ fa·*va*·ta rustic dish of broad beans, lard, pork, sausages, tomatoes & herbs

fave ⓕ pl *fa*·ve broad beans

fegato ⓜ *fe*·ga·to liver

felino ⓜ fe·*lee*·no type of salami

ferri, ai *fe*·ree, ai grilled on an open fire

fesa ⓕ *fe*·za veal (term used in northern Italy)

fetta ⓕ *fe*·ta slice (of meat/cheese)

fettuccine ⓕ pl fe·too·*chee*·ne long ribbon-shaped pasta

— alla romana *a*·la ro·*ma*·na 'Roman-style' – served with meat sauce, mushrooms & sheep's cheese

fiadoni ⓜ pl **alla trentina** fya·*do*·nee a·la tren·*tee*·na little sweets stuffed with almonds, honey, cinnamon & rum

fiandolein ⓜ fyan·do·*layn* 'egg flip' made with yolks, milk, sugar & lemon peel

fico ⓜ *fee*·ko fig

filoncino ⓜ fee·lon·*chee*·no breadstick

finanziera ⓕ fee·nan·*tsye*·ra sweetbreads, mushrooms & chicken livers in a creamy sauce

finocchio ⓜ fee·*no*·kyo fennel

fior di latte ⓜ fyor dee *la*·te fresh & very soft cheese • a **gelato** flavour

fiori ⓜ pl *fyo*·ree flowers – some are commonly eaten (eg zucchini flowers)

— di zucca farciti dee *tsoo*·ka far·*chee*·tee stuffed, fried zucchini or squash flowers

focaccia ⓕ fo·*ka*·cha flat bread often filled or topped with cheese, ham, vegetables & other ingredients

foglia ⓕ **d'alloro** *fo*·lya da·*lo*·ro bay leaf

fondo ⓜ *fon*·do stock

fondua ⓕ fon·*doo*·a cheese melted with butter & eggs & topped with thin slices of truffle

fontina ⓕ fon·*tee*·na sweet & creamy cheese, similar to Gruyère

formaggio ⓜ for·*ma*·jo cheese

forno, al *for*·no, al cooked in an oven

fragole ⓕ pl *fra*·go·le strawberries

freddo/a ⓜ/ⓕ *tre*·do/a cold

fresco/a ⓜ/ⓕ *fres*·ko/a fresh

fregola ⓕ *fre*·go·la type of coarse semolina

fregnacce ⓕ fre·*nya*·che thin rolled pancakes stuffed with meat

frisceu ⓕ free·*she*·oo fritters with lettuce, whitebait, zucchini, liver, brain, dried cod, pumpkin etc

frisedde ⓜ free·ze·de big ring-shaped cakes, boiled, baked then served with tomatoes, oil, salt & oregano

fritole ⓕ pl *free*·to·le fritters containing sultanas, pine nuts, candied lemon & liqueur

frittata ⓕ free·*ta*·ta thick omelette slice, served hot or cold

frittatensuppe ⓕ pl free·ta·ten·*soo*·pe thin omelettes cut into strips & served with meat stock

frittatine ⓕ pl **di farina al miele di fichi** free·ta·*tee*·ne dee fa·*ree*·na al *mye*·le dee *fee*·kee pancakes folded & stuffed with fig honey

frittelle ⓕ pl free·*te*·le fritters

frittelloni ⓜ pl free·te·*lo*·nee boiled spinach **tortellini** sauteed with butter, sultanas & cheese, then fried in lard

fritto/a ⓜ/ⓕ *free*·to/a fried

fritto ⓜ **misto** *free*·to *mees*·to a mixture of various ingredients, depending on the region & time of year, fried in olive oil (some versions contain offal)

— abruzzese a·broo·*tse*·ze diced artichokes & boiled fennel, breaded & fried

frumento ⓜ froo·*men*·to wheat

frutta ⓕ *froo*·ta fruit

— secca *se*·ka dried fruit

frutti ⓜ pl **di mare** *froo*·tee dee *ma*·re seafood

fugazza ⓕ foo·*ga*·tsa rich, sweet pastry

funghi ⓜ pl *foon*·gee mushrooms

fusilli ⓜ pl foo·*zee*·lee corkscrew-shaped pasta

galani ⓜ pl ga·*la*·nee layered strips of fried pastry sprinkled with icing sugar

gallina ⓕ ga·*lee*·na chicken • hen

gambero ⓜ *gam*·be·ro prawn • shrimp

gamberoni ⓜ pl gam·be·*ro*·nee prawns

gambon ⓜ gam·*bon* pig's leg, boned, pressed & matured

garagoli ⓜ pl ga·*ra*·go·lee shellfish similar to periwinkles

garganelli Ⓜ pl gar·ga·ne·lee short pasta served with various sauces

gattò Ⓜ **di patate e salsiccia** ga·to dee pa·ta·te e sal·see·cha baked meatloaf made with mashed potato, eggs, ham & cheeses

gelato Ⓜ je·la·to ice cream

genovese, alla je·no·ve·ze, a·la sauce including olive oil, garlic & herbs

gerstensuppe Ⓜ ger·sten·soo·pe barley soup with onions, parsley, spices & speck

gianduiotto Ⓜ jyan·doo·yo·to hazel-nut chocolate

giardiniera Ⓕ jar·dee·nye·ra pickled vegetables

girello Ⓜ jee·re·lo round cut of meat

gnocchi Ⓜ pl nyo·kee small (most commonly potato) dumplings

gnocchetti Ⓜ pl nyo·ke·tee small shell-shaped pasta

gnocco Ⓜ **di pane (al prosciutto)** nyo·ko dee pa·ne (al pro·shoo·to) pieces of bread fried in a mixture of butter, eggs, milk & ham

goregone Ⓜ go·re·go·ne freshwater lake fish

gorgonzola Ⓕ gor·gon·dzo·la spicy, sweet, creamy blue-vein cow's milk cheese

grana Ⓕ **(padano)** gra·na (pa·da·no) hard cheese, also refers to cheeses such as **parmigiano**

granchio Ⓜ gran·kyo crab

granita Ⓕ gra·nee·ta finely crushed flavoured ice

granseola Ⓕ gran·se·o·la spider crab

grano Ⓜ gra·no wheat

gran(o)turco Ⓜ gran(·o)·toor·ko maize

grappa Ⓕ gra·pa distilled grape must

grissini Ⓜ pl gree·see·nee bread-sticks

guanciale Ⓜ gwan·cha·le cheek, usually pig's

gubana Ⓕ goo·ba·na sweet pastry

~ I ~

impanada Ⓕ eem·pa·na·da savoury tart stuffed with vegetables & many kinds of meat & fish

impepata Ⓕ **di cozze** eem·pe·pa·ta dee ko·tse fish-based dish prepared with mussels & lemon

infarinata Ⓕ een·fa·ree·na·ta polenta as a soup, or fried in strips, with various meat & vegetable combinations

insalata Ⓕ een·sa·la·ta salad

— caprese ka·pre·ze with mozzarella, tomato & basil

— di carne cruda dee kar·ne kroo·da with raw minced meat

involtini Ⓜ pl een·vol·tee·nee stuffed rolls of meat or fish

— di carne dee kar·ne small veal slices, rolled up, stuffed, pierced on kebabs & baked or grilled

— siciliani see·chee·lya·nee meat rolled in breadcrumbs, stuffed with egg, ham & cheese

~ J ~

jota Ⓕ yo·ta soup with beans, milk, & polenta • soup with beans, potatoes, sauerkraut & smoked pork rinds

~ L ~

laganelle Ⓕ pl **e fagioli** la·ga·ne·le e fa·jo·lee sheets of pasta served in a bean soup

lamponi Ⓜ pl lam·po·nee raspberries

lasagne Ⓕ pl la·za·nye flat sheets of egg pasta

— alla bolognese a·la bo·lo·nye·ze baked lasagne with meat sauce, bechamel & parmesan

lattuga Ⓕ la·too·ga lettuce

lavarelli Ⓜ pl la·va·re·lee fresh water whitefish

lecca-lecca Ⓕ le·ka le·ka lollipop

lenticchie ① pl len·*tee*·kye lentils

lepre ① *lep*·re hare

lesso/a ⓜ/① *le*·so/a boiled

liscio/a ⓜ/① *lee*·sho/a smooth – describes pasta with a smooth surface

lianeddè ⓜ pl lya·ne·*de* noodles with chickpeas or rabbit sauce

lievito ⓜ *lye*·vee·to yeast

limone ⓜ lee·*mo*·ne lemon

lingua ① *leen*·gwa tongue

linguine ① pl leen·*gwee*·ne long thin ribbons of pasta

luccio ⓜ *loo*·cho pike

luganega ① loo·*ga*·ne·ga pork sausage

luganiga di verze ① loo·*ga*·nee·ga dee *ver*·dze cabbage sausage stuffed with mince, cheese, eggs & breadcrumbs

lumache ① pl loo·*ma*·ke snails

luppoli ⓜ pl *loo*·po·lee hops

~ **M** ~

maccaruni ⓜ pl **di casa con ragù** ma·ka·*roo*·nee dee *ka*·za kon ra·*goo* small pasta tubes served with tomato & meat sauce

maccheroni ⓜ pl ma·ke·*ro*·nee any tube pasta

— alla chitarra a·la kee·*ta*·ra square spaghetti, generally served with a meat sauce

— con la ricotta kon la ree·*ko*·ta pasta served with ricotta, sheep's cheese & sometimes also parmesan

magro/a ⓜ/① *mag*·ro/a thin • lean • meatless

maturo/a ⓜ/① ma·*too*·ro/a ripe

maiale ⓜ ma·*ya*·le pork

mais ⓜ *ma*·eez maize

malfatti ⓜ pl mal·*fa*·tee dumplings with spinach, eggs & cheese

malloreddus ⓜ pl ma·lo·re·*doos* dumplings with saffron in a meat sauce

maltagliati ⓜ pl mal·ta·*lya*·tee odd shapes of pasta

mandorle ① pl *man*·dor·le almonds

manteca ① man·*te*·ka fresh cheese rolled in a ball & stuffed with butter

mantecato ⓜ man·te·*ka*·to any ingredients pounded to a paste

manzo ⓜ *man*·dzo beef

maraschino ⓜ ma·ras·*kee*·no cherry liqueur

marcetto ⓜ mar·*che*·to very spicy cheese paste

marille ① pl ma·*ree*·le crazily shaped pasta designed to retain the maximum amount of sauce

marinara, alla ma·ree·*na*·ra, a·la dish containing seafood

maritozzi ⓜ pl ma·ree·*to*·tsee small, soft sweet cakes stuffed with pine nuts, sultanas, orange peel & fruit

marrone ⓜ ma·*rro*·ne large chestnut

marsala ① mar·*sa*·la fortified wine

marubini ⓜ pl ma·roo·*bee*·nee pasta stuffed with toasted bread, parmesan, marrow & eggs

mascarpone ⓜ mas·kar·*po*·ne very soft & creamy cheese

maturo/a ⓜ/① ma·*too*·ro/a ripe

mazzafegato ① pl ma·tsa·*fe*·ga·to matured dry-cured pork sausage, made with minced liver, kidney, tripe & lung

mela ① *me*·la apple

melagrana ① me·la·*gra*·na pomegranate

melanzanata ① **(di Lecce)** me·lan·dza·*na*·ta (dee *le*·che) eggplant pasta sauce • baked eggplant, tomato, onion, basil & sheep's cheese

melanzane ① pl me·lan·*dza*·ne eggplants • aubergines

— ripiene ree·*pye*·ne baked eggplants stuffed with their pulp, eggs, cheese, herbs, spices & bread

— violette vee·o·*le*·te purple eggplant

N

meringa ① me·*reen*·ga meringue
merlano ⑩ mer·*la*·no whiting
merluzzo ⑩ mer·*loo*·tso cod
mesta ① **e fasoi** ⑩ pl *mes*·ta e fa·*zoy* polenta cooked with beans
miele ⑩ *mye*·le honey
migliaccio ⑩ **'e cigule** ① pl mee·*lya*·cho e chee·*goo*·le baked polenta with pork, sausages, sheep's cheese & pepper
milanese, alla mee·la·*ne*·ze, *a*·la any sauce associated with Milan – normally includes butter
millecosedde ⑩ mee·le·ko·*ze*·de hearty soup with vegetables, legumes & short pasta
minestra ① mee·*ne*·stra soup
— **alla pignata** *a*·la pee·*nya*·ta with beans, pork & vegetables
— **cò i cece** ko ee *che*·che with chickpeas & pasta
minestrone ⑩ mee·ne·*stro*·ne trad·itional soup usually including many vegetables & sometimes pasta or rice, bacon cubes & pork rinds
misticanza ① mees·tee·*kan*·tsa salad with mixed greens
misto/a ⑩/① *mees*·to/a mixed
mollusco ⑩ mo·*loo*·sko mollusc
montasio ⑩ mon·*ta*·zyo hard cheese
montato/a ⑩/① mon·*ta*·to/a whipped
morbido/a ⑩/① *mor*·bee·do soft
mortadella ① **(di Bologna)** mor·ta·*de*·la (dee bo·*lo*·nya) salami made with minced pork, lard & black pepper
mostaccioli ⑩ pl mos·ta·*cho*·lee small chocolate-coated biscuits
mozzetta ① mo·*tse*·ta salami made with haunch of mountain-goat or chamois, salted & dried
mozzarella ① mo·tsa·*re*·la a soft, fresh white cheese made from cow's milk
— **di bufala** dee *boo*·fa·la made from buffalo's milk

— **in carrozza** een ka·*ro*·tsa on slices of bread, battered & fried
'mpanada ① m·pa·*na*·da see **impanada**
'mpepata ① **di cozze** m·pe·*pa*·ta dee *ko*·tse see **impepata di cozze**
muggine ⑩ *moo*·jee·ne mullet

~ N ~

napoletana, alla na·po·le·*ta*·na, *a*·la from or in the style of Naples – usually includes tomatoes & garlic
nasello ⑩ na·*ze*·lo hake
'ndugghia ① n·*doo*·gya dry-cured pork & fennel-seed sausage
nero ⑩ **di seppia/calamaro** *ne*·ro dee *se*·pya/ka·la·*ma*·ro squid/calamari ink
nocciola ① no·*cho*·la hazelnut
noce ⑩ *no*·che nut • walnut
— **di cocco** dee *ko*·ko coconut
— **moscata** mos·*ka*·ta nutmeg
norma, alla *nor*·ma, *a*·la pasta sauce with eggplant & tomato
nostrano ⑩ nos·*tra*·no hard cheese • local, home-made or domestic produce

~ O ~

oca ① *o*·ka goose
offelle ① pl o·*fe*·le sweet biscuits with mixed dried fruit
olio ⑩ *o*·lyo oil – almost always olive oil
ombrichelli ⑩ pl om·bree·*ke*·lee coarse home-made pasta spaghetti
opinus ⑩ o·*pee*·noos pine-cone-shaped biscuits sprinkled with melted sugar & egg whites
orata ① o·*ra*·ta bream • gilthead
orecchiette ① pl o·re·*kye*·te shell-shaped, hand-made pasta, served with vegetables & olive oil or a rich meat sauce

orzo ⓜ *or*-dzo barley
— e fagioli e fa*jo*-lee thick barley & bean broth
ossi di morti ⓜ pl o*-see dee *mor*-tee 'bones of the dead' – very hard crunchy biscuits
ossobuco ⓜ o-so-*boo*-ko veal shanks
— milanese mee-la-*ne*-ze cut into small pieces & cooked with spices
ostriche ⓕ pl os-tree-ke oysters

~ P ~

pagnottella ⓕ pa-nyo-*te*-la bread roll
palle ⓕ pl *pa*-le balls
— del nonno del *no*-no 'grandpa's balls' – sweet fried ricotta balls • crinkly pork sausages
— di riso dee *ree*-zo stuffed rice croquettes
palombo ⓜ pa-*lom*-bo dove • pigeon
— alla todina a-la to-*dee*-na roasted pigeon
pan ⓜ **biscotto condito** pan bees-*ko*-to kon-*dee*-to toasted bread with oil, tomatoes, herbs
panadas ⓕ pl pa-*na*-das see **pancotto**
pancetta ⓕ pan-*che*-ta salt-cured bacon
pancotto ⓜ pan-*ko*-to soup made with boiled bread, cheese & eggs or fresh tomatoes
pane ⓜ *pa*-ne bread
— a pasta acida a *pas*-ta *a*-chee-da sourdough bread
— all'olio a-*lo*-lyo bread with oil
— aromatico a-ro-*ma*-tee-ko herb or vegetable bread
— carasau ka-ra-*zow* long-lasting bread eaten by shepherds
— casereccio ka-ze-*re*-cho firm, floury loaf
— col mosto kol *mos*-to bread with nuts, anise, almonds, raisins, sugar & must

— di segale dee se-*ga*-le rye bread
— frattau fra-*tow* slices of bread with sheep's cheese, tomato or meat sauce, boiling broth & eggs
— fresa *fre*-za flat, crispy bread
— integrale een-te-*gra*-le wholemeal bread
— pugliese poo-*lye*-ze large, crusty loaf
— salato sa-*la*-to salty bread
— toscano tos-*ka*-no crumbly, unsalted bread
— unto *oon*-to slices of bread toasted with garlic, olive oil, salt & pepper
panelle ⓕ pl pa-*ne*-le fried chickpea fritters
panforte ⓜ **(senese)** pan-*for*-te (se-*ne*-ze) hard cake made with almonds, fruit & spices
panino ⓜ pa-*nee*-no bread roll
paniscia ⓕ **novarese** pa-*nee*-sha no-va-*re*-ze rice-based dish with onion, sausage & soup
panna ⓕ *pa*-na cream
— cotta *ko*-ta thick creamy dessert
panpepato ⓜ pan-pe-*pa*-to sweet, ring-shaped cake
pan ⓜ **speziale** pan spe-*cha*-le bread with honey, nuts, raisins & fruit
panzanella ⓕ pan-*tsa*-ne-la Tuscan bread served with tomato sauce, onion, lettuce, anchovies, basil, olive oil, vinegar & salt
panzerotti ⓜ pl pan-*tse*-ro-tee filled pasta or pastries in a half-moon shape
paparot pa-pa-*rot* spinach & corn soup
papassinas ⓜ pl pa-pa-*see*-nas small, sweet cone-shaped cakes
pappa ⓕ *pa*-pa baby food
— col pomodoro kol po-mo-*do*-ro soup made with thin slices of stale bread, tomatoes & spices

pappardelle ① pl pa·par·de·le wide, flat pasta ribbons
— alla lepre a·la le·pre with stewed hare, red wine & tomato sauce
parmigiana, alla par·mee·ja·na, a·la any type of cheesy sauce
parmigiana di melanzane par·mee·ja·na dee me·lan·dza·ne fried eggplant layered with eggs, basil, tomato sauce, onion & **mozzarella**
parmigiano ⓜ **(reggiano)** par·mee·ja·no (re·ja·no) parmesan cheese, often simply called **grana**
parrozzo ⓜ pa·ro·tso sweet bread, sometimes chocolate-coated
passatelli ⓜ pl pa·sa·te·lee small dumplings made with eggs, parmesan, ox marrow & nutmeg
pasta ① pas·ta general name for the numerous types of pasta shapes • dough • pastry (see also p170)
— col bianchetto kol byan·ke·to spaghetti with a whitebait, tomato, garlic & chilli sauce
— cresciuta kre·shoo·ta anchovy or courgette flower fritters
— e fagioli e fa·jo·lee bean soup with pasta
— fresca fres·ka freshly made pasta
pastasciutta ① pas·ta·shoo·ta dry pasta
pastissada/pastizzada ① pas·tee·sa·da/pas·tee·tsa·da stew prepared with beef, ox or horse meat & vegetables
patate ① pl pa·ta·te potatoes
pecorino ⓜ **(romano)** pe·ko·ree·no (ro·ma·no) hard & spicy cheese made from ewe's milk
penne ① pl pe·ne short & tubular pasta
pepe ⓜ pe·pe pepper
peperonata ① pe·pe·ro·na·ta capsicum, onion & tomato stew
peperoncini ⓜ pl pe·pe·ron·chee·nee hot chilli

peperoni ⓜ pl pe·pe·ro·nee peppers • capsicum
— ripieni ree·pye·nee stuffed with various fillings
pere ① pl pe·ra pears
— imbottite eem·bo·tee·te baked stuffed pears
persico ⓜ per·see·ko perch
pesca ① pe·ska peach
pesce ⓜ pe·she fish
pesto ⓜ pes·to sauce prepared with fresh basil, pine nuts, olive oil, garlic, cheese & salt
petto ⓜ pe·to breast
pettole ① pl pe·to·le home-made, long thin ribbons of pasta
piadina ① pya·dee·na flat round bread
piccagge ① pl pee·ka·je long ribbon pasta served with **pesto** or an artichoke & mushroom sauce
piccata ① pee·ka·ta veal with a lemon & **marsala** sauce
picchi pacchiu ① pee·kee pa·kyoo pasta sauce with tomato & chilli
pici ⓜ pl pee·chee fresh pasta, like thick spaghetti
piccione ⓜ pee·cho·ne squab • pigeon
picula ① **ad caval** pee·koo·la ad ka·val horse-meat stew
pinoli ⓜ pl pee·no·lee pine nuts
pinza ① **padovana** peen·tsa pa·do·va·na sweet pastry
pinzimonio ⓜ peen·tsee·mo·nyo seasoned virgin olive oil for dipping (see also **cazzimperio**)
piopparello ⓜ pyo·pa·re·lo common flat mushroom
pisarei ⓜ pl **e fasó** ⓜ pl pee·za·ray e fa·zo small dumplings flavoured with tomato sauce, bacon & boiled beans
piselli ① pl pee·ze·lee green peas
pistum ⓜ pees·toom sweet & sour dumplings served with pork stock
pitta ① pee·ta soft & flat loaf of bread

pitte ① *pee*·te fring-shaped cake

pizza ① *pee*·tsa there are more than 50 kinds, with varying bases & toppings

— a(l) taglio a(l) *ta*·lyo slice of pizza

— dolce di Pasqua *dol*·che dee *pas*·kwa sweet pizza dough with dried fruits

— Margherita mar·ge·*ree*·ta topped with simple ingredients such as oil, tomato, **mozzarella**, basil & oregano

— rustica roos·*tee*·ka topped with various combinations of ham, salami, sausage, egg or cheese

pizzaiola, alla pee·tsa·*yo*·la, a·la a tomato & oil sauce

pizzoccheri ⑩ pl pee·*tso*·ke·ree short, buckwheat pasta with cabbage & potatoes

polenta ① po·*len*·ta cornmeal porridge

— al ragù al ra·*goo* served with a meat sauce

— concia *kon*·cha flavoured with a variety of cheeses

— e osei e o·*zay* served with sparrows, thrushes or larks • sponge cake with jam

— pasticciata pas·tee·*cha*·ta baked with meat sauce, mushrooms & cheese

— sulla spianatoria soo·la spya·na·*to*·rya with sausages, tomato & sheep's cheese served from a pastry board in the middle of the table

— taragna ta·ra·*nya* originally buckwheat **polenta**

polipo ⑩ po·*lee*·po octopus (also called **polpi**)

pollo ⑩ *po*·lo chicken

— alla diavola a·la *dya*·vo·la grilled with red pepper or chilli

— con peperoni e patate al coccio kon pe·pe·*ro*·nee e pa·*ta*·te al *ko*·cho slowly cooked in a terracotta pot with sage, potatoes & capsicum

polpette ⑩ pol·*pe*·te meatballs

polpettine ① pl pol·pe·*tee*·ne small meatballs

— di carne con salsa di pomodoro dee *kar*·ne kon *sal*·sa dee po·mo·*do*·ro in tomato sauce

polpettone ⑩ pol·pe·*to*·ne meatloaf

polpi ⑩ pl *pol*·pee octopus (also called **polipo**)

— alla luciana a·la loo·*cha*·na sliced octopus with tomatoes, oil, garlic, parsley & lemon

— in purgatorio een poor·ga·*to*·ryo stewed with tomato, parsley, chilli & garlic

pomodori ⑩ pl po·mo·*do*·ree tomatoes

— secchi *se*·kee sun-dried tomatoes

pomodorini ⑩ pl po·mo·do·*ree*·nee tiny tomatoes • sun-dried tomatoes

pompelmo ⑩ pom·*pel*·mo grapefruit

porchetta ① por·*ke*·ta stuffed suckling pig

porcini ⑩ pl por·*chee*·nee ceps (type of mushrooms)

porco ⑩ *por*·ko pig

potizza ① po·*tee*·tsa soft cake prepared with leavened pastry

prataiolo ⑩ pra·ta·*yo*·lo popular button mushroom

preboggion ⑩ pre·bo·*jon* mixture of wild herbs

prosciutto ⑩ pro·*shoo*·to basic name for many types of thinly-sliced ham

— affumicato a·foo·mee·*ka*·to smoked salami

— San Daniele san da·*nye*·le sweet & delicate ham

provola ① *pro*·vo·la semi-hard cheese made from buffalo & cow's milk

provolone ⑩ pro·vo·*lo*·ne rich medium-hard cheese made from cow's milk

prugna ① *proo*·nya plum

puttanesca, alla poo·ta·*ne*·ska, *a*·la 'whore's style' – tomato, chilli, anchovies & black-olive pasta sauce

~ Q ~

quaglie ① pl *kwa*·lye quails
quartirolo ⓜ kwar·tee·*ro*·lo sweet & delicate soft cheese
quattro formaggi *kwa*·tro for·*ma*·jee pasta sauce with four different cheeses
quattro stagioni *kwa*·tro sta·*jo*·nee pizza with different toppings on each quarter

~ R ~

rabarbaro ⓜ ra·*bar*·ba·ro rhubarb
radicchio ⓜ ra·*dee*·kyo chicory
— rosso *ro*·so slightly bitter vegetable with long leaves
rafano ⓜ **tedesco** *ra*·fa·no te·*des*·ko horseradish
ragù ⓜ ra·*goo* generally a meat sauce but sometimes vegetarian
— alla bolognese *a*·la bo·lo·*nye*·ze sauce of minced veal & pork
— alla napoletana *a*·la na·po·le·*ta*·na sauce made with chunks of meat, vegetables & red wine
rambasicci ⓜ pl ram·ba·*zee*·chee stuffed cabbage leaves
rapa ① *ra*·pa turnip
ravioli ⓜ pl ra·vee·o·lee pasta squares usually stuffed with meat, parmesan cheese & breadcrumbs
— liguri lee·*goo*·ree sometimes filled with ricotta & herbs
raviolini ⓜ pl ra·vee·o·*lee*·nee small ravioli
ravioloni ⓜ pl ra·vee·o·*lo*·nee large ravioli
razza ① *ra*·tsa skate
ri(so) ⓜ **in cagnon** *ree*(·zo) een *ka*·nyon rice sauteed in garlic, butter, sage & sprinkled with parmesan

ribes ⓜ **nero** *ree*·bes *ne*·ro blackcurrant
ribes ⓜ **rosso** *ree*·bes *ro*·so redcurrant
ribollita ① ree·bo·*lee*·ta reheated & thickened vegetable soup
ricciarelli ⓜ pl ree·cha·*re*·lee almond biscuits
ricotta ① ree·*ko*·ta fresh, moist, white cheese
— affumicata a·foo·mee·*ka*·ta smoked
— infornata een·for·*na*·ta ovenbaked
rigaglie ① pl ree·*ga*·lye giblets
rigatoni ⓜ pl ree·ga·*to*·nee short, fat tubes of pasta
— con la pagliata kon la pa·*lya*·ta served with small intestines of calves
ripieno ree·*pye*·no stuffing
risi ⓜ pl **e bisi** ⓜ pl *ree*·zee e *bee*·zee thick rice-based soup with peas
risi ⓜ pl **e bruscandoli** ⓜ pl *ree*·zee e broos·*kan*·do·lee bitter hop sprouts cooked in a broth with rice
riso ⓜ *ree*·zo rice
— al salto al *sal*·to boiled rice sauteed with saffron
— comune ko·*moo*·ne lowest quality, usually used in soups
— fino *fee*·no good quality with large grains
— integrale een·te·*gra*·le brown rice
— semifino se·mee·*fee*·no slightly better quality than **comune**, with larger grains
— superfino soo·per·*fee*·no bestquality rice, used in risotto
risotto ⓜ ree·*zo*·to rice dish slowly cooked in broth to a creamy consistency
— alla milanese *a*·la mee·la·*ne*·ze with ox marrow, meat stock & saffron
— alla monzese *a*·la mon·*dze*·ze with sausage & saffron or red wine

— **alla piemontese** *a*·la pye·mon·*te*·ze with white wine & truffles (& sometimes tomato sauce)

— **alla sbirraglia** *a*·la sbee·*ra*·lya with chicken breasts

— **alla trevisana** *a*·la tre·vee·*za*·na with sausage or chicken livers

— **allo zafferano** *a*·lo dza·fe·*ra*·no see **risotto alla milanese**

— **con filetti di pesce persico** kon fee·*le*·tee dee *pe*·she *per*·see·ko with perch fillets

— **con le rane** kon le *ra*·ne with frog legs, frog broth & herbs

— **nero** *ne*·ro black risotto with chard, onion, cuttlefish & their ink

— **polesano** po·le·*za*·no with eel, grey mullet, bass, white wine & fish broth

robiola ① ro·*byo*·la soft cheese made mainly from cow's milk

romana, alla ro·*ma*·na, *a* la *sauce*, usually tomato-based

rombo ⓜ *rom*·bo turbot

rosolata ① ro·zo·*la*·ta saute

rosbif ⓜ *roz*·beef roast beef

rospo ⓜ *ros*·po angler fish

rosumada ① ro·zoo·*ma*·da egg-nog with red wine

rotolo ⓜ *ro*·to·lo folded sheet of pasta filled with spinach, ricotta or meat

ruchetta ① roo·*ke*·ta rocket

rucola ① *roo*·ko·la rocket

rum babà ① *room*·ba·ba *babà* sprinkled with rum & sugar

ruta ① *roo*·ta rue (bitter herb)

~ S ~

sa fregula ① sa *fre*·goo·la soup with small balls of flour & saffron

sagne chine ① sa·nye *kee*·ne baked pasta with meatballs, eggs & cheese

salama ① **da sugo ferrarese** sa·*la*·ma da soo·go fe·ra·*re*·ze pork sausage

salame ① **di Felino** sa·*la*·me dee fe·*lee*·no dry-cured pork sausage

salami ⓜ pl sa·*la*·mee (pork) sausage

salamino ⓜ sa·la·*mee*·no small salami

salato/a ⓜ/① sa·*la*·to/a salty

sale ⓜ *sa*·le salt

salmi ⓜ sal·*mee* marinade with spices & sometimes wine

salmone ⓜ sal·*mo*·ne salmon

salsa ① *sal*·sa sauce

— **alfredo** al·*fre*·do with butter, cream, parmesan & parsley

— **alla checca** *a*·la *ke*·ka cold sauce with tomatoes, olives, basil, capers & oregano

— **alla pizzaiola** *a*·la pee·tsa·*yo*·la pizza-style sauce

— **di cren** dee kren with grated radish & apples, onion, broth & white wine

— **di pomodoro al tonno e funghi** dee po·mo·*do*·ro al *to*·no e *foon*·gee with tuna, mushroom & tomato

— **di pomodoro alla siciliana** dee po·mo·*do*·ro *a*·la see·chee·*lya*·na with eggplant, anchovies, olives, capers, tomato & garlic

— **verde** *ver*·de green sauce with herbs, capers, olives, nuts, anchovies, breadcrumbs, garlic & vinegar

saltimbocca ① sal·teem·*bo*·ka 'jump into the mouth' – bite-sized

salumes ⓜ see *sa*·loo·me salami

sanguinaccio ⓜ sangween·*na*·cho black pudding made with pig's blood, olives & cocoa

saor, in sowr, een sweet & sour, vinegar-based marinade for fish

sarago ⓜ sa·*ra*·go white bream

sarde ① pl *sar*·de sardines

— **a scapece** a ska·*pe*·che fried sardines

— **alla marchigiana** *a*·la mar·kee·*ja*·na baked, marinated sardines

S

sardele in saor ① pl sar·*de*·le een sowr dish with fried, marinated pilchards

sartù 'e riso ⑩ sar·*too* e ree·zo savoury rice dish

sas melicheddas ⑩ pl sas me·lee·*ke*·das marzipan cakes sprinkled with sugar

sausa ① *sow*·sa da·*vee*·e honey, nut & mustard sauce

savoiardi ⑩ pl sa·vo·*yar*·dee lady-finger biscuits

sbrofadej ⑩ zbro·fa·*day* thin pasta

— in brodo een *bro*·do served in broth

scagliuozzoli ⑩ pl ska·lyoo·o·*tso*·lee fried **polenta** & **provolone**

scaloppine ① pl ska·lo·*pee*·ne thin cutlets, usually veal, pork or turkey

— al marsala al mar·*sa*·la lean veal cutlet with **marsala**

scamorza ① ska·*mor*·tsa soft, white cheese, similar to **mozzarella**, often smoked

scampi ⑩ pl *skam*·pee a small type of lobster

scapece ⑩ ska·*pe*·che vinegar-based marinade usually used for fish

— di Vasto dee *vas*·to dish prepared with sliced & fried fish, preserved in a marinade

scarole ⑩ ska·*ro*·le bitter leafy vegetable

schiaffettuni ⑩ pl **chini** skya·fe·*too*·nee *kee*·nee **maccheroni** with pork & eggs

schmorbraten ⑩ shmor·*bra*·ten veal marinated & cooked in wine & tomato sauce

sciatt ⑩ schat soft, round fritters containing **grappa**

scimú'd ⑩ shee·*mood* salted & spicy skim milk cheese

sciroppo ⑩ shee·*ro*·po syrup

scivateddi ⑩ shee·va·*te*·dee thick spaghetti served with meat sauce & ricotta

scottiglia ① sko·*tee*·lya rich stew with tomatoes & meat

sebadas se·*ba*·das large, round & sweet ravioli with cheese & honey

seccia ① **'mbuttunata** se·cha m·boo·too·*na*·ta stuffed cuttlefish stewed with tomato sauce

selvaggina ① sel·va·*jee*·na game

semifreddo ⑩ se·mee·*fre*·do cold, creamy desserts

— al torrone al to·*ro*·ne dessert with milk, vanilla, eggs & nougat

semola ① *se*·mo·la bran • semolina

semolino ⑩ se·mo·*lee*·no semolina

senape ① *se*·na·pe mustard

seno ⑩ *se*·no breast

seppia ① *se*·pya cuttlefish

serpe ⑩ *ser*·pe cake with marzipan, almonds, icing sugar or chocolate

sfogliatelle ① pl sfo·lya·*te*·le cake or pastry stuffed with **ricotta**, cinnamon, candied fruit & vanilla

sformato ⑩ sfor·*ma*·to flan

— di spinaci con cibreo al vinsanto dee spee·*na*·chee kon chee·*bre*·o al veen·*san*·to flan with spinach, served with liver

sgombro ⑩ sgom·bro mackerel

sogliola ① so·*lyo*·la sole

sopa ① **còada** *so*·pa ko·*a*·da soup of meat stock, pigeon, cheese & bread

soppressa ① so·*pre*·sa pork sausage

soppressata ① so·pre·*sa*·ta matured raw salami made with minced pig's tongue, lean pork & spices • soft salami made with pork & lard

— molisana mo·lee·*za*·na large pork sausage

sorbetto ⑩ sor·*be*·to sorbet

sott'aceti ⑩ pl so·ta·*che*·tee pickles

sott'olio ⑩ so·to·lyo preserved in oil

spaghetti ⑩ pl spa·*ge*·tee ubiquitous long thin pasta

spá'tzle ⑩ *spa*·tsle little dumplings that can be served in broth

speck ⑩ spek type of smoked ham

spiedino/spiedo ⓜ *spye·dee·no/ spye·do* skewer

spezie ⓕ pl *spe·tsye* spices

spigola ⓕ *spee·go·la* sea bass

spinaci ⓜ pl *spee·na·chee* spinach

sponga(r)da ⓕ *spon·ga(r)·da* sweet pastry with vanilla, egg & sometimes mixed dried fruits

spugnola ⓕ *spoo·nyo·la* morel (sponge-like mushroom)

stecchi ⓜ pl *ste·kee* sticks • kebabs

— alla ligure *a·la lee·goo·re* with veal, chicken, sweetbread, eggs, mushrooms, artichokes & spices

stiacciata ⓕ *stya·cha·ta* sweet bun

stinco ⓜ *steen·ko* shank

stoccafisso ⓜ *sto·ka·fee·so* stockfish (small air-dried cod)

— a brandacujun a *bran·da koo·yoon* creamy dish of potatoes & stockfish

— accomodato *a·ko·mo·da·to* stockfish cooked in a casserole with anchovies or mushrooms

stracchino ⓜ *stra·kee·no* soft & delicate cheese

stracciatella ⓕ *stra·cha·te·la* broth with whipped egg & parmesan

stracotto ⓜ *stra·ko·to* beef stew

stracotto/a ⓜ/ⓕ *stra·ko·to/a* cooked for a long time • overcooked

strangolapreti ⓜ pl *stran·go·la·pre·tee* 'priest throttlers' cheese & egg dumplings, varying from region to region

stravecchio ⓜ *stra·ve·kyo* 'very old' – aged for a long time

stringozzi ⓜ pl *streen·go·tsee* short pasta served with tomato or meat sauce

strinù ⓜ *stree·noo* tasty sausage, usually grilled

stroscia ⓕ **(di Pietrabruna)** *stro·sha (dee pye·tra·broo·na)* sweet cake

strozzapreti ⓜ pl *stro·tsa·pre·tee* long strips of pasta • dumplings made with spinach, chard & ricotta

strudel ⓜ *stroo·del* pastry with a stuffing including apples

stufatino ⓜ *stoo·fa·tee·no* lean veal stewed with tomatoes & spices

supa ⓕ **barbetta** *soo·pa bar·be·ta* rich meat & vegetable stock

suppa ⓕ *soo·pa* soup

supplì ⓜ *soo·plee* fried rice balls (similar to **crocchettes**)

suricitti ⓜ pl *soo·ree·chee·tee* flavoured polenta dumplings

susamelli ⓜ pl *soo·za·me·lee* 's'-shaped biscuits

~ T ~

tacchino ⓜ *ta·kee·no* turkey

— alla gosutta *a·la go·zoo·ta* turkey casserole with fennel & broth

— con sugo di melagrana kon *soo·go dee me·la·gra·na* with pomegranate sauce

tagliatelle ⓕ pl *ta·lya·te·le* long, ribbon-shaped pasta

— alla salsa di noci *a·la sal·sa dee no·chee* with nuts, oil, butter, ricotta & parmesan

— con finocchio selvatico kon *fee·no·kyo sel·va·tee·ko* served with a fennel, bacon & parsley sauce

taglierini ⓜ pl *ta·lye·ree·nee* thin strips of pasta

— al ragù *al ra·goo* served with meat sauce

tagliolini (blò blò) ⓜ pl *ta·lyo·lee·nee (blo blo)* thin strips of pasta in broth, with grated cheese

tajarin ⓜ pl *ta·ya·reen* thin pasta usually served with meat sauce

taleggio ⓜ *ta·le·jo* sweet, soft & fatty cheese with a soft rind

taralli ⓜ pl *ta·ra·lee* boiled & baked pretzel-like biscuits

T

MENU DECODER

U

tartufo ⑩ tar·*too*·fo truffle (very expensive kind of fungus)

tè ⑪ te tea

tegamata ⑪ **di maiale** te·ga·*ma*·ta dee ma·*ya*·le casserole of pork & fennel seed

tegame, in te·*ga*·me, een fried • braised

tegole ⑪ pl **d'Aosta** *te*·go·le da·*os*·ta almond biscuits

testaió ⑩ tes·ta·*yo* squares of pasta served with pesto & parmesan

testaroli ⑩ pl tes·ta·*ro*·lee discs of pasta, like pancakes

tiramisù ⑩ tee·ra·mee·*soo* sponge cake or savoiardi soaked in coffee & arranged in layers with mascarpone, then sprinkled with cocoa

tòcco ⑩ **di carne** *to*·ko dee *kar*·ne veal sauce

toma ⑪ *to*·ma firm cow or sheep's cheese

— piemontese pye·mon·*te*·ze a softer variety of **toma**

tomaxelle ⑪ pl to·ma·*kse*·le veal roulade in wine & broth

tomino ⑩ to·*mee*·no small fresh cheese

tonno ⑩ *to*·no tuna

torciarelli ⑩ pl **al tartufo** tor·cha·re·lee al tar·*too*·fo pasta served with a sauce containing minced lean pork, spices, mushrooms, truffles & cheese

torcinelli ⑩ pl tor·chee·*ne*·lee stewed lamb or kid entrails

torcolo ⑩ **di San Costanzo** *tor*·ko·lo dee san kos·*tan*·dzo ring-shaped cake

torresani ⑩ pl to·re·za·nee pigeon kebabs

torrone ⑩ to·*ro*·ne nougat

— al cioccolato al cho·ko·*la*·to very soft chocolate nougat

torroni ⑩ pl **di semi di sesamo** to·*ro*·nee dee *se*·mee dee *se*·za·mo crunchy sweets with sesame seeds

torta ⑪ *tor*·ta cake • tart • pie

tortelli ⑩ *tor*·te·lee fat, stuffed pasta

— di San Leo dee san *le*·o with spinach & cheeses

— di zucca dee *tsoo*·ka with pumpkin

tortellini ⑩ pl tor·te·*lee*·nee pasta filled with meat, parmesan & egg

tortelloni ⑩ pl tor·te·*lo*·nee large **tortellini**

tosella ⑪ to·*ze*·la fresh fried cheese

totano ⑩ to·*ta*·no type of squid

tramezzino ⑩ tra·me·*dzee*·no sandwich

Trebbiano ⑩ tre·*bya*·no white grape found throughout Italy

trenette ⑪ pl **al pesto** tre·*ne*·te al *pes*·to long, flat pasta with **pesto**

trifola ⑪ *tree*·fo·la white truffle

triglia ⑪ *tree*·lya red mullet

trota ⑪ *tro*·ta trout

tubetti ⑩ pl too·*be*·tee short pasta tubes

turcinelli ⑩ pl **arrostiti** toor·chee·*ne*·lee a·ro·*stee*·tee lamb-offal stew

~ U ~

uardi ⑩ pl **e fasoi** ⑩ pl *war*·dee e fa·*zoy* soup with beans, barley, ham bone & spices

umbrici ⑩ pl oom·*bree*·chee hand-made, thick spaghetti

uova ⑩ pl *wo*·va eggs

uva ⑪ pl oo·va grapes

— bianca *byan*·ka green grapes

— nera *ne*·ra red grapes

— passa *pa*·sa raisins

~ V ~

vapore, cotto/a a ⑩/⑪ va·*po*·re, *ko*·to/a a steamed

vecchio/a ⑩/⑪ *ve*·kyo/a old • aged

ventresca ⑪ **di tonno** ven·*tres*·ka dee *to*·no tuna belly

verdura/verdure ① ver·*doo*·ra/
ver·*doo*·re vegetable/vegetables
verza ① ver·dza savoy cabbage
vialone nano ⓜ vya·*lo*·ne na·no
short-grain rice used for risotto
vincisgrassi ⓜ pl veen·cheez·*gra*·see
rich, baked dish made of offal, cheese
& sometimes truffle
vino ⓜ *vee*·no wine
— bianco *byan*·ko white wine
— rosso ro·so red wine
— spumante spoo·*man*·te sparkling
wine
viscidu ⓜ vee·*shee*·doo dry, salty &
sour cheese, sliced & pickled
vitello ⓜ vee·*te*·lo veal
— tonnato to·*na*·to thin slices of
veal covered with a tuna, capers &
anchovy sauce
vongolo ① pl *vnn*·go·le clams

~ Z ~

zabaglione ⓜ dza·ba·*lyo*·ne mousse-
like dessert made of beaten egg,
marsala & sugar
zampetto ⓜ dzam·*pe*·to calf, lamb or
pig trotter
zenzero ⓜ dzen·dze·ro ginger
zeppule ① pl **'e cicenielli** ⓜ pl
dze·*poo*·le e chee·che·*nye*·lee fritters
with cheese & anchovies

zeppule ① pl **'e San Giuseppe**
dze·*poo*·le e san joo·ze·pe small, fried
ring-shaped cakes
zimin ⓜ pl *dzee*·meen soup with
beans, pork & chards • dish with
calamari & chard
ziti ⓜ pl dze·tee long fat hollow
pasta
zucca ① *tsoo*·ka pumpkin
— gialla in agrodolce *ja*·la een
a·gro·*dol*·che fried & served with
spices & capers
zucchero ⓜ *tsoo*·ke·ro sugar
zuccotto ⓜ **fiorentino** tsoo·*ko*·to
fyo·ren·*tee*·no sponge cake with
liqueur, custard, chocolate & whipped
cream
zuppa ① *tsoo*·pa soup, usually thick
— alla canavesana a·la
ka·na·ve·*za*·na soup base of bread,
cabbage, butter, lard, onions & garlic
— di ceci dee che·chee rich chickpea
soup
— di pesce alla marinara dee pe·she
a·la ma·ree·na·ra fish soup
— 'e zuffritto e tsoo·*free*·to sauce
prepared with pig's offal, red wine &
tomato sauce

V

MENU DECODER

A

Dictionary
ENGLISH *to* ITALIAN
Inglese–Italiano

Nouns in this dictionary, and adjectives affected by gender, have their gender indicated by ⓜ and/or ⓕ. If it's a plural noun, you'll also see pl. Where a word that could be either a noun or a verb has no gender indicated, it's a verb.

A

aboard a bordo a *bor*·do

abortion aborto ⓜ a·*bor*·to

above sopra *so*·pra

abroad all'estero a·*les*·te·ro

accident incidente ⓜ een·chee·*den*·te ·

accommodation alloggio ⓜ a·*lo*·jo

acupuncture agopuntura ⓕ a·go·poon·*too*·ra

adaptor spina ⓕ multipla *spee*·na *mool*·tee·pla

addicted dipendente ⓜ/ⓕ dee·pen·*den*·te

address indirizzo ⓜ een·dee·*ree*·tso

administration amministrazione ⓕ a·mee·nee·stra·*tsyo*·ne

admission price prezzo ⓜ d'ingresso *pre*·tso deen·*gre*·so

admit (let in) far entrare far en·*tra*·re

adult adulto/a ⓜ/ⓕ a·*dool*·to/a

adventure avventura ⓕ a·ven·*too*·ra

advertisement annuncio ⓜ a·*noon*·cho

aerobics aerobica ⓕ a·e·ro·*bee*·ka

after dopo *do*·po

afternoon pomeriggio ⓜ po·me·*ree*·jo

aftershave dopobarba ⓜ do·po·*bar*·ba

again di nuovo dee *nwo*·vo

age età ⓕ e·*ta*

aggressive aggressivo/a ⓜ/ⓕ a·gre·*see*·vo/a

agree essere d'accordo *e*·se·re da·*kor*·do

agriculture agricoltura ⓕ a·gree·kol·*too*·ra

AIDS AIDS ⓜ a·*eedz*

air aria ⓕ a·*rya*

airmail via ⓕ aerea *vee*·a a·e·re·a

air-conditioned ad aria condizionata ad a·rya kon·dee·*tsyo*·na·ta

airline linea ⓕ aerea *lee*·ne·a a·e·re·a

airport aeroporto ⓜ a·e·ro·*por*·to

airport tax tassa ⓕ aeroportuale *ta*·sa a·e·ro·por·*twa*·le

aisle (plane, train) corridoio ⓜ ko·ree·*do*·yo

alarm clock sveglia ⓕ *sve*·lya

alcohol alcol ⓜ *al*·kol

all (singular) tutto/a ⓜ/ⓕ *too*·to/a

B

all (plural) tutti/e ⓜ/ⓕ *too·tee/ too·te*

allergy allergia ⓕ *a·ler·jee·a*

almond mandorla ⓕ *man·dor·la*

alone da solo/a ⓜ/ⓕ *da so·lo/a*

already già *ja*

also anche *an·ke*

altar altare ⓜ *al·ta·re*

altitude quota ⓕ *kwo·ta*

always sempre *sem·pre*

ambassador ambasciatore/ ambasciatrice ⓜ/ⓕ *am·ba·sha·to·re/ am·ba·sha·tree·che*

ambulance ambulanza ⓕ *am·boo·lan·tsa*

amount quantità ⓕ *kwan·tee·ta*

ancient antico/a ⓜ/ⓕ *an·tee·ko/a*

and e *e*

angry arrabbiato/a ⓜ/ⓕ *a·ra·bya·to/a*

animal animale ⓜ *a·nee·ma·le*

ankle caviglia ⓕ *ka·vee·lya*

annual annuale *a·noo·a·le*

answer risposta ⓕ *rees·pos·ta*

ant formica ⓕ *for·mee·ka*

antibiotics antibiotici ⓜ pl *an·tee·bee·o·tee·chee*

antihistamines antistaminici ⓜ pl *an·tee·sta·mee·nee·chee*

antinuclear antinucleare *an·tee·noo·kle·a·re*

antique pezzo ⓜ di antiquariato *pe·tso dee an·tee·kwa·rya·to*

antiseptic antisettico ⓜ *an·tee·se·tee·ko*

appendix appendice ⓕ *a·pen·dee·che*

apple mela ⓕ *me·la*

appointment appuntamento ⓜ *a·poon·ta·men·to*

apricot albicocca ⓕ *al·bee·ko·ka*

archaeological archeologico/a ⓜ/ⓕ *ar·ke·o·lo·jee·ko/a*

architect architetto ⓜ *ar·kee·te·to*

architecture architettura ⓕ *ar·kee·te·too·ra*

argue litigare *lee·tee·ga·re*

arm braccio ⓜ *bra·cho*

aromatherapy aromaterapia ⓕ *a·ro·ma·te·ra·pee·a*

arrest arrestare *a·res·ta·re*

arrivals arrivi ⓜ pl *a·ree·vee*

arrive arrivare *a·ree·va·re*

art arte ⓕ *ar·te*

art gallery galleria ⓕ d'arte *ga·le·ree·a dar·te*

artist artista ⓜ&ⓕ *ar·tee·sta*

ashtray portacenere ⓜ *por·ta·che·ne·re*

ask (a question) domandare *do·man·da·re*

ask (for something) richiedere *ree·kye·de·re*

aspirin aspirina ⓕ *as·pee·ree·na*

asthma asma ⓕ *az·ma*

athletics atletica ⓕ *at·le·tee·ka*

aubergine melanzana ⓕ *me·lan·dza·na*

aunt zia ⓕ *tsee·a*

Australia Australia ⓕ *ow·stra·lya*

Austria Austria ⓕ *ow·stree·a*

automatic automatico/a ⓜ/ⓕ *ow·to·ma·tee·ko/a*

automatic teller machine (ATM) Bancomat ⓜ *ban·ko·mat*

autumn autunno ⓜ *ow·too·no*

avenue viale ⓜ *vee·a·le*

awful orrendo/a ⓜ/ⓕ *o·ren·do/a*

B

B&W (film) in bianco e nero *een byan·ko e ne·ro*

baby bimbo/a ⓜ/ⓕ *beem·bo/a*

baby food cibo ⓜ da bebè *chee·bo da be·be*

baby powder borotalco ⓜ *bo·ro·tal·ko*

back (body) schiena ⓕ *skye·na*

backpack zaino ⓜ *dzai·no*

bacon pancetta ⓕ *pan·che·ta*

bad cattivo/a ⓜ/ⓕ *ka·tee·vo/a*

bag (general) borsa ⓕ *bor·sa*

bag (shopping) sacchetto ⓜ *sa·ke·to*

baggage bagaglio ⓜ *ba·ga·lyo*

B

baggage allowance bagaglio ⓜ consentito ba·*ga*·lyo kon·sen·*tee*·to

baggage claim ritiro ⓜ bagagli ree·*tee*·ro ba·*ga*·lyee

bakery panetteria ⓕ pa·ne·te·*ree*·a

balance (account) saldo ⓜ *sal*·do

balcony balcone ⓜ bal·*ko*·ne

ball (dancing) ballo ⓜ *ba*·lo

ball (inflated) pallone ⓜ pa·*lo*·ne

ball (sports) palla ⓕ *pa*·la

ballet balletto ⓜ ba·*le*·to

band (music) gruppo ⓜ *groo*·po

bandage fascia ⓕ *fa*·sha

Band-Aids cerotti ⓜ pl che·*ro*·tee

bank (money) banca ⓕ *ban*·ka

bank account conto ⓜ in banca *kon*·to een *ban*·ka

banknote banconota ⓕ ban·ko·*no*·ta

baptism battesimo ⓜ ba·*te*·zee·mo

bar locale ⓜ lo·*ka*·le

bar fridge frigobar ⓜ *free*·go·bar

barber barbiere ⓜ bar·*bye*·re

basket cestino ⓜ ches·*tee*·no

basketball pallacanestro ⓕ pa·la·ka·*ne*·stro

bath bagno ⓜ *ba*·nyo

bathing suit costume ⓜ da bagno kos·*too*·me da *ba*·nyo

bathroom bagno ⓜ *ba*·nyo

battery (for car) batteria ⓕ ba·te·*ree*·a

battery (general) pila ⓕ *pee*·la

be essere *e*·se·re

beach spiaggia ⓕ *spya*·ja

beans fagioli ⓜ pl fa·*jo*·lee

beansprouts germogli ⓜ pl (di soia) jer·*mo*·lyee (dee *so*·ya)

beautician estetista ⓜ&ⓕ es·te·*tee*·sta

beautiful bello/a ⓜ/ⓕ *be*·lo/a

beauty salon parrucchiere ⓜ pa·roo·*kye*·re

because perché per·*ke*

bed letto ⓜ *le*·to

bedding coperte ⓕ pl e lenzuola ⓕ pl ko·*per*·te e len·*zwo*·la

bedroom camera ⓕ da letto *ka*·me·ra da *le*·to

bee ape ⓕ *a*·pe

beef manzo ⓜ *man*·dzo

beer birra ⓕ *bee*·ra

beetroot barbabietola ⓕ bar·ba·*bye*·to·la

before prima *pree*·ma

beggar mendicante ⓜ&ⓕ men·dee·*kan*·te

begin cominciare ko·meen·*cha*·re

behind dietro *dye*·tro

Belgium Belgio ⓜ *bel*·jo

below sotto *so*·to

best migliore mee·*lyo*·re

bet scommessa ⓕ sko·*me*·sa

better migliore mee·*lyo*·re

between fra fra

bible bibbia ⓕ *bee*·bya

bicycle bicicletta ⓕ bee·chee·*kle*·ta

big grande *gran*·de

bike chain catena ⓕ di bicicletta ka·*te*·na dee bee·chee·*kle*·ta

bike lock lucchetto ⓜ lo·*ke*·to

bike path ciclopista ⓕ chee·klo·*pee*·sta

bill (account) conto ⓜ *kon*·to

binoculars binocolo ⓜ bee·*no*·ko·lo

bird uccello ⓜ oo·*che*·lo

birthday compleanno ⓜ kom·ple·*a*·no

biscuit biscotto ⓜ bees·*ko*·to

bite (dog) morso ⓜ *mor*·so

bite (insect) puntura ⓕ poon·*too*·ra

black nero/a ⓜ/ⓕ *ne*·ro/a

blanket coperta ⓕ ko·*per*·ta

blind cieco/a ⓜ/ⓕ *chye*·ko/a

blister vescica ⓕ ve·*shee*·ka

blocked bloccato/a ⓜ/ⓕ blo·*ka*·to/a

blonde biondo/a ⓜ/ⓕ *byon*·do/a

blood sangue ⓜ *san*·gwe

blood group gruppo ⓜ sanguigno *groo*·po san·*gwee*·nyo

blood pressure pressione ⓕ del sangue pre·*syo*·ne del *san*·gwe

blood test analisi ⓕ del sangue a·*na*·lee·zee del *san*·gwe

blue (dark) blu bloo

blue (light) azzurro/a ⓜ/ⓕ
a·dzoo·ro/a

board (plane/ship) salire su
sa·lee·re soo

boarding house pensione ⓕ
pen·syo·ne

boarding pass carta ⓕ d'imbarco
kar·ta deem·bar·ko

boat barca ⓕ bar·ka

body corpo ⓜ kor·po

bone osso ⓜ o·so

book libro ⓜ lee·bro

book (make a booking) prenotare
pre·no·ta·re

booked out completo/a ⓜ/ⓕ
kom·ple·to/a

bookshop libreria ⓕ lee·bre·ree·a

boots stivali ⓜ pl stee·va·lee

boots (ski) scarponi ⓜ pl (da sci)
skar·po·nee (da shee)

boots (soccer) scarpette ⓕ pl
skar·pe·te

border confine ⓜ kon·fee·ne

bored annoiato/a ⓜ/ⓕ a·no·ya·to/a

boring noioso/a ⓜ/ⓕ no·yo·zo/a

borrow prendere in prestito pren·de·re
een pres·tee·to

bottle bottiglia ⓕ bo·tee·lya

bottle opener apribottiglie ⓜ
a·pree bo·tee·lye

(at the) bottom (in) fondo ⓜ (een)
fon·do

bowl piatto ⓜ fondo pya·to fon·do

box scatola ⓕ ska·to·la

boxing pugilato ⓜ poo·jee·la·to

boy bambino ⓜ bam·bee·no

boy(friend) ragazzo ⓜ ra·ga·tso

bra reggiseno ⓜ re·jee·se·no

brake freno ⓜ fre·no

brave coraggioso/a ⓜ/ⓕ ko·ra·jo·zo/a

bread pane ⓜ pa·ne

break rompere rom·pe·re

break down guastarsi gwas·tar·see

breakfast (prima) colazione ⓕ
(pree·ma) ko·la·tsyo·ne

breast seno ⓜ se·no

breathe respirare res·pee·ra·re

brewery fabbrica di birra ⓕ fa·bree·ka
dee bee·ra

bribe corrompere ko·rom·pe·re

bridge ponte ⓜ pon·te

briefcase valigetta ⓕ va·lee·je·ta

brilliant brillante ⓜ/ⓕ bree·lan·te

bring portare por·ta·re

broken rotto/a ⓜ/ⓕ ro·to/a

broken down guastato/a ⓜ/ⓕ
gwas·ta·to/a

bronchitis bronchite ⓕ bron·kee·te

brother fratello ⓜ fra·te·lo

brown marrone ⓜ/ⓕ ma·ro·ne

bruise livido ⓜ lee·vee·do

bucket secchio ⓜ se·kyo

Buddhist buddista ⓜ&ⓕ boo·dee·sta

budget bilancio ⓜ bee·lan·cho

buffet (meal) pasto ⓜ freddo pas·to
fre·do

bug insetto ⓜ een·se·to

build costruire kos·troo·ee·re

builder costruttore/costruttrice ⓜ/ⓕ
kos·troo·to·re/ko·stroo·tree·che

building edificio ⓜ e·de·fee·cho

burn bruciare broo·cha·re

bus (city) autobus ⓜ ow·to·boos

bus (coach) pullman ⓜ pool·man

bus station stazione ⓕ d'autobus
sta·tsyo·ne dow·to·boos

bus stop fermata ⓕ d'autobus
fer·ma·ta dow·to·boos

business affari ⓜ pl a·fa·ree

business class classe ⓕ business
kla·se beez·nes

business person uomo/donna
d'affari ⓜ/ⓕ wo·mo/do·na da·fa·ree

business studies commercio ⓜ
ko·mer·cho

business trip viaggio ⓜ d'affari
vee·a·jo da·fa·ree

busker musicista ⓜ&ⓕ di strada
moo·zee·chee·sta dee stra·da

but ma ma

butcher's shop macelleria ⓕ
ma·che·le·ree·a

C

butter burro ⓜ *boo*·ro
butterfly farfalla ⓕ far·*fa*·la
button bottone ⓜ bo·*to*·ne
buy comprare kom·*pra*·re

C

cabbage cavolo ⓜ *ka*·vo·lo
cable car funivia ⓕ foo·nee·*vee*·a
cafe bar ⓜ bar
cake torta ⓕ *tor*·ta
cake shop pasticceria ⓕ
pa·stee·che·*ree*·a
calculator calcolatrice ⓕ
kal·ko·la·*tree*·che
calendar calendario ⓜ ka·len·*da*·ryo
camera macchina ⓕ fotografica
ma·kee·na fo·to·*gra*·fee·ka
camera shop fotografo ⓜ
fo·*to*·gra·fo
camp campeggiare kam·pe·*ja*·re
camp site campeggio ⓜ kam·*pe*·jo
camping store negozio ⓜ da
campeggio ne·*go*·tsyo da kam·*pe*·jo
can (tin) scatola ⓕ *ska*·to·la
can potere po·*te*·re
can opener apriscatole ⓜ
a·pree·*ska*·to·le
cancel cancellare kan·che·*la*·re
cancer cancro ⓜ *kan*·kro
candle candela ⓕ kan·*de*·la
candy dolciumi ⓜ pl dol·*choo*·mee
cantaloupe melone ⓜ me·*lo*·ne
capsicum peperone ⓜ pe·pe·*ro*·ne
car macchina ⓕ *ma*·kee·na
car hire autonoleggio ⓜ
ow·to·no·*le*·jo
car owner's title libretto ⓜ
di circolazione lee·*bre*·to dee
cheer·ko·la·*tsyo*·ne
car park parcheggio ⓜ par·*ke*·jo
car racing automobilismo ⓜ
ow·to·mo·bee·*leez*·mo
car registration bollo ⓜ di circolazione
bo·lo dee cheer·ko·la·*tsyo*·ne
caravan roulotte ⓕ roo·*lot*
cards carte ⓕ pl *kar*·te

carpenter carpentiere ⓜ
kar·pen·*tye*·re
carrot carota ⓕ ka·*ro*·ta
carry portare por·*ta*·re
carry-on luggage bagaglio ⓜ a mano
ba·*ga*·lyo a *ma*·no
carton scatola ⓕ *ska*·to·la
cash soldi ⓜ pl *sol*·dee
cash a cheque riscuotere un assegno
ree·*skwo*·te·re oon a·*se*·nyo
cash register cassa ⓕ *ka*·sa
cashew noce ⓕ (di acagiù) *no*·che
(dee a·ka·*joo*)
cashier cassiere/a ⓜ/ⓕ ka·*sye*·re/a
casino casinò ⓜ ka·zee·*no*
cassette cassetta ⓕ ka·*se*·ta
castle castello ⓜ kas·*te*·lo
cat gatto ⓜ *ga*·to
cathedral duomo ⓜ *dwo*·mo
Catholic cattolico/a ⓜ/ⓕ
ka·*to*·lee·ko/a
cauliflower cavolfiore ⓜ
ka·vol·*fyo*·re
cave grotta ⓕ *gro*·ta
caviar caviale ⓜ ka·*vya*·le
CD cidi ⓜ chee·*dee*
celebration celebrazione ⓕ
che·le·bra·*tsyo*·ne
cell phone (telefono) cellulare ⓜ
(te·*le*·fo·no) che·loo·*la*·re
cent centesimo ⓜ chen·*te*·zee·mo
centimetre centimetro ⓜ
chen·*tee*·me·tro
central heating riscaldamento ⓜ
centrale rees·kal·da·*men*·to chen·*tra*·le
centre centro ⓜ *chen*·tro
cereal cereali ⓜ pl che·re·*a*·lee
certificate certificato ⓜ
cher·tee·fee·*ka*·to
chain catena ⓕ ka·*te*·na
chair sedia ⓕ *se*·dya
chairlift (skiing) seggiovia ⓕ
se·jo·*vee*·a
championships campionato ⓜ
kam·pyo·*na*·to
chance fortuna ⓕ for·*too*·na

C

change (coins) spiccioli ⓜ pl
spee·cho·lee

change (money) resto ⓜ res·to

change cambiare kam·bya·re

change room (sport) spogliatoio ⓜ
spo·lya·to·yo

charming affascinante
a·fa·shee·nan·te

chat up agganciare a·gan·cha·re

cheap economico/a ⓜ/ⓕ
e·ko·no·mee·ko/a

cheat imbrogliare eem·bro·lya·re

check (bill) conto ⓜ kon·to

check controllare kon·tro·la·re

check-in (airport) accetazione ⓕ
a·che·ta·tsyo·ne

check-in (hotel) registrazione ⓕ
re·jee·stra·tsyo·ne

cheese formaggio ⓜ for·ma·jo

chef cuoco/a ⓜ/ⓕ kwo·ko/a

chemist farmacista ⓜ&ⓕ
far·ma·chee·sta

cheque assegno ⓜ a·se·nyo

chess scacchi ⓜ pl ska·kee

chest petto ⓜ pe·to

chicken pollo ⓜ po·lo

chickpeas ceci ⓜ pl che·chee

child bambino/a ⓜ/ⓕ bam·bee·no/a

child seat seggiolino ⓜ se·jo·lee·no

child minding (group) asilo nido ⓜ
a·zee·lo nee·do

chilli peperoncino ⓜ
pe·pe·ron·chee·no

chilli sauce salsa ⓕ di peperoncino
rosso sal·sa dee pe·pe·ron·chee·no
ro·so

chiropractor chiropratico ⓜ
kee·ro·pra·tee·ko

chocolate cioccolato ⓜ cho·ko·la·to

Christian cristiano/a ⓜ/ⓕ
krees·tya·no/a

Christmas Natale ⓜ na·ta·le

church chiesa ⓕ kye·za

cider sidro ⓜ see·dro

cigar sigaro ⓜ see·ga·ro

cigarette sigaretta ⓕ see·ga·re·ta

cigarette lighter accendino ⓜ
a·chen·dee·no

cinema cinema ⓜ chee·ne·ma

circus circo ⓜ cheer·ko

citizenship cittadinanza ⓕ
chee·ta·dee·nan·tsa

city città ⓕ chee·ta

class classe ⓕ kla·se

classical classico/a ⓜ/ⓕ
kla·see·ko/a

clean pulito/a ⓜ/ⓕ poo·lee·to/a

cleaning pulizia ⓕ poo·lee·tsee·a

client cliente ⓜ&ⓕ klee·en·te

cliff scogliera ⓕ sko·lye·ra

climb scalare ska·la·re

cloakroom guardaroba ⓜ
gwar·da·ro·ba

clock orologio ⓜ o·ro·lo·jo

close (nearby) vicino/a ⓜ/ⓕ
vee·chee·no/a

close (shut) chiudere kyoo·de·re

closed chiuso/a ⓜ/ⓕ kyoo·zo/a

clothes line corda ⓕ del bucato
kor·da del boo·ka·to

clothing abbigliamento ⓜ
a·bee·lya·men·to

clothing store negozio ⓜ di
abbigliamento ne·go·tsyo dee
a·bee·lya·men·to

cloud nuvola ⓕ noo·vo·la

cloudy nuvoloso/a ⓜ/ⓕ
noo·vo·lo·zo/a

clutch frizione ⓕ free·tsyo·ne

coach (bus) pullman ⓜ pool·man

coast costa ⓕ kos·ta

coat cappotto ⓜ ka·po·to

cocaine cocaina ⓕ ko·ka·ee·na

cockroach scarafaggio ⓜ
ska·ra·fa·jo

cocoa cacao ⓜ ka·ka·o

coffee caffè ⓜ ka·fe

coins monete ⓕ pl mo·ne·te

cold freddo/a ⓜ/ⓕ fre·do/a

(have a) cold essere raffreddato/a
ⓜ/ⓕ e·se·re ra·fre·da·to/a

colleague collega ⓜ&ⓕ ko·le·ga

collect call chiamata ① a carico del destinatario kya·*ma*·ta a *ka*·ree·ko del des·tee·na·ta·ryo

college collegio ⓜ universitario ko·*le*·jo oo·nee·ver·see·*ta*·ryo

colour colore ⓜ ko·*lo*·re

comb pettine ⓜ *pe*·tee·ne

come venire ve·*nee*·re

comedy commedia ① comica ko·*me*·dya ko·mee·ka

comfortable comodo/a ⓜ/①
ko·mo·do/a

commission commissione ①
ko·mee·*syo*·ne

communion comunione ①
ko·moo·*nyo*·ne

communist comunista ⓜ&①
ko·moo·*nee*·sta

companion compagno/a ⓜ/①
kom·*pa*·nyo/a

company (firm) ditta ① *dee*·ta

compass bussola ① *boo*·so·la

complain lamentarsi la·men·*tar*·see

complimentary (free) gratuito/a
ⓜ/① gra·*too*·ee·to/a

computer game gioco ⓜ elettronico
jo·ko e·le·*tro*·nee·ko

concert concerto ⓜ kon·*cher*·to

conditioner balsamo ⓜ per i capelli
bal·sa·mo per ee ka·*pe*·lee

condom preservativo ⓜ
pre·zer·va·*tee*·vo

confession (religious) confessione
① kon·fe·*syo*·ne

confirm (a booking) confermare
kon·fer·*ma*·re

connection (transport) coincidenza
① ko·een·chee·*den*·tsa

conservative conservatore/
conservatrice ⓜ/① kon·ser·va·*to*·re/
kon·ser·va·*tree*·che

constipation stitichezza ①
stee·tee·*ke*·tsa

consulate consolato ⓜ kon·so·*la*·to

contact lenses lenti ① pl a contatto
len·tee a kon·*ta*·to

contraceptive contraccettivo ⓜ
kon·tra·che·*tee*·vo

contract contratto ⓜ kon·*tra*·to

convenience store alimentari ⓜ
a·lee·men·*ta*·ree

convent convento ⓜ kon·*ven*·to

cook cuoco/a ⓜ/① *kwo*·ko/a

cook cucinare koo·chee·*na*·re

cookie biscotto ⓜ bees·*ko*·to

corn flakes fiocchi ⓜ pl di mais
fyo·kee dee *ma*·ees

corner angolo ⓜ *an*·go·lo

correct giusto/a ⓜ/① *joo*·sto/a

corrupt corrotto/a ⓜ/① ko·*ro*·to/a

cost costare kos·*ta*·re

cot culla ① *koo*·la

cotton cotone ⓜ ko·*to*·ne

cotton balls batuffoli ⓜ pl di cotone
ba·*too*·fo·lee dee ko·*to*·ne

cough tossire to·*see*·re

cough medicine sciroppo ⓜ per la
tosse shee·*ro*·po per la *to*·se

count contare kon·*ta*·re

counter (at bar) bancone ⓜ ban·*ko*·ne

country (nation) paese ⓜ pa·*e*·ze

countryside campagna ① kam·*pa*·nya

courgette zucchini ⓜ pl
tsoo·*kee*·nee

court (legal) corte ① *kor*·te

court (tennis) campo ⓜ da tennis
kam·po da *te*·nees

cover charge (restaurant) coperto ⓜ
ko·*per*·to

cover charge (venue) ingresso ⓜ
een·*gre*·so

cow mucca ① *moo*·ka

craft (product) pezzo ⓜ
d'artigianato *pe*·tso dar·tee·ja·*na*·to

craft (trade) mestiere ⓜ mes·*tye*·re

crash (accident) incidente ⓜ
een·chee·*den*·te

crazy pazzo/a ⓜ/① *pa*·tso/a

cream (food) panna ① *pa*·na

cream cheese formaggio ⓜ fresco
for·*ma*·jo *fres*·ko

creche asilo ⓜ nido a·*zee*·lo *nee*·do

credit card carta ⓕ di credito *kar*·ta dee *kre*·dee·to

crime (infringment) delitto ⓜ de·*lee*·to

crime (issue) criminalità ⓕ kree·mee·na·lee·*ta*

Croatia Croazia ⓜ kro·a·*tsya*

cross (religious) croce ⓕ *kro*·che

crowded affollato/a ⓜ/ⓕ a·fo·la·to/a

cucumber cetriolo ⓜ che·tree·o·lo

cup tazza ⓕ *ta*·tsa

currency exchange cambio ⓜ valuta *kam*·byo va·*loo*·ta

current (electricity) corrente ⓕ ko·*ren*·te

current affairs attualità ⓕ a·too·a·lee·*ta*

curry powder polvere ⓕ da curry *pol*·ve·ro da *kuu*·ree

customs dogana ⓕ do·*ga*·na

cut tagliare ta·*lya*·re

cutlery posate ⓕ pl po·*za*·te

cycle andare in bicicletta an·*da*·re een bee·chee·*kle*·ta

cycling ciclismo ⓜ chee·*kleez*·mo

cyclist ciclista ⓜ&ⓕ chee·*klee*·sta

cystitis cistite ⓕ chees·*tee*·te

D

dad papà ⓜ pa·*pa*

damage danno ⓜ *da*·no

dance ballare ba·*la*·re

dancing ballo ⓜ *ba*·lo

dangerous pericoloso/a ⓜ/ⓕ pe·ree·ko·lo·zo/a

dark scuro/a ⓜ/ⓕ *skoo*·ro/a

date (appointment) appuntamento ⓜ a·poon·ta·*men*·to

date (day) data ⓕ *da*·ta

date (go out with) uscire con oo·*shee*·re kon

date of birth data ⓕ di nascita *da*·ta dee *na*·shee·ta

daughter figlia ⓕ *fee*·lya

day giorno ⓜ *jor*·no

day after tomorrow dopodomani do·po·do·*ma*·nee

day before yesterday altro ieri ⓜ *al*·tro *ye*·ree

dead morto/a ⓜ/ⓕ *mor*·to/a

deaf sordo/a ⓜ/ⓕ *sor*·do/a

deep profondo/a ⓜ/ⓕ pro·*fon*·do/a

delay ritardo ⓜ ree·*tar*·do

delicatessen salumeria ⓕ sa·loo·me·*ree*·a

democracy democrazia ⓕ de·mo·kra·*tsee*·a

demonstration (protest) manifestazione ⓕ ma·nee·fes·ta·*tsyo*·ne

Denmark Danimarca ⓕ da·nee·*mar*·ka

dental floss filo ⓜ dentario *fee*·lo den·*ta*·ree·o

dentist dentista ⓜ&ⓕ den·*tee*·sta

deodorant deodorante ⓜ de·o·do·*ran*·te

depart partire par·*tee*·re

department store grande magazzino ⓜ *gran*·de ma·ga·*dzee*·no

departure partenza ⓕ par·*ten*·tsa

deposit (bank) deposito ⓜ de·po·*zee*·to

deposit (refundable) caparra ⓕ ka·*pa*·ra

derailleur deragliatore ⓜ de·ra·lya·*to*·re

dessert dolce ⓜ *dol*·che

destination destinazione ⓕ des·tee·na·*tsyo*·ne

diabetes diabete ⓜ dee·a·*be*·te

dial tone segnale ⓜ (acustico) se·*nya*·le (a·*koos*·tee·ko)

diaper pannolino ⓜ pa·no·*lee*·no

diaphragm diaframma ⓜ dee·a·*fra*·ma

diarrhoea diarrea ⓕ dee·a·*re*·a

diary agenda ⓕ a·*jen*·da

dictionary vocabolario ⓜ vo·ka·bo·*la*·ryo

die morire mo·*ree*·re

diet dieta ⓕ *dye*·ta

different diverso/a dee·*ver*·so/a
different (from) differente (da) dee·fe·*ren*·te (da)
difficult difficile dee·*fee*·chee·le
digital digitale dee·jee·*ta*·le
dining car carrozza ⓕ ristorante ka·ro·tsa rees·to·*ran*·te
dinner cena ⓕ *che*·na
direct diretto/a ⓜ/ⓕ dee·*re*·to/a
direct-dial telefono ⓜ diretto te·*le*·fo·no dee·*re*·to
direction direzione ⓕ dee·re·*tsyo*·ne
director (films) regista ⓜ&ⓕ re·*jee*·sta
dirty sporco/a ⓜ/ⓕ *spor*·ko/a
disabled disabile dee·*za*·bee·le
discount sconto ⓜ *skon*·to
discrimination discriminazione ⓕ dees·kree·mee·na·*tsyo*·ne
disease malattia ⓕ ma·la·*tee*·a
disinfectant disinfettante ⓜ deez·een·fe·*tan*·te
disk (computer) dischetto ⓜ dees·*ke*·to
disposable usa e getta oo·za e *je*·ta
dive tuffarsi ⓜ pl too·*far*·see
diving (sea) immersioni ⓕ pl ee·mer·*syo*·ne
divorced divorziato/a ⓜ/ⓕ dee·vor·*tsya*·to/a
dizzy stordito/a ⓜ/ⓕ stor·*dee*·to/a
do fare *fa*·re
doctor medico ⓜ *me*·dee·ko
dog cane ⓜ *ka*·ne
dole sussidio ⓜ di disoccupazione soo·*see*·dyo dee dee·zo·koo·pa·*tsyo*·ne
doll bambola ⓕ *bam*·bo·la
dollar dollaro ⓜ *do*·la·ro
door porta ⓕ *por*·ta
dope (drugs) roba ⓕ *ro*·ba
double doppio/a ⓜ/ⓕ *do*·pyo/a
double bed letto ⓜ matrimoniale *le*·to ma·tree·mo·*nya*·le
double room camera ⓕ doppia *ka*·mer·a *do*·pya
down giù joo

dozen dozzina ⓕ do·*dzee*·na
drag queen travestito ⓜ tra·ves·*tee*·to
drama dramma ⓜ *dra*·ma
dream sogno ⓜ *so*·nyo
dream sognare so·*nya*·re
dress abito ⓜ *a*·bee·to
drink bevanda ⓕ be·*van*·da
drink bere *be*·re
drinkable potabile po·*ta*·bee·le
drive guidare gwee·*da*·re
drivers licence patente ⓕ (di guida) pa·*ten*·te (dee gwee·da)
drug (medicinal) medicina ⓕ me·dee·*chee*·na
drug addiction tossicodipendenza ⓕ to·see·ko·dee·pen·*den*·tsa
drug dealer spacciatore/spacciatrice ⓜ/ⓕ spa·cha·to·re/spa·cha·*tree*·che
drugs (illegal) droga ⓕ sg *dro*·ga
drums batteria ⓕ ba·te·*ree*·a
drunk ubriaco/a ⓜ/ⓕ oo·bree·*a*·ko/a
dry secco/a ⓜ/ⓕ *se*·ko/a
dry asciugare a·shoo·*ga*·re
dry cleaning lavaggio ⓜ a secco la·*va*·jo a *se*·ko
duck anatra ⓕ *a*·na·tra
dummy (pacifier) ciucciotto ⓜ choo·*cho*·to
during durante doo·*ran*·te

E

each ciascuno/a ⓜ/ⓕ chas·*koo*·no/a
ear orecchio ⓜ o·*re*·kyo
early presto ⓜ/ⓕ *pres*·to
earplugs tappi ⓜ pl per le orecchie *ta*·pee per le o·*re*·kye
earrings orecchini ⓜ pl o·re·*kee*·nee
Earth Terra ⓕ *te*·ra
earthquake terremoto ⓜ te·re·*mo*·to
east est ⓜ est
Easter Pasqua ⓕ *pas*·kwa
easy facile *fa*·chee·le
eat mangiare man·*ja*·re
economy class classe ⓕ turistica *kla*·se too·*ree*·stee·ka

eczema eczema Ⓜ ek·dze·ma
education istruzione Ⓕ
ees·troo·tsyo·ne
egg uovo Ⓜ wo·vo
eggplant melanzana Ⓕ me·lan·dza·na
elections elezioni Ⓕ pl e·le·tsyo·nee
electrician elettricista Ⓜ&Ⓕ
e·le·tree·chee·sta
electricity elettricità Ⓕ
e·le·tree·chee·ta
elevator ascensore Ⓜ a·shen·so·re
email email Ⓜ e·mayl
embarrassed imbarazzato/a Ⓜ/Ⓕ
eem·ba·ra·tsa·to/a
embassy ambasciata Ⓕ am·ba·sha·ta
emergency emergenza Ⓕ
e·mer·jen·tsa
emotional emotivo/a Ⓜ/Ⓕ
e·mo·tee·vo/a
employee impiegato/a Ⓜ/Ⓕ
eem·pye·ga·to/a
employer datore/datrice Ⓜ/Ⓕ di
lavoro da·to·re/da·tree·ce dee la·vo·ro
empty vuoto/a Ⓜ/Ⓕ vwo·to/a
end fine Ⓕ fee·ne
end finire fee·nee·re
endangered species specie Ⓕ in via
di estinzione spe·che een vee·a dee
es·teen·tsyo·ne
engagement (couple) fidanzamento
Ⓜ fee·dan·tsa men·to
engine motore Ⓜ mo·to·re
engineer ingegnere Ⓜ&Ⓕ
een·je·nye·re
England Inghilterra Ⓕ een·geel·te·ra
English inglese een·gle·ze
enjoy (oneself) divertirsi
dee·ver·teer·see
enough abbastanza a·bas·tan·tsa
enter entrare en·tra·re
entertainment guide guida Ⓕ agli
spettacoli gwee·da a·lyee spe·ta·ko·lee
entry entrata Ⓕ en·tra·ta
(padded) envelope busta Ⓕ
(imbottita) boo·sta eem·bo·tee·ta
environment ambiente Ⓜ am·byen·te

epilepsy epilessia Ⓕ e·pee·le·see·a
equipment attrezzatura Ⓕ
a·tre·tsa·too·ra
escalator scala Ⓕ mobile ska·la
mo·bee·le
euro euro Ⓜ e·oo·ro
Europe Europa Ⓕ e·oo·ro·pa
European europeo/a Ⓜ/Ⓕ
e·oo·ro·pe·o/a
euthanasia eutanasia Ⓕ
e·oo·ta·na·zee·a
evening sera Ⓕ se·ra
everything tutto Ⓜ too·to
example esempio Ⓜ e·zem·pyo
excellent ottimo/a Ⓜ/Ⓕ o·tee·mo/a
excess bagage bagaglio Ⓜ in
eccedenza ba·ga·lyo een e·che·den·tsa
exchange cambio Ⓜ kam·byo
exchange cambiare kam·bya·re
exchange rate tasso Ⓜ di cambio
ta·so dee kam·byo
excluded escluso/a Ⓜ/Ⓕ es·kloo·zo/a
exhaust (car) tubo Ⓜ di scappamento
too·bo dee ska·pa·men·to
exhibition esposizione Ⓕ
es·po·zee·tsyo·ne
exit uscita Ⓕ oo·shee·ta
expensive caro/a Ⓜ/Ⓕ ka·ro/a
experience esperienza Ⓕ
es·pe·ryen·tsa
exploitation sfruttamento Ⓜ
sfroo·la·men·to
express espresso/a Ⓜ/Ⓕ es·pre·so/a
express mail posta Ⓕ prioritaria
pos·la pree·o·ree·ta·rya
extension (visa) proroga Ⓕ pro·ro·ga
eye occhio Ⓜ o·kyo
eye drops collirio Ⓜ ko·lee·ryo

F

fabric stoffa Ⓕ sto·fa
face faccia Ⓕ fa·cha
factory fabbrica Ⓕ fa·bree·ka
factory worker operaio/a Ⓜ/Ⓕ
o·pe·ra·yo/a
fall (autumn) autunno Ⓜ ow·too·no

F

family famiglia ① fa·*mee*·lya
family name cognome ⑩ ko·*nyo*·me
famous famoso/a ⑩/① fa·*mo*·zo/a
fan (person) tifoso/a ⑩/① tee·*fo*·zo/a
fan (machine) ventilatore ⑩ ven·tee·la·*to*·re
fan belt cinghia ① della ventola *cheen*·gya de·la ven·to·la
far lontano/a ⑩/① lon·*ta*·no/a
farm fattoria ① fa·to·*ree*·a
farmer agricoltore/agricoltrice ⑩/① a·gree·kol·*to*·re/a·gree·kol·*tree*·che
fashion moda ① *mo*·da
fast veloce ve·*lo*·che
fat grasso/a ⑩/① *gra*·so/a
father padre ⑩ *pa*·dre
father-in-law suocero ⑩ *swo*·che·ro
faucet rubinetto ⑩ roo·bee·*ne*·to
fault (someone's) colpa ① *kol*·pa
faulty difettoso/a ⑩/① dee·fe·*to*·zo/a
favourite preferito/a ⑩/① pre·fe·*ree*·to/a
fee compenso ⑩ kom·*pen*·so
feel sentire sen·*tee*·re
feelings sentimenti ⑩ pl sen·tee·*men*·tee
fence recinto ⑩ re·*cheen*·to
fencing (sport) scherma ① *sker*·ma
ferry traghetto ⑩ tra·*ge*·to
festival festa ① *fes*·ta
fever febbre ① *fe*·bre
few pochi/e ⑩/① *po*·kee/*po*·ke
fiance(e) fidanzato/a ⑩/① fee·dan·*tsa*·to/a
fiction narrativa ① na·ra·*tee*·va
fig fico ⑩ *fee*·ko
fight lite ① *lee*·te
film (cinema) film ⑩ feelm
film (roll for camera) rullino ⑩ roo·*lee*·no
film speed ASA *a*·za
find trovare tro·*va*·re
fine (payment) multa ① *mool*·ta
finger dito ⑩ *dee*·to
finish finire fee·*nee*·re

fire fuoco ⑩ *fwo*·ko
firewood legna ① da ardere *le*·nya da ar·*de*·re
first primo/a ⑩/① *pree*·mo/a
first class prima classe ① *pree*·ma *kla*·se
first-aid kit valigetta ① del pronto soccorso va·lee·*je*·ta del *pron*·to so·*kor*·so
fish pesce ⑩ *pe*·she
fish shop pescheria ① pe·ske·*ree*·a
fishing pesca ① *pe*·ska
flag bandiera ① ban·*dye*·ra
flashlight (torch) torcia ① elettrica *tor*·cha e·*le*·tree·ka
flat appartamento ⑩ a·par·ta·*men*·to
flat piatto/a ⑩/① *pya*·to/a
flea pulce ① *pool*·che
flight volo ⑩ *vo*·lo
flood inondazione ① ee·non·da·*tzyo*·nee
floor (ground) pavimento ⑩ pa·vee·*men*·to
floor (storey) piano ⑩ *pya*·no
florist fioraio ⑩&① fyo·*ra*·yo
flour farina ① fa·*ree*·na
flower fiore ① *fyo*·re
flu influenza ① een·floo·*en*·tsa
fly mosca ① *mos*·ka
fly volare vo·*la*·re
foggy nebbioso/a ⑩/① ne·*byo*·zo/a
follow seguire se·*gwee*·re
food cibo ⑩ *chee*·bo
food poisoning intossicazione ① alimentare een·to·see·ka·*tsyo*·ne a·lee·men·*ta*·re
food supplies provviste ⑩ pl alimentari pro·vee·ste a·lee·men·*ta*·ree
foot piede ⑩ *pye*·de
football (soccer) calcio ⑩ *kal*·cho
footpath marciapiede ⑩ mar·cha·*pye*·de
foreign straniero/a ⑩/① stra·*nye*·ro/a
forest foresta ① fo·*res*·ta
forever per sempre per *sem*·pre

forget dimenticare dee·men·tee·ka·re

forgive perdonare per·do·na·re

fork forchetta ① for·ke·ta

form (paper) modulo ⓜ mo·doo·lo

fortnight quindici giorni ⓜ pl kween·dee·chee jor·nee

foyer atrio ⓜ a·tryo

fragile fragile fra·jee·le

France Francia ① fran·cha

free (gratis) gratuito/a ⓜ/① gra·too·ee·to/a

free (not bound) libero/a ⓜ/① lee·be·ro/a

freeze congelare kon·je·la·re

fresh fresco/a ⓜ/① fres·ko/a

fridge frigorifero ⓜ free·go·ree·fe·ro

friend amico/a ⓜ/① a·mee·ko/a

frozen congelato/a ⓜ/① kon·je·la·to/a

frozen foods surgelati ⓜ pl soor·je·la·tee

fruit frutta ① froo·ta

fruit juice (bottled) succo ⓜ di frutta soo·ko dee froo·ta

fruit juice (fresh) spremuta ① spre·moo·ta

fry friggere free·je·re

frying pan padella ① pa·de·la

full pieno/a ⓜ/① pye·no/a

full-time a tempo pieno a tem·po pye·no

fun divertimento ⓜ dee·ver·tee·men·to

(have) fun divertirsi dee·ver·teer·see

funeral funerale ⓜ foo·ne·ra·le

funny divertente dee·ver·ten·te

furniture mobili ⓜ pl mo·bee·lee

future futuro ⓜ foo·too·ro

G

game (play) gioco ⓜ jo·ko

game (sport) partita ① par·tee·ta

garage garage ⓜ ga·raj

garbage spazzatura ① pl spa·tsa·too·ra

garden giardino ⓜ jar·dee·no

gardening giardinaggio ⓜ jar·dee·na·jo

garlic aglio ⓜ a·lyo

gas (for cooking) gas ⓜ gaz

gas (petrol) benzina ① ben·dzee·na

gas cartridge cartuccia ① di ricambio del gas kar·too·cha dee ree·kam·byo del gaz

gastroenteritis gastroenterite ① gas·tro·en·te·ree·te

gate cancello ⓜ kan·che·lo

gay gay gei

gears (bicycle) cambio ⓜ kam·byo

general generale je·ne·ra·le

Germany Germania ① jer·ma·nya

gift regalo ⓜ re·ga·lo

ginger zenzero ⓜ dzen·dze·ro

girl(friend) ragazza ① ra·ga·tsa

give dare da·re

glandular fever mononucleosi ⓜ mo·no·noo·kle·o·zo

glass (material) vetro ⓦ ve·tro

glass (drinking) bicchiere ⓜ bee·kye·re

glasses (spectacles) occhiali ⓜ pl o·kya·lee

gloves guanti ⓜ pl gwan·tee

go andare an·da·re

go out with uscire con oo·shee·re kon

goat capra ① ka·pra

god (general) dio/dea ⓜ/① dee·o/de·a

goggles (skiing) occhiali ⓜ pl (da sci) o·kya·lee (da shee)

gold oro ⓜ o·ro

golf ball palla ① da golf pa·la da golf

golf course campo ⓜ da golf kam·po da golf

good buono/a ⓜ/① bwo·no/a

government governo ⓜ go·ver·no

grams grammi ⓜ pl gra·mee

grandchild nipote ⓜ&① nee·po·te

grandfather nonno ⓜ no·no

grandmother nonna ① no·na

grapefruit pompelmo ⓜ pom·pel·mo

grapes uva ① pl oo·va

H

grass erba ⓕ *er·*ba
grave (tomb) tomba ⓕ *tom·*ba
great ottimo/a ⓜ/ⓕ *o·*tee·mo/a
green verde *ver·*de
greengrocer fruttivendolo/a ⓜ/ⓕ
froo·tee·*ven·*do·lo/a
grey grigio/a ⓜ/ⓕ *gree·*jo/a
grocery drogheria ⓕ dro·ge·*ree·*a
groundnut arachide ⓕ a·*ra·*kee·de
grow crescere *kre·*she·re
guesthouse pensione ⓕ pen·*syo·*ne
guide (audio) guida ⓕ audio *gwee·*da
*ow·*dyo
guide (person) guida ⓕ *gwee·*da
guide dog cane ⓜ guida *ka·*ne
*gwee·*da
guidebook guida ⓕ (turistica)
*gwee·*da (too·*ree·*stee·ka)
guided tour visita ⓕ guidata
*vee·*zee·ta gwee·*da·*ta
guilty colpevole kol·*pe·*vo·le
guitar chitarra ⓕ kee·*ta·*ra
gum (mouth) gengiva ⓕ jen·*jee·*va
gum (chewing) gomma ⓕ da
masticare *go·*ma da ma·stee·*ka·*re
gym palestra ⓕ pa·*le·*stra
gymnastics ginnastica ⓕ
jee·*nas·*tee·ka
gynaecologist ginecologo/a ⓜ/ⓕ
jee·ne·ko·*lo·*go/a

H

hail grandine ⓕ *gran·*dee·ne
hailstorm grandinata ⓕ
gran·dee·*na·*ta
haircut taglio ⓜ di capelli *ta·*lyo dee
ka·*pe·*lee
hairdresser parrucchiere/a ⓜ/ⓕ
pa·roo·*kye·*re/a
halal halal a·*lal*
half mezzo ⓜ *me·*dzo
hallucinate allucinare
a·loo·chee·*na·*re
ham (boiled) prosciutto ⓜ (cotto)
pro·*shoo·*to (*ko·*to)
hammer martello ⓜ mar·*te·*lo

hammock amaca ⓕ a·*ma·*ka
hand mano ⓕ *ma·*no
handbag borsetta ⓕ bor·*se·*ta
handball pallamuro ⓕ pa·la·*moo·*ro
handicrafts oggetti ⓜ pl
d'artigianato o·*je·*tee dar·tee·ja·*na·*to
handkerchief fazzoletto ⓜ
fa·tso·*le·*to
handlebars manubrio ⓜ ma·*noo·*bryo
handmade fatto/a ⓜ/ⓕ a mano
*fa·*to/a *ma·*no
handsome bello/a ⓜ/ⓕ *be·*lo/a
happy felice ⓜ/ⓕ fe·*lee·*che
harassment molestia ⓕ mo·*les·*tya
harbour porto ⓜ *por·*to
hard (not easy) difficile
dee·*fee·*chee·le
hard (not soft) duro/a ⓜ/ⓕ *doo·*ro/a
hardware store ferramenta ⓕ
fe·ra·*men·*ta
hash hashish ⓜ a·*sheesh*
hat cappello ⓜ ka·*pe·*lo
have avere a·*ve·*re
hay fever febbre ⓕ da fieno *fe·*bre
da *fye·*no
he lui *loo·*ee
head testa ⓕ *tes·*ta
headache mal ⓜ di testa mal dee
*tes·*ta
headlights fari ⓜ pl *fa·*ree
health salute ⓕ sa·*loo·*te
hear sentire sen·*tee·*re
hearing aid apparecchio ⓜ acustico
a·pa·*re·*kyo a·*koos·*tee·ko
heart cuore ⓜ *kwo·*re
heart condition problema ⓜ
cardiaco pro·*ble·*ma kar·*dee·*a·ko
heat caldo ⓜ *kal·*do
heater stufa ⓕ *stoo·*fa
heating riscaldamento ⓜ
rees·kal·da·*men·*to
heavy pesante pe·*zan·*te
height altezza ⓕ al·*te·*tsa
helmet casco ⓜ *kas·*ko
help aiutare a·yoo·*ta·*re
hepatitis epatite ⓕ e·pa·*tee·*te

herbalist erborista ⓜ&ⓕ
er·bo·ree·sta

herbs erbe ⓕ pl er·be

here qui kwee

heroin eroina ⓕ e·ro·ee·na

herring aringa ⓕ a·reen·ga

high alto/a ⓜ/ⓕ al·to/a

high school scuola ⓕ superiore
skwo·la soo·pe·ryo·re

hike escursione ⓕ a piedi
es·koor·syo·ne a pye·de

hiking escursionismo ⓜ a piedi
es·koor·syo·neez·mo a pye·de

hiking boots scarponi ⓜ pl
skar·po·nee

hiking route itinerario ⓜ
escursionistico e·tee·ne·ra·ryo
es·koor·syo·nee·stee·ko

hill collina ⓕ ko·lee·na

Hindu indù ⓜ&ⓕ een·doo

hire noleggiare no·le·ja·re

historical storico/a ⓜ/ⓕ
sto·ree·ko/a

history storia ⓕ sto·rya

hitchhike fare l'autostop fa·re
low·to·stop

HIV positive sieropositivo/a ⓜ/ⓕ
sye·ro·po·zee·tee·vo/a

hobby passatempo ⓜ pa·sa·tem·po

hockey hockey ⓜ o·kee

holidays vacanze ⓕ pl va·kan·tse

Holy Week settimana ⓕ santa
se·tee·ma·na san·ta

home casa ⓕ ka·za

homeless senzatetto ⓜ&ⓕ
sen·tsa·te·to

homemaker casalingo/a ⓕ
ka·za·leen·go/a

homeopathy omeopatia ⓕ
o·me·o·pa·tee·a

homosexual omosessuale ⓜ&ⓕ
o·mo·se·swa·le

honey miele ⓜ mye·le

honeymoon luna ⓕ di miele loo·na
dee mye·le

horse cavallo ⓜ ka·va·lo

horse riding andare a cavallo an·da·re
a ka·va·lo

horseradish rafano ⓜ ra·fa·no

hospital ospedale ⓜ os·pe·da·le

hospitality ospitalità ⓕ
os·pee·ta·lee·ta

hot caldo/a ⓜ/ⓕ kal·do/a

hot water acqua ⓕ calda a·kwa kal·da

hotel albergo ⓜ al·ber·go

hour ora ⓕ o·ra

house casa ⓕ ka·za

how come ko·me

how much quanto/a ⓜ/ⓕ kwan·to/a

hug abbracciare a·bra·cha·re

huge enorme e·nor·me

human rights diritti ⓜ pl umani
dee·ree·tee oo·ma·nee

(to be) hungry avere fame a·ve·re
fa·me

hunting caccia ⓕ ka·cha

(to be in a) hurry avere fretta a·ve·re
fre·ta

hurt fare male fa·re ma·le

husband marito ⓜ ma·ree·to

hydrating fluid fluido ⓜ idratante
floo·ee·do ee·dra·tan·te

I

I io ee·o

ice ghiaccio ⓜ gya·cho

ice axe piccozza ⓕ pee·ko·tsa

ice cream gelato ⓜ jo·la·to

ice-cream parlour gelateria ⓕ
je·la·te·ree·a

ice hockey hockey ⓜ su ghiaccio
o·kee soo gya·cho

identification documento ⓜ
d'identità do·koo·men·to dee·den·tee·ta

identification card (ID) carta ⓕ
d'identità kar·ta dee·den·tee·ta

idiot idiota ⓜ&ⓕ ee·dyo·ta

if se se

ill malato/a ⓜ/ⓕ ma·la·to/a

illegal illegale ee·le·ga·le

immigration immigrazione ⓕ
ee·mee·gra·tsyo·ne

J

DICTIONARY

important importante
eem·por·*tan*·te

impossible impossibile
eem·po·*see*·bee·le

included compreso/a ⓜ/ⓕ
kom·*pre*·zo/a

indicator (car) freccia ⓕ *fre*·cha

indigestion indigestione ⓕ
een·dee·je·*styo*·ne

industry industria ⓕ een·*doos*·trya

infection infezione ⓕ een·fe·*tsyo*·ne

inflammation infiammazione ⓕ
een·fya·ma·*tsyo*·ne

influenza influenza ⓕ een·floo·*en*·tsa

information informazioni ⓕ pl
een·for·ma·*tsyo*·nee

ingredient ingrediente ⓜ
een·gre·*dyen*·te

inhaler inalatore ⓜ ee·na·la·*to*·re

injection iniezione ⓕ ee·nye·*tsyo*·ne

injured ferito/a ⓜ/ⓕ fe·*ree*·to/a

injury ferita ⓕ fe·*ree*·ta

innocent innocente ee·no·*chen*·te

insect insetto ⓜ een·*se*·to

inside dentro *den*·tro

instructor (general) istruttore/
istruttrice ⓜ/ⓕ ee·stroo·*to*·re/
ee·stroo·*tree*·che

instructor (skiing) maestro/a ⓜ/ⓕ
ma·*es*·tro/a

insurance assicurazione ⓕ
a·see·koo·ra·*tsyo*·ne

interesting interessante
een·te·re·*san*·te

intermission intervallo ⓜ een·ter·*va*·lo

international internazionale
een·ter·na·tsyo·*na*·le

internet (cafe) Internet (point) ⓜ
een·ter·net (poynt)

interpreter interprete ⓜ/ⓕ
een·ter·*pre*·te

intersection incrocio ⓜ een·*kro*·cho

interview colloquio ⓜ (selettivo)
ko·*lo*·kwyo (se·le·*tee*·vo)

invite invitare een·vee·*ta*·re

Ireland Irlanda ⓕ eer·*lan*·da

iron (for clothes) ferro ⓜ da stiro
fe·ro da *stee*·ro

island isola ⓕ *ee*·zo·la

IT informatica ⓕ een·for·*ma*·tee·ka

Italian italiano/a ⓜ/ⓕ ee·ta·*lya*·no/a

Italy Italia ⓕ ee·*ta*·lya

itch prurito ⓜ proo·*ree*·to

itinerary itinerario ⓜ ee·tee·ne·*ra*·ryo

IUD spirale ⓕ spee·*ra*·le

J

jacket giacca ⓕ *ja*·ka

jail prigione ⓕ pree·*jo*·ne

jam marmellata ⓕ mar·me·*la*·ta

Japan Giappone ⓜ ja·*po*·ne

jar barattolo ⓜ ba·*ra*·to·lo

jealous geloso/a ⓜ/ⓕ je·*lo*·zo/a

jet lag disturbi ⓜ pl da fuso orario
dees·*toor*·bee da *foo*·zo o·*ra*·ryo

jewellery gioielli ⓜ pl jo·*ye*·lee

Jewish ebreo/a ⓜ/ⓕ e·*bre*·o/a

job lavoro ⓜ la·*vo*·ro

jockey fantino ⓜ fan·*tee*·no

jogging footing ⓜ *foo*·teeng

joke scherzo ⓜ *sker*·tso

journalist giornalista ⓜ&ⓕ
jor·na·*lee*·sta

judge giudice ⓜ/ⓕ *joo*·dee·che

judo giudò ⓜ pl *joo*·do

juice succo ⓜ *soo*·ko

jump saltare sal·*ta*·re

jumper maglione ⓜ ma·*lyo*·ne

jumper leads cavi ⓜ pl con morsetti
ka·vee kon mor·*se*·tee

K

key chiave ⓕ *kya*·ve

keyboard tastiera ⓕ tas·*tye*·ra

kick dare un calcio *da*·re oon *kal*·cho

kill ammazzare a·ma·*tsa*·re

kilogram chilo ⓜ *kee*·lo

kilometre chilometro ⓜ kee·*lo*·me·tro

kind gentile jen·*tee*·le

kindergarten asilo ⓜ a·*zee*·lo

king re ⓜ re

L

kiss bacio ⓜ *ba*·cho
kiss baciare ba·*cha*·re
kitchen cucina ⓕ koo·*chee*·na
kitten gattino ⓜ ga·*tee*·no
knapsack zaino ⓜ *dzai*·no
knee ginocchio ⓜ jee·*no*·kyo
knife coltello ⓜ kol·*te*·lo
know (a person) conoscere
ko·*no*·she·re
know (how to) sapere sa·*pe*·re
kosher kasher *ka*·sher

L

labourer lavoratore/lavoratrice ⓜ/ⓕ
la·vo·ra·*to*·re/la·vo·ra·*tree*·che
lace merletto ⓜ mer·*le*·to
lager birra ⓕ chiara *bee*·ra *kya*·ra
lake lago ⓜ *la*·go
lamb agnello ⓜ a·*nye*·lo
land terra ⓕ *te*·ra
lane vicolo ⓜ *vee*·ko·lo
landlady padrona ⓕ di casa
pa·*dro*·na dee *ka*·za
landlord padrone ⓜ di casa pa·*dro*·ne
dee *ka*·za
language lingua ⓕ *leen*·gwa
laptop (computer) portatile ⓜ
(kom·*pyoo*·ter) por·ta·*tee*·le
lard lardo ⓜ *lar*·do
large grande *gran*·de
last ultimo/a ⓜ/ⓕ *ool*·tee·mo/a
late in ritardo een ree·*tar*·do
laugh ridere *ree*·de·re
laundrette lavanderia ⓕ a gettone
la·van·de·*ree*·a a je·*to*·ne
laundry lavanderia ⓕ la·van·de·*ree*·a
law legge ⓕ *le*·je
lawyer avvocato/a ⓜ/ⓕ a·vo·*ka*·to/a
laxatives lassativi ⓜ pl la·sa·*tee*·vee
lazy pigro/a ⓜ/ⓕ *pee*·gro/a
leader capo ⓜ *ka*·po
leaf foglia ⓕ *fo*·lya
learn imparare eem·pa·*ra*·re
leather cuoio ⓜ *kwo*·yo
leave partire par·*tee*·re
leek porro ⓜ *po*·ro

left (direction) sinistra ⓕ
see·*nee*·stra
left luggage (office) deposito ⓜ
bagagli de·*po*·zee·to ba·*ga*·lyee
left wing (di) sinistra (dee)
see·*nee*·stra
leg (body part) gamba ⓕ *gam*·ba
leg (in race) tappa ⓕ *ta*·pa
legal legale le·*ga*·le
legume legume ⓜ le·*goo*·me
lemon limone ⓜ lee·*mo*·ne
lemonade limonata ⓕ lee·mo·*na*·ta
lens obiettivo ⓜ o·bye·*tee*·vo
Lent quaresima ⓕ kwa·*re*·zee·ma
lentil lenticchia ⓕ len·*tee*·kya
lesbian lesbica ⓕ *lez*·bee·ka
less (di) meno (dee) *me*·no
letter lettera ⓕ *le*·te·ra
lettuce lattuga ⓕ la·*too*·ga
level (tier) livello ⓜ lee·*ve*·lo
liar bugiardo/a ⓜ/ⓕ boo·*jar*·do/a
library biblioteca ⓕ bee·blyo·*te*·ka
lice pidocchi ⓜ pl pee·*do*·kee
licence plate number numero ⓜ di
targa *noo*·me·ro dee *tar*·ga
lie (not stand) stendersi *sten*·der·see
life vita ⓕ *vee*·ta
life jacket giubbotto ⓜ di salvataggio
joo·*bo*·to dee sal·va·*ta*·jo
lift (elevator) ascensore ⓜ
a·shen·*so*·re
light luce ⓕ *loo*·che
light (colour) chiaro/a ⓜ/ⓕ *kya*·ro/a
light (not heavy) leggero/a ⓜ/ⓕ
le·*je*·ro/a
light bulb lampadina ⓕ
lam·pa·*dee*·na
light meter esposimetro ⓜ
es·po·*zee*·me·tro
lighter accendino ⓜ a·chen·*dee*·no
lights (on car) fari ⓜ pl *fa*·ree
like piacere pya·*che*·re
lime limetta ⓕ lee·*me*·ta
line linea ⓕ *lee*·ne·a
lip balm burro ⓜ per le labbra *boo*·ro
per le *la*·bra

M

lips labbra ① pl *la·*bra
lipstick rossetto ⑩ ro·*se·*to
liquor store bottiglieria ①
bo·tee·lye·*ree·*a
list elenco ⑩ e·*len·*ko
listen ascoltare as·kol·*ta·*re
litre litro ⑩ *lee·*tro
(a) little un po' oon po
live vivere vee·*ve·*re
liver fegato ⑩ *fe·*ga·to
lizard lucertola ① loo·*cher·*to·la
local locale lo·*ka·*le
lock (door) serratura ① se·ra·*too·*ra
locked chiuso/a ⑩/① (a chiave)
*kyoo·*zo/a (a *kya·*ve)
locker armadietto ⑩ ar·ma·*dye·*to
lollies caramelle ① pl ka·ra·*me·*le
long lungo/a ⑩/① *loon·*go/a
long-distance (bus) interurbano/a
⑩/① een·ter·oor·*ba·*no/a
look guardare gwar·*da·*re
look after curare koo·*ra·*re
look for cercare cher·*ka·*re
lookout veduta ① ve·*doo·*ta
loose change spiccioli ⑩ pl
*spee·*cho·lee
lose perdere per·*de·*re
lost perso/a ⑩/① *per·*so/a
lost-property office ufficio ⑩
oggetti smarriti oo·*fee·*cho o·*je·*tee
sma·*ree·*tee
(a) lot molto/a ⑩/① *mol·*to/a
loud forte ⑩/① *for·*te
love amare a·*ma·*re
lover amante ⑩/① a·*man·*te
low basso/a ⑩/① *ba·*so/a
lubricant lubrificante ⑩
loo·bree·fee·*kan·*te
luck fortuna ① for·*too·*na
lucky fortunato/a ⑩/①
for·too·*na·*to/a
luggage bagaglio ⑩ ba·*ga·*lyo
luggage lockers armadietti ⑩ pl
per i bagagli ar·ma·*dye·*tee per ee
ba·*ga·*lyee
luggage tag etichetta ① e·tee·*ke·*ta

lump nodulo ⑩ *no·*doo·lo
lunch pranzo ⑩ *pran·*dzo
lungs polmoni ⑩ pl pol·*mo·*nee
luxurious di lusso dee *loo·*so

M

machine macchina ① *ma·*kee·na
made of (cotton) fatto/a ⑩/① di
(cotone) *fa·*to/a dee (ko·*to·*ne)
magazine rivista ① ree·*vee·*sta
mail posta ① *pos·*ta
mail box buca ① delle lettere *boo·*ka
*de·*le *le·*te·re
main principale preen·chee·*pa·*le
make fare *fa·*re
make-up trucco ⑩ *troo·*ko
mallet mazzuolo ⑩ ma·*tswo·*lo
mammogram mammografia ①
ma·mo·gra·*fee·*a
man uomo ⑩ *wo·*mo
manager manager ⑩ *me·*nee·je
mandarin mandarino ⑩
man·da·*ree·*no
manual manuale ma·noo·*a·*le
manual worker manovale ⑩&①
ma·no·*va·*le
many molti/e ⑩/① pl *mol·*tee/*mol·*te
map pianta ① *pyan·*ta
marble marmo ⑩ *mar·*mo
margarine margarina ① mar·ga·*ree·*na
marijuana marijuana ① ma·ree·*wa·*na
marital status stato ⑩ civile *sta·*to
chee·*vee·*le
market mercato ⑩ mer·*ka·*to
marmalade marmellata ①
mar·me·*la·*ta
marriage matrimonio ⑩
ma·tree·*mo·*nyo
married sposato/a ⑩/① spo·*za·*to/a
marry sposare spo·*za·*re
martial arts arti ① pl marziali *ar·*tee
mar·*tsya·*lce
mass (Catholic) messa ① *me·*sa
massage massaggio ⑩ ma·*sa·*jo
mat tappeto ⑩ ta·*pe·*to
match (sport) partita ① par·*tee·*ta

M

matches fiammiferi ⓜ pl
fya·mee·fe·ree
mattress materasso ⓜ ma·te·ra·so
maybe forse for·se
mayonnaise maionese ① ma·yo·ne·ze
mayor sindaco ⓜ seen·da·ko
measles morbillo ⓜ mor·bee·lo
meat carne ① kar·ne
mechanic meccanico ⓜ&①
me·ka·nee·ko
media mezzi ⓜ pl di comunicazione
me·tsee dee ko·moo·nee·ka·tsyo·ne
medicine medicina ①
me·dee·chee·na
meditation meditazione ①
me·dee·ta·tsyo·ne
meet incontrare een·kon·tra·re
melon melone ⓜ me·lo·ne
member socio/a ⓜ/① so·cho/a
menstruation mestruazione ①
me·stroo·a·tsyo·ne
menu menu ⓜ me·noo
message messaggio ⓜ me·sa·jo
metal metallo ⓜ me·ta·lo
metre (distance) metro ⓜ me·tro
metro station stazione ①
della metropolitana sta·tsyo·ne de·la
me·tro·po·lee·ta·na
microwave oven forno ⓜ a
microonde for·no a mee·kro·on·de
midnight mezzanotte ① me·dza·no·te
migraine emicrania ① e·mee·kra·nya
military le forze ① pl armate le
for·tse ar·ma·te
military service servizio ⓜ militare
ser·vee·tsyo mee·lee·ta·re
milk latte ⓜ la·te
millimetre millimetro ⓜ
mee·lee·me·tro
mince carne ① tritata kar·ne
tree·ta·ta
mineral water acqua ① minerale
a·kwa mee·ne·ra·le
minibar frigobar ⓜ free·go·bar
mints caramelle ① pl alla menta
ka·ra·me·le a·la men·ta

minute minuto ⓜ mee·noo·to
mirror specchio ⓜ spe·kyo
miscarriage aborto ⓜ spontaneo
a·bor·to spon·ta·ne·o
miss (feel absence of) mancare
man·ka·re
mistake sbaglio ⓜ sba·lyo
mix mescolare mes·ko·la·re
mobile phone (telephone) cellulare ⓜ
(te·le·fo·no) che·loo·la·re
modern moderno/a ⓜ/①
mo·der·no/a
moisturiser idratante ⓜ ee·dra·tan·te
monastery monastero ⓜ
mo·nas·te·ro
money denaro ⓜ de·na·ro
month mese ⓜ me·ze
monument monumento ⓜ
mo·noo·men·to
(full) moon luna ① (piena) loo·na
(pye·na)
more (di) più (dee) pyoo
morning mattina ① ma·tee·na
morning after pill la pillola ①
del mattino dopo la pee·lo·la del
ma·tee·no do·po
morning sickness nausea ①
mattutina now·ze·a ma·too·tee·na
mosque moschea ① mos·ke·a
mosquito zanzara ① tsan·tsa·ra
mother madre ① ma·dre
mother-in-law suocera ① swo·che·ra
motorboat motoscafo ⓜ
mo·to·ska·fo
motorbike moto ① mo·to
motorway (tollway) autostrada ①
ow·to·stra·da
mountain montagna ① mon·ta·nya
mountain path sentiero ⓜ di
montagna sen·tye·ro dee mon·ta·nya
mountain range catena ① di
montagne ka·te·na dee mon·ta·nye
mountaineering alpinismo ⓜ
al·pee·neez·mo
mouse (rodent) topo ⓜ to·po
mouth bocca ① bo·ka

N

movie film ⓜ feelm
mud fango ⓜ fan·go
mum mamma ⓕ ma·ma
muscle muscolo ⓜ moo·sko·lo
museum museo ⓜ moo·ze·o
mushroom fungo ⓜ foon·go
music musica ⓕ moo·zee·ka
musician musicista ⓜ&ⓕ moo·zee·chee·sta
Muslim musulmano/a ⓜ/ⓕ moo·sool·ma·no/a
mussels cozze ⓕ pl ko·tse
mustard senape ⓕ se·na·pe
mute muto/a ⓜ/ⓕ moo·to/a

N

nail clippers tagliaunghie ⓜ ta·lya·oon·gye
name nome ⓜ no·me
napkin tovagliolo ⓜ to·va·lyo·lo
nappy pannolino ⓜ pa·no·lee·no
nappy rash sfogo ⓜ da pannolino sfo·go da pa·no·lee·no
national nazionale na·tsyo·na·le
national park parco ⓜ nazionale par·ko na·tsyo·na·le
nationality nazionalità ⓕ na·tsyo·na·lee·ta
nature natura ⓕ na·too·ra
naturopathy naturopatia ⓕ na·too·ro·pa·tee·a
near (to) vicino (a) vee·chee·no (a)
nearby vicino/a ⓜ/ⓕ vee·chee·no/a
necessary necessario/a ⓜ/ⓕ ne·che·sa·ryo/a
neck collo ⓜ ko·lo
need avere bisogno di a·ve·re bee·zo·nyo dee
needle (sewing) ago ⓜ a·go
needle (syringe) ago ⓜ da siringa a·go da see·reen·ga
neither nessuno/a ⓜ/ⓕ ne·soo·no/a
net rete ⓕ re·te
Netherlands Paesi Bassi ⓜ pl pa·e·zee ba·see
never mai mai

new nuovo/a ⓜ/ⓕ nwo·vo/a
New Year's Day Capodanno ⓜ ka·po da·no
New Year's Eve San Silvestro ⓜ san seel·ves·tro
New Zealand Nuova Zelanda ⓕ nwo·va dze·lan·da
news notizie ⓕ pl no·tee·tsye
newsagency edicola ⓕ e·dee·ko·la
newspaper giornale ⓜ jor·na·le
next prossimo/a ⓜ/ⓕ pro·see·mo/a
next to accanto a a·kan·to a
nice (meal) buono/a ⓜ/ⓕ bwo·no/a
nice (person) gentile jen·tee·le
nice (weather) bello/a ⓜ/ⓕ be·lo/a
nickname soprannome ⓜ so·pra·no·me
night notte ⓕ no·te
no no no
noisy rumoroso/a ⓜ/ⓕ roo·mo·ro·zo/a
nondirect non-diretto/a ⓜ/ⓕ non·dee·re·to/a
none niente nyen·te
nonsmoking non fumatore foo·ma·to·re
noodles pasta ⓕ pas·ta
noon mezzogiorno ⓜ me·dzo jor·no
north nord ⓜ nord
nose naso ⓜ na·zo
notebook quaderno ⓜ kwa·der·no
nothing niente nyen·te
novel romanzo ⓜ ro·man·dzo
now adesso a·de·so
nuclear energy energia ⓕ nucleare en·er·jee·a noo·kle·a·re
nuclear testing esperimenti ⓜ pl nucleari es·pe·ree·men·tee noo·kle·a·ree
nuclear waste scorie ⓕ pl radioattive sko·rye ra·dyo·a·tee·ve
number numero ⓜ noo·me·ro
number plate targa ⓕ tar·ga
nun suora ⓕ swo·ra
nurse infermiere/a ⓜ/ⓕ een·fer·mye·re/a
nut noce ⓕ no·che

O

oats avena ① a·ve·na
occupation (work) mestiere ⓜ mes·tye·re
ocean oceano ⓜ o·che·a·no
off (spoiled) guasto/a ⓜ/① gwa·sto/a
office ufficio ⓜ oo·fee·cho
office worker impiegato/a ⓜ/① eem·pye·ga·to/a
often spesso spe·so
oil olio ⓜ o·lyo
old vecchio/a ⓜ/① ve·kyo/a
old city centro ⓜ storico chen·tro sto·ree·ko
olive oliva ① o·lee·va
olive oil olio ⓜ d'oliva o·lyo do·lee·va
on su soo
once una volta ① oo·na vol·ta
one-way (ticket) (un biglietto di) solo andata (oon bee·lye·to dee) so·lo an·da·ta
onion cipolla ① chee·po·la
only solo so·lo
open aperto/a ⓜ/① a·per·to/a
open aprire a·pree·re
opening hours orario ⓜ di apertura o·ra·ryo dee a·per·too·ra
opera opera ① lirica o·pe·ra lee·ree·ka
opera house teatro ⓜ dell'opera te·a·tro del·o·pe·ra
operation (medical) intervento ⓜ een·ter·ven·to
operator operatore/operatrice ⓜ/① o·pe·ra·to·re/o·pe·ra·tree·che
opinion opinione ① o·pee·nyo·ne
opposite di fronte a dee fron·te a
or o o
orange (colour) arancione a·ran·cho·ne
orange (fruit) arancia ① a·ran·cha
orange juice (bottled) succo ⓜ d'arancia soo·ko da·ran·cha
orange juice (fresh) spremuta ① d'arancia spre·moo·ta da·ran·cha

orchestra orchestra ① or·kes·tra
order ordine ⓜ or·dee·ne
order ordinare or·dee·na·re
ordinary ordinario/a ⓜ/① or·dee·na·ryo/a
original originale ⓜ/① o·ree·jee·na·le
other altro/a ⓜ/① al·tro/a
outside fuori fwo·ree
ovarian cyst cisti ① ovarica chee·stee o·va·ree·ka
oven forno ⓜ for·no
over (above) sopra so·pra
overdose dose ① eccessiva do·ze e·che·see·va
owner proprietario/a ⓜ/① pro·prye·ta·ryo/a
oxygen ossigeno ⓜ o·see·je·no
oyster ostrica ① o·stree·ka
ozone layer strato ⓜ d'ozono stra·to do·dzo·no

P

pacifier ciucciotto ⓜ choo·cho·to
package pacchetto ⓜ pa·ke·to
packet (general) pacchetto ⓜ pa·ke·to
padded envelope busta ① imbottita boos·ta eem·bo·tee·ta
padlock lucchetto ⓜ loo·ke·to
page pagina ① pa·jee·na
pain dolore ⓜ do·lo·re
painful doloroso/a ⓜ/① do·lo·ro·zo/a
painkillers analgesico ⓜ an·al·je·zee·ko
paint dipingere dee·peen·je·re
painter pittore/pittrice ⓜ/① pee·to·re/pee·tree·che
painting (the art) pittura ① pee·too·ra
painting (canvas) quadro ⓜ kwa·dro
pair paio ⓜ pa·yo
palace palazzo ⓜ pa·la·tso
pan pentola ① pen·to·la
pants pantaloni ⓜ pl pan·ta·lo·nee
panty liners salva slip ⓜ pl sal·va sleep

P

pantyhose collant ① pl ko·*lant*

pap smear pap test ⑩ pap test

paper carta ① *kar*·ta

papers documenti ⑩ pl
do·koo·*men*·tee

paperwork moduli ⑩ pl *mo*·doo·lee

parcel pacchetto ⑩ pa·*ke*·to

parents genitori ⑩ pl je·nee·*to*·ree

park parco ⑩ *par*·ko

parliament parlamento ⑩
par·la·*men*·to

part parte ① *par*·te

part-time ad orario ridotto ad o·*ra*·ryo
ree·*do*·to

partner (intimate) compagno/a ⑩/①
kom·*pa*·nyo/a

party (celebration) festa ① *fes*·ta

party (politics) partito ⑩ par·*tee*·to

pass (document) tessera ① *te*·se·ra

pass (mountain) passo ⑩ *pa*·so

pass (sport) passaggio ⑩ pa·*sa*·jo

passenger passeggero/a ⑩/①
pa·se·*je*·ro/a

passport passaporto ⑩ pa·sa·*por*·to

past passato ⑩ pa·*sa*·to

pate (food) paté ⑩ pa·*te*

path sentiero ⑩ sen·*tye*·ro

pay pagare pa·*ga*·re

payment pagamento ⑩
pa·ga·*men*·to

pea pisello ⑩ pee·*ze*·lo

peace pace ① *pa*·che

peach pesca ① *pe*·ska

peak cima ① *chee*·ma

peanuts arachidi ① pl a·ra·*kee*·dee

pear pera ① *pe*·ra

pedal pedale ⑩ pe·*da*·le

pedestrian pedone ⑩/① pe·*do*·ne

pegs (tent) picchetti ⑩ pl pee·*ke*·tee

pen (ballpoint) penna ① (a sfera)
pe·na (a *sfe*·ra)

pencil matita ① ma·*tee*·ta

penis pene ⑩ *pe*·ne

penicillin penicillina ①
pe·nee·chee·*lee*·na

penknife temperino ⑩ tem·pe·*ree*·no

pensioner pensionato/a ⑩/①
pen·syo·*na*·to/a

people gente ① *jen*·te

pepper pepe ⑩ *pe*·pe

per (day) al (giorno) al (*jor*·no)

per cent per cento ① per·*chen*·to

performance spettacolo ⑩
spe·*ta*·ko·lo

perfume profumo ⑩ pro·*foo*·mo

period pain dolori ⑩ pl mestruali
do·*lo*·ree me·*stroo*·a·lee

permanent permanente ⑩/①
per·ma·*nen*·te

permission permesso ⑩ per·*me*·so

permit permesso ⑩ per·*me*·so

person persona ① per·*so*·na

personal personale ⑩/① per·so·*na*·le

petition petizione ① pe·tee·*tsyo*·ne

petrol benzina ① ben·*dzee*·na

petrol station distributore ⑩
dee·stree·boo·*to*·re

pharmacy farmacia ① far·ma·*chee*·a

phone book elenco ⑩ telefonico
e·*len*·ko te·le·*fo*·nee·ko

phone box cabina ① telefonica
ka·*bee*·na te·le·*fo*·nee·ka

phone call chiamata ① kya·*ma*·ta

phonecard scheda ① telefonica
ske·da te·le·*fo*·nee·ka

photo foto ① *fo*·to

photographer fotografo ⑩
fo·*to*·gra·fo

photography fotografia ①
fo·to·gra·*fee*·a

phrasebook vocabolarietto ⑩
vo·ka·bo·la·*rye*·to

pick (up) raccogliere ra·ko·*lye*·re

pickaxe piccone ⑩ pee·*ko*·ne

pickles sottoaceti ⑩ pl
so·to·a·*che*·tee

pie torta ① *tor*·ta

piece pezzo ⑩ *pe*·tso

pig maiale ⑩ ma·*ya*·le

pill pillola ① *pee*·lo·la

(the) Pill la pillola ① (anticoncezionale)
la *pee*·lo·la (an·tee·kon·che·*tsyo*·na·le)

P

pillow cuscino ⓜ koo·*shee*·no
pillowcase federa ⓕ *fe*·de·ra
pineapple ananas ⓜ a·na·nas
pink rosa ⓜ&ⓕ *ro*·za
pistachio pistacchio ⓜ pee·*sta*·kyo
place (location) luogo ⓜ *lwo*·go
place (seat) posto ⓜ *pos*·to
place of birth luogo ⓜ di nascita
lwo·go de *na*·shee·ta
plane aereo ⓜ a·e·re·o
planet pianeta ⓜ pya·*ne*·ta
plant pianta ⓕ *pyan*·ta
plastic plastica ⓕ *pla*·stee·ka
plate piatto ⓜ *pya*·to
plateau altopiano ⓜ al·to·*pya*·no
platform binario ⓜ bee·*na*·ryo
play (a game) giocare jo·*ka*·re
play (guitar) suonare (la chitarra)
swo·*na*·re (la kee·*ta*·ra)
play (soccer) giocare (a calcio)
jo·*ka*·re (a *kal*·cho)
play (sport) praticare pra·tee·*ka*·re
play (theatre) commedia ⓕ
ko·*me*·dya
playground parco ⓜ giochi *par*·ko
jo·kee
plug (bath) tappo ⓜ *ta*·po
plug (electricity) spina ⓕ *spee*·na
plum prugna ⓕ *proo*·nya
pocket tasca ⓕ *tas*·ka
poetry poesia ⓕ po·e·*zee*·a
point punto ⓜ *poon*·to
point indicare een·dee·*ka*·re
poisonous velenoso/a ⓜ/ⓕ
ve·le·*no*·zo/a
police (civilian) polizia ⓕ po·lee·*tsee*·a
police (military) carabinieri ⓜ pl
ka·ra·bee·*nye*·ree
police station posto ⓜ di polizia
pos·to dee po·lee·*tsee*·a
politician politico ⓜ po·*lee*·tee·ko
politics politica ⓕ po·*lee*·tee·ka
pollen polline ⓜ *po*·lee·ne
polls elezioni ⓕ pl e·le·*tsyo*·nee
pollution inquinamento ⓜ
een·kwee·na·*men*·to

pony cavallino ⓜ ka·va·*lee*·no
pool (game) biliardo ⓜ beel·*yar*·do
pool (swimming) piscina ⓕ
pee·*shee*·na
poor povero/a ⓜ/ⓕ *po*·ve·ro/a
popular popolare po·po·*la*·re
pork maiale ⓜ ma·*ya*·le
port porto ⓜ *por*·to
possible possibile po·*see*·bee·le
post code codice ⓜ postale
ko·dee·che pos·*ta*·le
poste restante fermo ⓜ posta *fer*·mo
pos·ta
post office ufficio ⓜ postale
oo·*fee*·cho pos·*ta*·le
postage tariffa ⓕ postale ta·*ree*·fa
pos·*ta*·le
postcard cartolina ⓕ kar·to·*lee*·na
pot (ceramics) pignatta ⓕ pee·*nya*·ta
pot (dope) erba ⓕ *er*·ba
pot (cooking) pentola ⓕ *pen*·to·la
potato patata ⓕ pa·*ta*·ta
pottery oggetti ⓜ pl in ceramica
o·*je*·tee een che·*ra*·mee·ka
pound (money) sterlina ⓕ ster·*lee*·na
poverty povertà ⓕ po·ver·*ta*
power potere ⓜ po·*te*·re
prawn gambero ⓜ *gam*·be·ro
prayer preghiera ⓕ pre·*gye*·ra
prefer preferire pre·fe·*ree*·re
pregnancy test kit test ⓜ di
gravidanza test dee gra·vee·*dan*·tsa
pregnant incinta een·*cheen*·ta
premenstrual tension tensione ⓕ
premestruale ten·*syo*·ne
pre·me·*stroo*·a·le
prepare preparare pre·pa·*ra*·re
prescription ricetta ⓕ ree·*che*·ta
present (gift) regalo ⓜ re·*ga*·lo
president presidente ⓜ/ⓕ
pre·zee·*den*·te
pressure pressione ⓕ pre·*syo*·ne
pretty carino/a ⓜ/ⓕ ka·*ree*·no/a
previous precedente pre·che·*den*·te
price prezzo ⓜ *pre*·tso
priest prete ⓜ *pre*·te

prime minister primo ministro ⓜ/ⓕ
*pree·*mo mee·*nee·*stro

printer (computer) stampante ⓕ
stam·*pan·*te

prison prigione ⓕ pree·*jo·*ne

prisoner prigioniero/a ⓜ/ⓕ
pree·jo·*nye·*ro/a

private privato/a ⓜ/ⓕ pree·*va·*to/a

produce produrre pro·*doo·*re

profit profitto ⓜ pro·*fee·*to

program programma ⓜ pro·*gra·*ma

projector proiettore ⓜ pro·ye·*to·*re

promise promessa ⓕ pro·*me·*sa

protect proteggere pro·*te·*je·re

protected (species) (specie) ⓕ
protetta (*spe·*che) pro·*te·*ta

protest manifestazione ⓕ
ma·nee·fes·ta·*tsyo·*ne

protest protestare pro·tes·*ta·*re

provisions provviste ⓕ pl pro·*vee·*ste

prune prugna ⓕ *proo·*nya

pub pub ⓜ poob

public holiday festa ⓕ *fes·*ta

public telephone telefono ⓜ
pubblico te·*le·*fo·no *poo·*blee·ko

public toilet gabinetto ⓜ pubblico
ga·bee·*ne·*to *poo·*blee·ko

pull tirare tee·*ra·*re

pump pompa ⓕ pom·*pa*

pumpkin zucca ⓕ *tsoo·*ka

puncture bucatura ⓕ boo·ka·*too·*ra

puppy cucciolo ⓜ *koo·*cho·lo

pure puro/a ⓜ/ⓕ *poo·*ro/a

purple viola vee·*o·*la

push spingere *speen·*je·re

put mettere *me·*te·re

Q

qualifications titoli ⓜ pl di studio
*tee·*to·lee dee *stoo·*dee·o

quality qualità ⓕ kwa·lee·*ta*

quantity quantità ⓕ kwan·tee·*ta*

quarantine quarantena ⓕ
kwa·ran·*te·*na

quarrel bisticcio ⓜ bees·*tee·*cho

quarter quarto ⓜ *kwar·*to

queen regina ⓕ re·*jee·*na

question domanda ⓕ do·*man·*da

queue coda ⓕ *ko·*da

quick rapido/a ⓜ/ⓕ *ra·*pee·do/a

quiet tranquillo/a ⓜ/ⓕ
tran·*kwee·*lo/a

R

rabbit coniglio ⓜ ko·*nee·*lyo

race (sport) gara ⓜ *ga·*ra

racetrack pista ⓕ *pee·*sta

racing bike bici ⓕ da corsa *bee·*chee
da *kor·*sa

racism razzismo ⓜ ra·*tseez·*mo

racquet racchetta ⓕ ra·*ke·*ta

radiator radiatore ⓜ ra·dya·*to·*re

railway station stazione ⓕ
ferroviaria sta·*tsyo·*ne fe·ro·vee·a·*ree·*a

rain pioggia ⓜ *pyo·*ja

raincoat impermeabile ⓜ
eem·per·me·a·*bee·*le

raisin uva ⓕ passa *oo·*va pa·*sa*

rape stupro ⓜ *stoo·*pro

rare raro/a ⓜ/ⓕ *ra·*ro/a

rash sfogo ⓜ *sfo·*go

raspberry lampone ⓜ lam·*po·*ne

rat topo ⓜ *to·*po

raw crudo/a ⓜ/ⓕ *kroo·*do/a

razor rasoio ⓜ ra·*zo·*yo

razor blades lamette ⓕ pl (da barba)
la·*me·*te (da *bar·*ba)

read leggere *le·*je·re

ready pronto/a ⓜ/ⓕ *pron·*to/a

realistic realistico/a ⓜ/ⓕ
re·a·*lee·*stee·ko/a

reason ragione ⓕ ra·*jo·*ne

receipt ricevuta ⓕ ree·che·*voo·*ta

receive ricevere ree·*che·*ve·re

recently di recente dee re·*chen·*te

recommend raccomandare
ra·ko·man·*da·*re

recyclable riciclabile
ree·chee·*kla·*bee·le

recycle riciclare ree·chee·*kla·*re

red rosso/a ⓜ/ⓕ *ro·*so/a

referee arbitro ⓜ *ar·*bee·tro

reflexology riflessologia ⓕ
ree·fle·so·lo·jee·a

refrigerator frigo ⓜ free·go

refugee rifugiato/a ⓜ/ⓕ
ree·foo·gya·to/a

refund rimborso ⓜ reem·bor·so

refuse rifiutare ree·fyoo·ta·re

region regione ⓕ re·jo·ne

registered mail posta raccomandata
ⓕ pos·ta ra·ko·man·da·ta

regular normale nor·ma·le

relationship rapporto ⓜ ra·por·to

relax rilassarsi ree·la·sar·see

relic reliquia ⓕ re·lee·kwee·a

religion religione ⓕ re·lee·jo·ne

religious religioso/a ⓜ/ⓕ
re·lee·jo·zo/a

remote remoto/a ⓜ/ⓕ re·mo·to/a

remote control telecomando ⓜ
te·le·ko·man·do

rent affitto ⓜ a·fee·to

rent prendere in affitto pren·de·re een
a·fee·to

repair riparare ree·pa·ra·re

reservation prenotazione ⓕ
pre·no·ta·tsyo·ne

rest riposare ree·po·za·re

restaurant ristorante ⓜ rees·to·ran·te

retired pensionato/a ⓜ/ⓕ
pen·syo·na·to/a

return ritornare ree·tor·na·re

return (ticket) (biglietto) di andata
e ritorno (bee·lye·tô) dee un da·ta e
ree·tôr·no

reverse-charges call chiamata ⓕ
a carico del destinatario kya·ma·ta ⓕ
a·ka·ree·ko del des·tee·na·ta·ryo

rhythm ritmo ⓜ reet·mo

rice riso ⓜ ree·zo

rich (wealthy) ricco/a ⓜ/ⓕ ree·ko/a

ride (a bike) andare in bicicletta
an·da·re een bee·chee·kle·ta

ride (a horse) cavalcare ka·val·ka·re

right (correct) giusto/a ⓜ/ⓕ
joo·sto/a

right (direction) a destra a de·stra

right-wing (di) destra (dee) de·stra

ring (on finger) anello ⓜ a·ne·lo

ring (by phone) telefonare
te·le·fo·na·re

rip-off bidone ⓜ bee·do·ne

risk rischio ⓜ rees·kyo

river fiume ⓜ fyoo·me

road strada ⓕ stra·da

rob derubare de·roo·ba·re

rock roccia ⓕ ro·cha

rock (music) (musica) ⓕ rock
(moo·zee·ka) rok

rock climbing (andare su) roccia ⓕ
(an·da·re soo) ro·cha

rock group gruppo ⓜ rock groo·po rok

roll (bread) panino ⓜ pa·nee·no

romantic romantico/a ⓜ/ⓕ
ro·man·tee·ko/a

room camera ⓕ ka·me·ra

rope corda (ⓕ) kor·da

round rotondo/a ⓜ/ⓕ ro·tôn·do/a

roundabout rotonda ⓜ ro·ton·da

route itinerario ⓜ ee·tee·ne·ra·ryo

rowing canottaggio ⓜ ka·no·ta·jo

rubbish spazzatura ⓕ spa·tsa·too·ra

rug tappeto ⓜ ta·pe·to

rugby rugby ⓜ roog·bee

ruins rovine ⓜ pl ro·vee·ne

rules regole ⓕ pl re·go·le

run correre ko·re·re

running (sport) footing ⓜ foo·teeng

S

sad triste tree·ste

saddle sella ⓕ se·la

safe cassaforte ⓕ ka·sa·for·te

safe sicuro/a ⓜ/ⓕ see·koo·ro/a

safe sex rapporti ⓜ pl protetti
ra·por·tee pro·te·tee

safety gear corredo ⓜ
antinfortunistico ko·re·do
an·teen·for·too·nee·stee·ko

saint santo/a ⓜ/ⓕ san·to/a

salad insalata ⓕ een·sa·la·ta

salami salame ⓜ sa·la·me

salary stipendio ⓜ stee·*pen*·dyo
(on) sale in vendita een *ven*·dee·ta
sales tax IVA ⓕ *ee*·va
salmon salmone ⓜ sal·*mo*·ne
salt sale ⓜ *sa*·le
same stesso/a ⓜ/ⓕ *ste*·so/a
sand sabbia ⓕ *sa*·bya
sandals sandali ⓜ pl *san*·da·lee
sandwich tramezzino ⓜ
tra·me·*dzee*·no
sanitary napkins assorbenti ⓜ pl
igienici as·or·*ben*·tee ee·je·*nee*·chee
sardines sardine ⓕ pl sar·*dee*·ne
sauce sugo ⓜ *soo*·go
sauna sauna ⓕ *sow*·na
sausage salsiccia ⓕ sal·*see*·cha
say dire *dee*·re
scanner scanner ⓜ *ska*·ner
scarf sciarpa ⓕ *shar*·pa
school scuola ⓕ *skwo*·la
science scienza ⓕ *shen*·tsa
scissors forbici ⓕ pl *for*·bee·chee
score punteggio ⓜ poon·*te*·jo
score segnare se·*nya*·re
scoreboard tabellone ⓜ segnapunti
ta·be·*lo*·ne se·nya·*poon*·tee
Scotland Scozia ⓕ *sko*·tsya
sculpture scultura ⓕ skool·*too*·ra
sea mare ⓜ *ma*·re
seasickness mal ⓜ di mare mal dee
ma·re
seaside al mare al *ma*·re
season stagione ⓕ sta·*jo*·ne
seat (chair) sedile ⓜ se·*dee*·le
seat (place) posto ⓜ *pos*·to
seatbelt cintura ⓕ di sicurezza
cheen·*too*·ra dee see·koo·*re*·tsa
second secondo ⓜ se·*kon*·do
second secondo/a ⓜ/ⓕ se·*kon*·do/a
second class seconda classe ⓕ
se·*kon*·da *kla*·se
secondhand di seconda mano ⓜ/ⓕ
dee se·*kon*·da *ma*·no
secretary segretario/a ⓜ/ⓕ
se·gre·*ta*·ryo/a
see vedere ve·*de*·re

(to be) self-employed lavorare in
proprio la·vo·*ra*·re een *pro*·pryo
selfish egoista ⓜ/ⓕ e·go·*ee*·sta
sell vendere *ven*·de·re
send mandare man·*da*·re
sensual sensuale ⓜ/ⓕ sen·soo·*a*·le
separate separato/a ⓜ/ⓕ
se·pa·*ra*·to/a
(TV) series serie ⓕ (televisiva)
se·ree·e (te·le·vee·*see*·va)
serious serio/a ⓜ/ⓕ *se*·ryo/a
service servizio ⓜ ser·*vee*·tsyo
service charge servizio ⓜ
ser·*vee*·tsyo
service station stazione ⓕ di servizio
sta·*tsyo*·ne dee ser·*vee*·tsyo
several diversi/e ⓜ/ⓕ pl dee·*ver*·see/
dee·*ver*·se
sew cucire koo·*chee*·re
sex sesso ⓜ *se*·so
sexism sessismo ⓜ se·*seez*·mo
sexy erotico/a ⓜ/ⓕ e·ro·*tee*·ko/a
shade ombra ⓕ *om*·bra
shadow ombra ⓕ *om*·bra
shape forma ⓕ *for*·ma
share (with) condividere
kon·dee·*vee*·de·re
sharp affilato/a ⓜ/ⓕ a·fee·*la*·to/a
shave rasatura ⓕ ra·za·*too*·ra
shave fare la barba *fa*·re la *bar*·ba
shaving cream crema ⓕ da barba
kre·ma da *bar*·ba
she lei lay
sheep pecora ⓕ *pe*·ko·ra
sheet (bed) lenzuolo ⓜ len·*tswo*·lo
ship nave ⓕ *na*·ve
shirt camicia ⓕ ka·*mee*·cha
shoe shop negozio ⓜ di scarpe
ne·*go*·tsyo dee *skar*·pe
shoes scarpe ⓕ pl *skar*·pe
shop negozio ⓜ ne·*go*·tsyo
shopping centre centro ⓜ
commerciale *chen*·tro ko·mer·*cha*·le
short (height) basso/a ⓜ/ⓕ
ba·so/a
short (length) corto/a ⓜ/ⓕ *kor*·to/a

shorts pantaloncini ⓜ pl
pan·ta·lon·chee·nee
shoulder spalla ⓕ spa·la
shout urlare oor·la·re
show spettacolo ⓜ spe·ta·ko·lo
show mostrare mos·tra·re
shower doccia ⓕ do·cha
shrine santuario ⓜ san·too·a·ryo
shut chiuso/a ⓜ/ⓕ kyoo·zo/a
shy timido/a ⓜ/ⓕ tee·mee·do/a
sick malato/a ⓜ/ⓕ ma·la·to/a
side lato ⓜ la·to
sign segno ⓜ se·nyo
signature firma ⓕ feer·ma
silk seta ⓕ se·ta
silver argento ⓜ ar·jen·to
similar simile ⓜ/ⓕ see·mee·le
simple semplice ⓜ/ⓕ
sem·plee·che
since (time) da da
sing cantare kan·ta·re
singer cantante ⓜ/ⓕ kan·tan·te
single (man) celibe ⓜ che·lee·be
single (woman) nubile ⓕ noo·bee·le
single room camera ⓕ singola
ka·me·ra seen·go·la
singlet canottiera ⓕ ka·no·tye·ra
sister sorella ⓕ so·re·la
sit sedere se·de·re
size (clothes) taglia ⓕ ta·lya
size (general) dimensioni ⓕ pl
dee·men·syo·nee
ski sciare shee·a·re
ski lift sciovia ⓕ shee·o·vee·a
skiing sci ⓜ shee
ski(s) sci ⓜ sg&pl shee
skimmed milk latte ⓜ scremato la·te
skre·ma·to
skin pelle ⓕ pe·le
skirt gonna ⓕ go·na
sky cielo ⓜ che·lo
sleep dormire dor·mee·re
sleeping bag sacco ⓜ a pelo sa·ko
a pe·lo
sleeping car vagone ⓜ letto va·go·ne
le·to

sleeping pills sonniferi ⓜ pl
so·nee·fe·ree
(to be) sleepy avere sonno ⓜ a·ve·re
so·no
slice fetta ⓕ fe·ta
slide (film) diapositiva ⓜ
dee·a·po·zee·tee·va
slope pista ⓕ pee·sta
Slovenia Slovenia ⓕ slo·ve·nya
slow lento/a ⓜ/ⓕ len·to/a
slowly lentamente len·ta·men·te
small piccolo/a ⓜ/ⓕ pee·ko·lo/a
smell odore ⓜ o·do·re
smile sorridere so·ree·de·re
smoke fumare foo·ma·re
snack spuntino ⓜ spoon·tee·no
snail lumaca ⓕ loo·ma·ka
snake serpente ⓜ ser·pen·te
snorkel boccaglio ⓜ bo·ka·lyo
snow neve ⓕ ne·ve
snowboarding surf ⓜ da neve soorf
da ne·ve
snow chains catene ⓕ pl da neve
ka·te·ne da ne·ve
soap sapone ⓜ sa·po·ne
soap opera telenovela ⓕ te·le·no·ve·la
soccer calcio ⓜ kal·cho
social welfare assistenza ⓕ sociale
a·sees·ten·tsa so·cha·le
socialist socialista ⓜ&ⓕ
so·cha·lee·sta
socks calzini ⓜ pl cal·tsee·nee
soft morbido/a ⓜ/ⓕ mor·bee·do/a
soft drink bibita ⓕ bee·bee·ta
soldier soldato ⓜ sol·da·to
some alcuni/e ⓜ/ⓕ pl al·koo·nee/
al·koo·ne
someone qualcuno/a ⓜ/ⓕ
kwal·koo·no/a
something qualcosa kwal·ko·za
sometimes a volte a vol·te
son figlio ⓜ fee·lyo
song canzone ⓕ kan·tso·ne
soon fra poco fra po·ko
sore doloroso/a ⓜ/ⓕ do·lo·ro·zo/a
soup minestra ⓕ mee·nes·tra

S

S

sour cream panna ⓕ acida *pa*·na a·chee·da

south sud ⓜ sood

souvenir ricordino ⓜ ree·kor·*dee*·no

souvenir shop negozio ⓜ di souvenir ne·*go*·tsyo dee soo·ve·neer

soy milk latte ⓜ di soia *la*·te dee *so*·ya

soy sauce salsa ⓕ di soia *sal*·sa dee *so*·ya

space spazio ⓜ *spa*·tsyo

spade vanga ⓕ *van*·ga

Spain Spagna ⓕ *spa*·nya

speak parlare par·*la*·re

special speciale spe·*cha*·le

specialist specialista ⓜ&ⓕ spe·cha·*lee*·sta

speed velocità ⓕ ve·lo·chee·*ta*

speed limit limite ⓜ di velocità *lee*·mee·te dee ve·lo·chee·*ta*

speedometer tachimetro ⓜ ta·*kee*·me·tro

spermicide spermicida ⓕ sper·mee·*chee*·da

spider ragno ⓜ *ra*·nyo

spinach spinaci ⓜ pl spee·*na*·chee

spoke(s) raggio/raggi ⓜ *ra*·jo/*ra*·jee

spoon cucchiaio ⓜ koo·*kya*·yo

sports store negozio ⓜ di articoli sportivi ne·*go*·tsyo dee ar·*tee*·ko·lee spor·*tee*·vee

sportsperson sportivo/a ⓜ/ⓕ spor·*tee*·vo·a

sprain storta ⓕ *stor*·ta

spring (season) primavera ⓕ pree·ma·*ve*·ra

square (town) piazza ⓕ *pya*·tsa

stadium stadio ⓜ *sta*·dyo

stage (theatre) palcoscenico ⓜ pal·ko·*she*·nee·ko

stage (in race) tappa ⓕ *ta*·pa

stairway scale ⓕ pl *ska*·le

stamp francobollo ⓜ fran·ko·*bo*·lo

standby (ticket) (in lista) d'attesa (een *lee*·sta) da·*te*·za

(four-)star (a quattro) stelle (a *kwa*·tro) *ste*·le

stars stelle ⓕ pl *ste*·le

start inizio ⓜ ee·*nee*·tsyo

start cominciare ko·meen·*cha*·re

station stazione ⓕ sta·*tsyo*·ne

stationer cartolaio ⓜ kar·to·*la*·yo

statue statua ⓕ *sta*·too·a

stay (at a hotel) fermarsi fer·*mar*·see

steak (beef) bistecca ⓕ bees·*te*·ka

steal rubare roo·*ba*·re

steep ripido/a ⓜ/ⓕ *ree*·pee·do/a

stingy avaro/a ⓜ/ⓕ a·*va*·ro/a

stockings calze ⓕ pl *kal*·tse

stolen rubato/a ⓜ/ⓕ roo·*ba*·to/a

stomach stomaco ⓜ *sto*·ma·ko

stomachache mal ⓜ di pancia mal dee *pan*·cha

stone pietra ⓕ *pye*·tra

stoned (drugged) fumato/a ⓜ/ⓕ foo·*ma*·to/a

stop fermata ⓕ fer·*ma*·ta

stop fermare fer·*ma*·re

storm temporale ⓜ tem·po·*ra*·le

story racconto ⓜ ra·*kon*·to

stove stufa ⓕ (a gas) *stoo*·fa a gaz

straight diritto/a ⓜ/ⓕ dee·*ree*·to/a

strange strano/a ⓜ/ⓕ *stra*·no/a

stranger sconosciuto/a ⓜ/ⓕ sko·no·*shoo*·to/a

strawberry fragola ⓕ *fra*·go·la

stream ruscello ⓜ roo·*she*·lo

street strada ⓕ *stra*·da

(on) strike (in) sciopero ⓜ een *sho*·pe·ro

string spago ⓜ *spa*·go

strong forte ⓜ/ⓕ *for*·te

student studente/studentessa ⓜ/ⓕ stoo·*den*·te/stoo·den·*te*·sa

stupid stupido/a ⓜ/ⓕ *stoo*·pee·do/a

style stile ⓜ *stee*·le

subtitles sottotitoli ⓜ pl so·to·*tee*·to·lee

suburb quartiere ⓜ kwar·*tye*·re

subway metropolitana ⓕ me·tro·po·lee·*ta*·na

sugar zucchero ⓜ *tsoo·ke·ro*
suitcase valigia ⓕ *va·lee·ja*
summer estate ⓕ es·*ta·te*
sun sole ⓜ *so·le*
sunblock crema ⓕ solare *kre·ma so·la·re*
sunburn scottatura ⓕ sko·ta·*too·ra*
sunglasses occhiali ⓜ pl da sole o·*kya·*lee da *so·le*
sunny soleggiato/a ⓜ/ⓕ so·le·*ja·to/a*
sunrise alba ⓕ *al·ba*
sunscreen crema ⓕ solare *kre·ma so·la·re*
sunset tramonto ⓜ tra·*mon·to*
supermarket supermercato ⓜ soo·per·mer·*ka·to*
superstition superstizione ⓕ soo·por·stee·*tsyo·ne*
supplies provviste ⓕ pl pro·*vee·ste*
support (cheer on) fare il tifo *fa·re* eel *tee·fo*
supporters tifosi ⓜ pl tee·*fo·zee*
surf praticare il surf pra·tee·*ka·re* eel soorf
surface mail posta ⓕ ordinaria *pos·ta* or·dee·*na·rya*
surfboard tavola da surf *ta·vo·la* da soorf
surname cognome ⓜ ko·*nyo·me*
surprise sorpresa ⓕ sor·*pre·sa*
sweater maglione ⓜ ma·*lyo·ne*
Sweden Svezia ⓕ *sve·tsee·a*
sweet dolce *dol·che*
swelling gonfiore ⓜ gon·*fyo·re*
swim nuotare nwo·*ta·re*
swimming nuoto ⓜ *nwo·to*
swimming pool piscina ⓕ pee·*shee·na*
swimsuit costume ⓜ da bagno ko·*stoo·me* da *ba·*nyo
Switzerland Svizzera ⓕ *svee·tse·ra*
synagogue sinagoga ⓕ see·na·*go·ga*
synthetic sintetico/a ⓜ/ⓕ seen·*te·tee·ko/a*
syringe siringa ⓕ see·*reen·ga*

T

table tavola ⓕ *ta·vo·la*
table tennis ping-pong ⓜ peeng·*pong*
tablecloth tovaglia ⓕ to·*va·lya*
tailor sarto ⓜ *sar·to*
take prendere *pren·*de·re
take (photo) fare *fa·re*
talk parlare par·*la·re*
tall alto/a ⓜ/ⓕ *al·to/a*
tampons tamponi ⓜ pl tam·*po·nee*
tanning lotion lozione ⓕ abbronzante lo·*tsyo·ne* a·bron·*dzan·te*
tap (faucet) rubinetto ⓜ roo·bee·*ne·to*
tasty gustoso/a ⓜ/ⓕ goo·*sto·zo/a*
tax tassa ⓕ *ta·sa*
taxi tassì ⓜ ta·*see*
taxi stand posteggio ⓜ di tassì po·*ste·ju* dee ta·*see*
tea tè ⓜ te
teacher (general) insegnante ⓜ&ⓕ een·sen·*yan·te*
teacher (primary) maestro/a ⓜ/ⓕ ma·*es·tro/a*
teacher (secondary) professore/professoressa ⓜ/ⓕ pro·fe·*so·re/* pro·fe·so·*re·sa*
team squadra ⓕ *skwa·dra*
teaspoon cucchiaino ⓜ koo·kya·*ee·no*
teeth denti ⓜ pl *den·tee*
telegram telegramma ⓜ te·le·*gra·ma*
telephone telefono ⓜ te·*le·fo·no*
telephone telefonare te·le·fo·*na·re*
telephone centre centro ⓜ telefonico *chen·tro* te·le·*fo·nee·ko*
telephoto lens teleobiettivo ⓜ te·le·o·bye·*tee·vo*
television televisione ⓕ te·le·vee·*zyo·ne*
tell raccontare ra·kon·*ta·re*
temperature (fever) febbre ⓕ *fe·bre*
temperature (weather) temperatura ⓕ tem·pe·ra·*too·ra*

temple tempio ⓜ *tem*·pyo
tennis court campo ⓜ da tennis *kam*·po da te·nees
tent tenda ⓕ *ten*·da
tent pegs picchetti ⓜ pl (per la tenda) pee·*ke*·tee (per la *ten*·da)
terrible terribile ⓜ/ⓕ te·*ree*·bee·le
test esame ⓜ e·*za*·me
thank ringraziare reen·gra·*tsya*·re
theatre teatro ⓜ te·*a*·tro
there là la
they loro *lo*·ro
thick spesso/a ⓜ/ⓕ *spe*·so/a
thief ladro/a ⓜ/ⓕ *la*·dro/a
thin magro/a ⓜ/ⓕ *ma*·gro/a
think pensare pen·*sa*·re
third terzo/a ⓜ/ⓕ *ter*·tso/a
(to be) thirsty avere sete ⓕ a·*ve*·re *se*·te
this (one) questo/a ⓜ/ⓕ *kwe*·sto/a
thread (sewing) filo ⓜ *fee*·lo
throat gola ⓕ *go*·la
thrush (medical) mughetto ⓜ moo·*ge*·to
ticket biglietto ⓜ bee·*lye*·to
ticket collector controllore ⓜ kon·tro·*lo*·re
ticket machine distributore ⓜ automatico di biglietti dee·stree·boo·to·re ow·to·*ma*·tee·ko dee bee·*lye*·tee
ticket office biglietteria ⓕ bee·lye·te·*ree*·a
tide marea ⓕ ma·*re*·a
tight stretto/a ⓜ/ⓕ *stre*·to/a
time tempo ⓜ *tem*·po
time difference differenza ⓕ di fuso orario dee·fe·*ren*·tsa dee *foo*·zo o·*ra*·ryo
timetable orario ⓜ o·*ra*·ryo
tin (can) scatoletta ⓕ ska·to·*le*·ta
tin opener apriscatole ⓜ a·pree·*ska*·to·le
tiny minuscolo/a ⓜ/ⓕ mee·*noos*·ko·lo/a
tip (gratuity) mancia ⓕ *man*·cha

tired stanco/a ⓜ/ⓕ *stan*·ko/a
tissues fazzolettini ⓜ pl di carta fa·tso·le·*tee*·nee dee *kar*·ta
toast pane ⓜ tostato *pa*·ne tos·*ta*·to
toaster tostapane ⓜ tos·ta·*pa*·ne
tobacco tabacco ⓜ ta·*ba*·ko
tobacconist tabaccheria ⓕ ta·ba·ke·*ree*·a
toboganing andare in slitta an·*da*·re een *slee*·ta
today oggi o·jee
toe dito ⓜ del piede *dee*·to del *pye*·de
together insieme een·*sye*·me
toilet gabinetto ⓜ ga·bee·*ne*·to
toilet paper carta ⓕ igienica *kar*·ta ee·*je*·nee·ka
toilets servizi ⓜ pl igienici ser·*vee*·tse ee·*je*·nee·chee
token gettone ⓜ je·*to*·ne
tomato pomodoro ⓜ po·mo·*do*·ro
tomato sauce salsa ⓕ di pomodoro *sal*·sa dee po·mo·*do*·ro
tomorrow domani do·*ma*·nee
tonight stasera sta·*se*·ra
too (expensive) troppo (caro/a) *tro*·po (*ka*·ro/a)
too many troppi/e ⓜ/ⓕ pl *tro*·pee/ *tro*·pe
too much troppo/a ⓜ/ⓕ sg *tro*·po/a
tooth (front) dente ⓜ *den*·te
toothache mal ⓜ di denti mal dee *den*·tee
toothbrush spazzolino ⓜ da denti spa·tso·*lee*·no da *den*·tee
toothpaste dentifricio ⓜ den·tee·*free*·cho
toothpick stuzzicadenti ⓜ stoo·tsee·ka·*den*·tee
torch (flashlight) torcia ⓕ elettrica *tor*·cha e·*le*·tree·ka
touch toccare to·*ka*·re
tour gita ⓕ *jee*·ta
tourist turista ⓜ&ⓕ too·*ree*·sta
tourist office ufficio ⓜ del turismo oo·*fee*·cho del too·*reez*·mo

towel asciugamano ⓜ
a·shoo·ga·ma·no

tower torre ⓕ to·re

toxic waste rifiuti ⓜ pl tossici
ree·fyoo·tee to·see·chee

toyshop negozio ⓜ di giocattoli
ne·go·tsyo dee jo·ka·to·lee

track (path) sentiero ⓜ sen·tye·ro

track (sports) pista ⓕ pee·sta

trade commercio ⓜ ko·mer·cho

traffic traffico ⓜ tra·fee·ko

traffic jam ingorgo ⓜ een·gor·go

traffic lights semaforo ⓜ se·ma·fo·ro

trail pista ⓕ pee·sta

train treno ⓜ tre·no

train station stazione ⓕ (ferroviaria)
sta·tsyo·ne (fe·ro·vyar·ya)

tram tram ⓜ tram

transit lounge sala ⓕ di transito
sa·la dee tran·zee·to

translate tradurre tra·doo·re

transport trasporto ⓜ tras·por·to

travel viaggiare vee·a·ja·re

travel agency agenzia ⓕ di viaggio
a·jen·tsee·a dee vee·a·jo

travel sickness (air) mal ⓜ di aereo
mal dee a·e·re·o

travel sickness (car) mal ⓜ di
macchina mal dee ma·kee·na

travel sickness (sea) mal ⓜ di mare
mal dee ma·re

travellers cheque assegno ⓜ di
viaggio a·se·nyo dee vee·a·jo

tree albero ⓜ al·be·ro

trip gita ⓕ jee·ta

trolley (luggage) carrello ⓜ ka·re·lo

trousers pantaloni ⓜ pl pan·ta·lo·nee

truck camion ⓜ ka·myon

true vero/a ⓜ/ⓕ ve·ro/a

try (attempt) provare pro·va·re

T-shirt maglietta ⓕ ma·lye·ta

tube (tyre) camera ⓕ d'aria ka·me·ra
da·rya

tuna tonno ⓜ to·no

tune melodia ⓕ me·lo·dee·a

turkey tacchino ⓜ ta·kee·no

turn girare jee·ra·re

TV TV ⓕ tee·voo

tweezers pinzette ⓕ pl peen·tse·te

twice due volte doo·e vol·te

twin beds due letti doo·e le·tee

twins gemelli/e ⓜ/ⓕ pl je·me·lee/
je·me·le

type tipo ⓜ tee·po

typical tipico/a ⓜ/ⓕ tee·pee·ko/a

tyre gomma ⓕ go·ma

U

ugly brutto/a ⓜ/ⓕ broo·to/a

ultrasound ecografia ⓕ e·ko·gra·fee·a

umbrella ombrello ⓜ om·bre·lo

uncomfortable scomodo/a ⓜ/ⓕ
sko·mo·do/a

understand capire ka·pee·re

underwear biancheria ⓕ intima
byan·ke·ree·a een·tee·ma

unemployed disoccupato/a ⓜ/ⓕ
dee·zo·koo·pa·to/a

uniform divisa ⓕ dee·vee·za

universe universo ⓜ oo·nee·ver·so

university università ⓕ
oo·nee·ver·see·ta

unleaded senza piombo sen·tsa
pyom·bo

unsafe pericoloso/a ⓜ/ⓕ
pe·ree·ko·lo·zo/a

until fino a fee·no a

unusual insolito/a ⓜ/ⓕ
een·so·lee·to/a

up su soo

uphill in salita een sa·lee·ta

urgent urgente ⓜ/ⓕ oor·jen·te

USA Stati ⓜ pl Uniti d'America
sta·tee oo·nee·tee da·me·ree·ka

useful utile oo·tee·le

V

vacant libero/a ⓜ/ⓕ lee·be·ro/a

vacation vacanza ⓕ va·kan·tsa

vaccination vaccinazione ⓕ
va·chee·na·tsyo·ne

W

vagina vagina ⓕ va·*jee*·na
validate convalidare kon·va·lee·*da*·re
valley valle ⓕ *va*·le
valuable prezioso/a ⓜ/ⓕ pre·*tsyo*·zo/a
valuables oggetti ⓜ pl di valore o·*je*·tee dee va·*lo*·re
value (price) valore ⓜ va·*lo*·re
van furgone ⓜ foor·*go*·ne
veal vitello ⓜ vee·*te*·lo
vegetable verdura ⓕ ver·*doo*·ra
vegetarian vegetariano/a ⓜ/ⓕ ve·je·ta·*rya*·no/a
venereal disease malattia ⓕ venerea ma·la·*tee*·a ve·ne·re·a
venue locale ⓜ lo·*ka*·le
very molto *mol*·to
video videoregistratore ⓜ vee·de·o·re·jee·stra·*to*·re
video camera videocamera ⓕ vee·de·o·*ka*·me·ra
video tape videonastro ⓜ vee·de·o·*nas*·tro
view vista ⓕ *vee*·sta
village villaggio ⓜ vee·*la*·jo
vinegar aceto ⓜ a·*che*·to
vineyard vigneto ⓜ vee·*nye*·to
virus virus ⓜ *vee*·roos
visa visto ⓜ *vee*·sto
visit (person) andare a trovare an·*da*·re a tro·*va*·re
visit (place) fare una visita *fa*·re oo·na *vee*·see·ta
vitamins vitamine ⓕ pl vee·ta·*mee*·ne
voice voce ⓕ *vo*·che
volleyball pallavolo ⓜ pa·la·*vo*·lo
vomit vomitare vo·mee·*ta*·re
vote votare vo·*ta*·re

W

wage salario ⓜ sa·*la*·ryo
wait aspettare as·pe·*ta*·re
waiter cameriere/a ⓜ/ⓕ ka·mer·*ye*·re/a
waiting room sala ⓕ d'attesa *sa*·la da·*te*·sa

wake up svegliarsi sve·*lyar*·see
Wales Galles ⓜ *ga*·les
walk passeggiata ⓕ pa·se·*ja*·ta
walk camminare ka·mee·*na*·re
wall (external) muro ⓜ *moo*·ro
wall (internal) parete ⓕ pa·*re*·te
wallet portafoglio ⓜ por·ta·*fo*·lyo
want volere vo·*le*·re
war guerra ⓕ *gwe*·ra
wardrobe armadio ⓜ ar·*ma*·dyo
warm tiepido/a ⓜ/ⓕ *tye*·pee·do/a
warn avvertire a·ver·*tee*·re
wash (oneself) lavarsi la·*var*·see
wash (something) lavare la·*va*·re
washing machine lavatrice ⓕ la·va·*tree*·che
washing powder detersivo ⓜ de·ter·*see*·vo
watch orologio ⓜ o·ro·*lo*·jo
watch guardare gwar·*da*·re
water acqua ⓕ *a*·kwa
water bottle borraccia ⓕ bo·*ra*·cha
waterfall cascata ⓕ kas·*ka*·ta
watermelon anguria ⓕ an·*goo*·rya
waterproof impermeabile eem·per·me·a·bee·le
water skiing sci ⓜ acquatico shee a·*kwa*·tee·ko
watersports sport ⓜ acquatici sport a·*kwa*·tee·chee
wave onda ⓕ *on*·da
way via ⓕ *vee*·a
we noi noy
weak debole *de*·bo·le
wealthy ricco/a ⓜ/ⓕ *ree*·ko/a
wear indossare een·do·*sa*·re
weather tempo ⓜ *tem*·po
wedding matrimonio ⓜ ma·tree·*mo*·nyo
wedding present regalo ⓜ di nozze re·*ga*·lo dee *no*·tse
week settimana ⓕ se·tee·*ma*·na
weekend fine settimana ⓜ *fee*·ne se·tee·*ma*·na
weight peso ⓜ *pe*·zo

welcome dare il benvenuto a *da*·re eel ben·ve·*noo*·to a

well in buona salute een *bwo*·na sa·*loo*·te

west ovest ⓜ o·vest

wet bagnato/a ⓜ/ⓕ ba·*nya*·to/a

wetsuit muta ⓕ *moo*·ta

what che (cosa) ke (*ko*·za)

wheel ruota ⓕ *rwo*·ta

wheelchair sedia ⓕ a rotelle *se*·dya a ro·*te*·le

when quando *kwan*·do

where dove *do*·ve

white bianco/a ⓜ/ⓕ *byan*·ko/a

who chi kee

why perché per·*ke*

wide largo/a ⓜ/ⓕ *lar*·go/a

widow vedova ⓕ ve·*do*·va

widower vedovo ⓜ ve·*do*·vo

wife moglie ⓕ *mo*·lye

win vincere *veen*·che·re

wind vento ⓜ *ven*·to

window (car, plane) finestrino ⓜ fee·nes·*tree*·no

window (general) finestra ⓕ fee·*nes*·tra

windscreen parabrezza ⓜ pa·ra·*bre*·dza

wine vino ⓜ *vee*·no

wine cellar cantina ⓕ kan·*tee*·na

wine tasting degustazione ⓕ dei vini de·goos·ta·*tsyo*·ne day *vee*·nee

winery cantina ⓕ kan·*tee*·na

wings ali ⓕ pl *a*·lee

winner vincitore/vincitrice ⓜ/ⓕ veen·chee·*to*·re/veen·chee·*tree*·che

winter inverno ⓜ een·*ver*·no

wish desiderare de·see·de·*ra*·re

with con kon

within (an hour) entro (un'ora) *en*·tro (oon·*o*·ra)

without senza *sen*·tsa

woman donna ⓕ *do*·na

wonderful meraviglioso/a ⓜ/ⓕ me·ra·vee·*lyo*·zo/a

wood legno ⓜ *le*·nyo

wool lana ⓕ *la*·na

word parola ⓕ pa·*ro*·la

work (occupation) lavoro ⓜ la·*vo*·ro

work (of art) opera ⓕ (d'arte) *o*·pe·ra (*dar*·te)

work lavorare la·vo·*ra*·re

workout allenamento ⓜ a·le·na·*men*·to

workshop laboratorio ⓜ la·bo·ra·*to*·ryo

world mondo ⓜ *mon*·do

World Cup Coppa ⓕ del Mondo *ko*·pa del *mon*·do

worried preoccupato/a ⓜ/ⓕ pre·o·koo·*pa*·to/a

worship (pray) pregare pre·*ga*·re

wrist polso ⓜ *pol*·so

write scrivere skree·ve·re

writer scrittore/scrittrice ⓜ/ⓕ skree·*to*·re/skree·*tree*·che

wrong sbagliato/a ⓜ/ⓕ sba·*lya*·to/a

Y

year anno ⓜ *a*·no

yellow giallo/a ⓜ/ⓕ *ja*·lo/a

yes sì see

yesterday ieri ye·ree

(not) yet (non) ancora (non) an·*ko*·ra

you sg inf tu too

you sg pol Lei lay

you pl inf voi voy

you pl pol Loro *lo*·ro

young giovane jo·va·ne

youth hostel ostello ⓜ della gioventù os·*te*·lo *de*·la jo·ven·*too*

Z

zoo giardino ⓜ zoologico jar·*dee*·no dzo·o·*lo*·jee·ko

Dictionary

ITALIAN *to* ENGLISH

Italiano–Inglese

Nouns in this dictionary, and adjectives affected by gender, have their gender indicated by Ⓜ and/or Ⓕ. If it's a plural noun, you'll also see pl. Where a word that could be either a noun or a verb has no gender indicated, it's a verb.

A

a a in • at • to • until • per
a bordo a *bor*·do aboard
abbastanza a·bas·*tan*·tsa enough
abbigliamento Ⓜ a·bee·lya·*men*·to clothing
abbracciare a·bra·*cha*·re hug
abitare a·bee·*ta*·re live (somewhere)
abito Ⓜ *a*·bee·to dress
aborto Ⓜ a·*bor*·to abortion
— spontaneo spon·*ta*·ne·o miscarriage
accanto a·*kan*·to nearby
accanto a a·*kan*·to a next to
accendino Ⓜ a·chen·*dee*·no (cigarette) lighter
accetazione Ⓕ a·che·ta·*tsyo*·ne check-in (airport)
aceto Ⓜ a·*che*·to vinegar
acqua Ⓕ *a*·kwa water
— bollita bo·*lee*·ta boiled water
— calda *kal*·da hot water
— del rubinetto del roo·bee·*ne*·to tap water
— minerale mee·ne·*ra*·le mineral water
— non gassata non ga·*sa*·ta still water

adesso a·*de*·so now
adulto/a Ⓜ/Ⓕ a·*dool*·to/a adult
aereo Ⓜ a·e·re·o plane
aerobica Ⓕ a·e·ro·bee·ka aerobics
aeroporto Ⓜ a·e·ro·*por*·to airport
affari Ⓜ pl a·*fa*·ree business
affascinante a·fa·shee·*nan*·te charming • attractive
affilato/a Ⓜ/Ⓕ a·fee·*la*·to/a sharp
affitto Ⓜ a·*fee*·to rent
affollato/a Ⓜ/Ⓕ a·fo·*la*·to/a crowded
agenda Ⓕ a·*jen*·da diary
agenzia Ⓕ **di viaggio** a·jen·*tsee*·a dee vee·a·jo travel agency
agganciare a·gan·*cha*·re chat up
aggiustare a·joo·*sta*·re repair
aggressivo/a Ⓜ/Ⓕ a·gre·*see*·vo/a aggressive
aglio Ⓜ *a*·lyo garlic
agnello Ⓜ a·*nye*·lo lamb
ago Ⓜ *a*·go needle (sewing)
agopuntura Ⓕ a·go·poon·*too*·ra acupuncture
agricoltore/agricoltrice Ⓜ/Ⓕ a·gree·kol·*to*·re/a·gree·kol·*tree*·che farmer

agricoltura ① a·gree·kol·*too*·ra agriculture

aiutare a·yoo·*ta*·re help

alba ① *al*·ba sunrise

albergo ⓜ al·*ber*·go hotel

albero ⓜ *al*·be·ro tree

albicocca ① al·bee·*ko*·ka apricot

alcuni/e ⓜ/① pl al·*koo*·nee/al·*koo*·ne some

ali ① pl *a*·lee wings

alimentari ⓜ a·lee·men·*ta*·ree grocery store • convenience store

alimento ⓜ a·lee·*men*·to food

al giorno al *jor*·no per day

al mare al *ma*·re seaside

all'estero a·*les*·te·ro abroad

allenamento ⓜ a·le·na·*men*·to workout

allergia ① a·ler·*jee*·a allergy

alloggio ⓜ a·*lo*·jo accommodation

allucinare a·loo·chee·*na*·re hallucinate

alpinismo ⓜ al·pee·*neez*·mo mountaineering

altare ⓜ al·*ta*·re altar

altezza ① al·*te*·tsa height

alto/a ⓜ/① *al*·to/a high • tall

altopiano ⓜ al·to·*pya*·no plateau

altro/a ⓜ/① *al*·tro/a other

— ieri *ye*·ree day before yesterday

amaca ① a·*ma*·ka hammock

amante ⓜ/① a·*man*·te lover

amaro a·*ma*·re love

ambasciata ① am·ba·*sha*·ta embassy

ambasciatore/ambasciatrice ⓜ/① am·ba·sha·*to*·re/am·ba·sha·*tree*·che ambassador

ambiente ⓜ am·*byen*·te environment

ambulanza ① am·boo·*lan*·tsa ambulance

amico/a ⓜ/① a·*mee*·ko/a friend

ammazzare a·ma·*tsa*·re kill

amministrazione ① a·mee·nee·stra·*tsyo*·ne administration

analgesico ⓜ an·al·*je*·zee·ko painkillers

analisi ① **del sangue** a·*na*·lee·zee del *san*·gwe blood test

ananas ① *a*·na·nas pineapple

anatra ① *a*·na·tra duck

anche *an*·ke also

ancora an·*ko*·ra still • yet

andare an·*da*·re go

— a cavallo a ka·*va*·lo horse riding

— a vedere a ve·*de*·re visit

— in bicicletta een bee·chee·*kle*·ta cycle • ride (a bike)

— in slitta een *slee*·ta tobogganing

— su roccia soo *ro*·cha rock climbing

andata ① an·*da*·ta outward journey

anello ⓜ a·*ne*·lo ring (on finger)

angolo ⓜ *an*·go·lo corner

anguria ① an·*goo*·rya watermelon

animale ⓜ a·nee·*ma*·le animal

anno ⓜ *a*·no year

annoiato/a ⓜ/① a·no·*ya*·to/a bored

annuale a·noo·*a*·le annual

annuncio ⓜ a·*noon*·cho advertisement

antibiotici ⓜ pl an·tee·bee·o·*tee*·chee antibiotics

antico/a ⓜ/① an·*tee*·ko/a ancient

antinucleare an·tee·noo·kle·*a*·re antinuclear

antisettico ⓜ an·tee·*se*·tee·ko antiseptic

antistaminici ⓜ pl an·tee·sta·*mee*·nee·chee antihistamines

ape ① *a*·pe bee

aperto/a ⓜ/① a·*per*·to/a open

apparecchio ⓜ **acustico** a·pa·*re*·kyo a·*koos*·tee·ko hearing aid

appartamento ⓜ a·par·ta·*men*·to flat

appendice ① a·pen·*dee*·che appendix

appuntamento ⓜ a·poon·ta·*men*·to appointment • date

apribottiglie ⓜ a·pree·bo·*tee*·lye bottle opener

aprire a·*pree*·re open

apriscatole ⓜ a·pree·*ska*·to·le can opener

B

arachidi ⓕ pl a·*ra*·kee·dee peanuts • groundnuts

arancia ⓕ a·*ran*·cha orange (fruit)

arancione a·ran·*cho*·ne orange (colour)

arbitro ⓜ ar·bee·tro referee

archeologico/a ⓜ/ⓕ ar·ke·o·*lo*·jee·ko/a archaeological

architetto ⓜ ar·kee·*te*·to architect

architettura ⓕ ar·kee·te·*too*·ra architecture

argento ⓜ ar·*jen*·to silver

aria ⓕ a·rya air

— condizionata kon·dee·*tsyo*·na·ta air-conditioning

aringa ⓕ a·*reen*·ga herring

armadietti ⓜ pl ar·ma·*dye*·tee lockers

— per i bagagli per ee ba·*ga*·lyee luggage lockers

armadio ⓜ ar·*ma*·dyo wardrobe

arrabbiato/a ⓜ/ⓕ a·ra·*bya*·to/a angry

arrestare a·res·*ta*·re arrest

arrivare a·ree·*va*·re arrive

arrivi ⓜ pl a·*ree*·vee arrivals

arte ⓕ *ar*·te art

arti ⓕ pl **marziali** *ar*·tee mar·*tsya*·lee martial arts

artista ⓜ&ⓕ ar·*tee*·sta artist

ASA a·za film speed

ascensore ⓜ a·shen·*so*·re elevator

asciugamano ⓜ a·shoo·ga·*ma*·no towel

asciugare a·*shoo*·ga·re dry

ascoltare as·kol·*ta*·re listen

asilo ⓜ a·*zee*·lo kindergarten

— nido *nee*·do creche

asma ⓕ *az*·ma asthma

asparagi ⓜ pl as·*pa*·ra·jee asparagus

aspettare as·pe·*ta*·re wait

aspirina ⓕ as·pee·*ree*·na aspirin

assegno ⓜ a·*se*·nyo cheque

— di viaggio dee vee·*a*·jo travellers cheque

assicurazione ⓕ a·see·koo·ra·*tsyo*·ne insurance

assistenza ⓕ **sociale** a·sees·*ten*·tsa so·*cha*·le (social) welfare

assorbenti ⓜ pl **igienici** a·sor·*ben*·tee ee·je·*nee*·chee sanitary napkins

atletica ⓕ at·*le*·tee·ka athletics

atrio ⓜ a·tryo foyer

attesa ⓕ a·*te*·sa wait

attrezzatura ⓕ a·tre·tsa·*too*·ra equipment

attualità ⓕ a·too·a·lee·*ta* current affairs

autobus ⓜ ow·to·boos bus (city)

autostop ⓜ ow·to·stop hitchhiking

automatico/a ⓜ/ⓕ ow·to·*ma*·tee·ko/a automatic

automobilismo ⓜ ow·to·mo·bee·*leez*·mo car racing

autonoleggio ⓜ ow·to·no·*le*·jo car hire

autostrada ⓕ ow·to·*stra*·da motorway • tollway

autunno ⓜ ow·*too*·no autumn

a volte a *vol*·te sometimes

avaro/a ⓜ/ⓕ a·*va*·ro/a stingy

avena ⓕ a·*ve*·na oats

avere a·*ve*·re have

— bisogno di bee·*zo*·nyo dee need

— fame ⓕ *fa*·me (to be) hungry

— fretta ⓕ *fre*·ta (to be) in a hurry

— mal ⓜ **di mare** mal dee *ma*·re (to be) seasick

— sete ⓕ *se*·te (to be) thirsty

— sonno ⓜ *so*·no (to be) sleepy

avventura ⓕ a·ven·*too*·ra adventure

avvertire a·ver·*tee*·re warn

avvocato/a ⓜ/ⓕ a·vo·*ka*·to/a lawyer

azzurro/a ⓜ/ⓕ a·*dzoo*·ro/a blue (light)

B

baciare ba·*cha*·re kiss

bacio ⓜ *ba*·cho kiss

bagaglio ⓜ ba·*ga*·lyo luggage

— a mano a *ma*·no carry-on luggage

B

— **consentito** kon·sen·tee·to baggage allowance

— **in eccedenza** een e·che·den·tsa excess bagage

bagnato/a ⓜ/ⓕ ba·nya·to/a wet

bagno ⓜ ba·nyo bath • bathroom

balcone ⓜ bal·ko·ne balcony

ballare ba·la·re dance

balletto ⓜ ba·le·to ballet

ballo ⓜ ba·lo ball (dancing) • dancing

balsamo ⓜ **per i capelli** bal·sa·mo per ee ka·pe·lee conditioner

bambino/a ⓜ/ⓕ bam·bee·no/a child

bambola ⓕ bam·bo·la doll

banca ⓕ ban·ka bank (money)

Bancomat ⓜ ban·ko·mat automatic teller machine (ATM)

bancone ⓜ ban·ko·ne counter (at bar)

banconota ⓕ ban·ko·no·ta banknote

bandiera ⓕ ban·dye·ra flag

bar ⓜ bar cafe

barattolo ⓜ ba·ra·to·lo jar

barbabietola ⓕ bar·ba·bye·to·la beetroot

barbiere ⓜ bar·bye·re barber

barca ⓕ bar·ka boat

basso/a ⓜ/ⓕ ba·so/a low • short (height)

batteria ⓕ ba·te·ree·a battery (for car) • drums

battesimo ⓜ ba·te·zee·mo baptism

batuffoli ⓜ pl **di cotone** ba·too·fo·lee dee ko·to·ne cotton balls

bebè ⓜ&ⓕ be·be baby

bello/a ⓜ/ⓕ be·lo/a beautiful • handsome • good (weather)

benessere ⓜ be·ne·se·re welfare (well-being)

benzina ⓕ ben·dze·na gas (petrol)

bere be·re drink

bevanda ⓕ be·van·da drink

biancheria ⓕ **intima** byan·ke·ree·a een·tee·ma underwear

bianco/a ⓜ/ⓕ byan·ko/a white

bibbia ⓕ bee·bya bible

bibita ⓕ bee·bee·ta soft drink

biblioteca ⓕ beeb·lyo·te·ka library

bicchiere ⓜ bee·kye·re glass (drinking)

bici ⓕ **(da corsa)** bee·chee (da kor·sa) (racing) bike

bicicletta ⓕ bee·chee·kle·ta bicycle

bidone ⓜ bee·do·ne rip-off • bin

biglietteria ⓕ bee·lye·te·ree·a ticket office

biglietto ⓜ bee·lye·to ticket

— **di andata e ritorno** dee an·da·ta e ree·tor·no return ticket

— **di solo andata** dee so·lo an·da·ta one-way ticket

bilancio ⓜ bee·lan·cho budget

biliardo ⓜ beel·yar·do pool (game)

bimbo/a ⓜ/ⓕ beem·bo/a baby

binario ⓜ bee·na·ryo platform

binocolo ⓜ bee·no·ko·lo binoculars

biondo/a ⓜ/ⓕ byon·do/a blonde

birra ⓕ bee·ra beer

— **chiara** kya·ra lager

biscotto ⓜ bees·ko·to biscuit • cookie

bisogno ⓜ bee·zo·nyo need • necessity

bistecca ⓕ bees·te·ka steak (beef)

bisticcio ⓜ bees·tee·cho quarrel

bloccato/a ⓜ/ⓕ blo·ka·to/a blocked

blu bloo blue (dark)

bocca ⓕ bo·ka mouth

boccaglio ⓜ bo·ka·lyo snorkel

bollo ⓜ bo·lo stamp • seal

— **di circolazione** dee cheer·ko·la·tsyo·ne car registration

bordo ⓜ bor·do edge • border

borotalco ⓜ bo·ro·tal·ko baby powder

borraccia ⓕ bo·ra·cha water bottle

borsa ⓕ bor·sa bag (general)

borsetta ⓕ bor·se·ta handbag

bottiglia ⓕ bo·tee·lya bottle

bottiglieria ⓕ bo·tee·lye·ree·a liquor store

bottone ⓜ bo·to·ne button

braccio ⓜ bra·cho arm

C

brillante ⓜ/ⓕ bree·*lan*·te brilliant
bronchite ⓕ bron·*kee*·te bronchitis
bruciare broo·*cha*·re burn
brutto/a ⓜ/ⓕ *broo*·to/a ugly
buca ⓕ *boo*·ka hole • pit
— delle lettere de·le *le*·te·re mail box
bucatura ⓕ boo·ka·*too*·ra puncture
buddista ⓜ&ⓕ boo·*dee*·sta Buddhist
bugiardo/a ⓜ/ⓕ boo·*jar*·do/a liar
buono/a ⓜ/ⓕ *bwo*·no/a good • nice (meal)
burro ⓜ *boo*·ro butter
— per le labbra per le *la*·bra lip balm
bussola ⓕ *boo*·so·la compass
busta ⓕ **(imbottita)** *boo*·sta (eem·bo·*tee*·ta) (padded) envelope

C

cabina ⓕ ka·*bee*·na cabin • cubicle
— telefonica te·le·*fo*·nee·ka phone box
cacao ⓜ ka·*ka*·o cocoa
caccia ⓕ *ka*·cha hunting
caffè ⓜ ka·*fe* coffee
calcio ⓜ *kal*·cho soccer
calcolatrice ⓕ kal·ko·la·*tree*·che calculator
caldo ⓜ *kal*·do heat
caldo/a ⓜ/ⓕ *kal*·do/a hot
calendario ⓜ ka·len·*da*·ryo calendar
calze ⓕ pl *kal*·tse stockings
calzini ⓜ pl kal·*tsee*·nee socks
cambiare kam·*bya*·re change
cambio ⓜ *kam*·byo exchange
— valuta ⓕ va·*loo*·ta currency exchange
camera ⓕ *ka*·me·ra room
— d'aria *da*·rya tube (tyre)
— da letto da *le*·to bedroom
— doppia *do*·pya double room
— singola *seen*·go·la single room
cameriere/a ⓜ/ⓕ ka·mer·*ye*·re/a waiter
camicia ⓕ ka·*mee*·cha shirt
camion ⓜ *ka*·myon truck
camminare ka·mee·*na*·re walk

camminata ⓕ ka·mee·*na*·ta (long) walk
campagna ⓕ kam·*pa*·nya countryside
campeggiare kam·pe·*ja*·re camp
campeggio ⓜ kam·*pe*·jo campsite
campionato ⓜ kam·pyo·*na*·to championships
campo ⓜ *kam*·po field • pitch • court
— da golf da golf golf course
— da tennis da *te*·nees tennis court
cancellare kan·che·*la*·re cancel
cancello ⓜ kan·*che*·lo gate
cancro ⓜ *kan*·kro cancer
candela ⓕ kan·*de*·la candle • spark plug
cane ⓜ *ka*·ne dog
— guida *gwee*·da guide dog
canottaggio ⓜ ka·no·*ta*·jo rowing • canoeing
canottiera ⓕ ka·no·*tye*·ra singlet
cantante ⓜ/ⓕ kan·*tan*·te singer
cantare kan·*ta*·re sing
cantina ⓕ kan·*tee*·na wine cellar • winery
canzone ⓕ kan·*tso*·ne song
caparra ⓕ ka·*pa*·ra deposit (refundable)
capire ka·*pee*·re understand
capo ⓜ *ka*·po leader
Capodanno ⓜ *ka*·po·*da*·no New Year's Day
cappello ⓜ ka·*pe*·lo hat
cappotto ⓜ ka·*po*·to coat
capra ⓕ *ka*·pra goat
carabinieri ⓜ pl ka·ra·bee·*nye*·ree police (military)
caramelle ⓕ pl ka·ra·*me*·le lollies
— alla menta a·la *men*·ta mints
carcere ⓜ *kar*·che·re jail
carino/a ⓜ/ⓕ ka·*ree*·no/a pretty • cute
carne ⓕ *kar*·ne meat
— tritata tree·*ta*·ta mince meat
caro/a ⓜ/ⓕ *ka*·ro/a expensive
carota ⓕ ka·*ro*·ta carrot

carpentiere ⓜ kar·pen·*tye*·re carpenter

carrello ⓜ ka·*re*·lo trolley

carrozza ⓕ ka·*ro*·tsa carriage

— ristorante rees·to·*ran*·te dining car

carta ⓕ *kar*·ta paper

— d'identità dee·den·tee·*ta* identification card (ID)

— d'imbarco deem·*bar*·ko boarding pass

— di credito dee *kre*·dee·to credit card

— igienica ee·*je*·nee·ka toilet paper

— telefonica te·le·*fo*·nee·ka phone card

carte ⓕ pl *kar*·te cards

cartolaio ⓜ kar·to·*la*·yo stationer

cartolina ⓕ kar·to·*lee*·na postcard

cartuccia ⓕ kar·*too*·cha cartridge

— di ricambio del gas dee ree·*kam*·byo del gaz gas cartridge

casa ⓕ *ka*·za house • home

casalingo/a ⓜ/ⓕ ka·za·*leen*·go/a homemaker

cascata ⓕ kas·*ka*·ta waterfall

casco ⓜ *kas*·ko helmet

casinò ⓜ ka·zee·*no* casino

cassa ⓕ *ka*·sa cash register

cassaforte ⓕ ka·sa·*for*·te safe

cassetta ⓕ ka·*se*·ta cassette

cassiere/a ⓜ/ⓕ ka·*sye*·re/a cashier

castello ⓜ kas·*te*·lo castle

catena ⓕ ka·*te*·na chain

— di montagne dee mon·*ta*·nye mountain range

catene ⓕ pl **da neve** ka·*te*·ne da *ne*·ve snow chains

cattivo/a ⓜ/ⓕ ka·*tee*·vo/a bad

cattolico/a ⓜ/ⓕ ka·*to*·lee·ko/a Catholic

cavalcare ka·val·*ka*·re ride (horse)

cavallino ⓜ ka·va·*lee*·no pony

cavallo ⓜ ka·*va*·lo horse

cavi ⓜ pl **con morsetti** *ka*·vee kon mor·*se*·tee jumper leads

caviale ⓜ ka·*vya*·le caviar

caviglia ⓕ ka·*vee*·lya ankle

cavo ⓜ *ka*·vo cable

cavoletti ⓜ pl **di Bruxelles** ka·vo·*le*·tee dee brook·*sel* Brussels sprouts

cavolfiore ⓜ ka·vol·*fyo*·re cauliflower

cavolo ⓜ *ka*·vo·lo cabbage

ceci ⓜ pl *che*·chee chickpeas

celebrazione ⓕ che·le·bra·*tsyo*·ne celebration

celibe ⓜ *che*·lee·be single (man)

cellulare ⓜ che·loo·*la*·re mobile phone

cena ⓕ *che*·na dinner

centesimo ⓜ chen·*te*·zee·mo cent

centimetro ⓜ chen·*tee*·me·tro centimetre

centro ⓜ *chen*·tro centre

— commerciale ko·mer·*cha*·le shopping centre

— storico *sto*·ree·ko old city

— telefonico te·le·*fo*·nee·ko telephone centre

cercare cher·*ka*·re look for

cereali ⓜ pl che·re·*a*·lee cereal

cerotti ⓜ pl che·*ro*·tee Band-aids

certificato ⓜ cher·tee·fee·*ka*·to certificate

cestino ⓜ ches·*tee*·no basket

cetriolo ⓜ che·tree·*o*·lo cucumber

che (cosa) ke (*ko*·za) what

chi kee who

chiamata ⓕ kya·*ma*·ta phone call

— a carico del destinatario a ka·*ree*·ko del dee·*tee*·na·*ta*·ryo reverse-charges call • collect call

chiaro/a ⓜ/ⓕ *kya*·ro/a light (colour)

chiave ⓕ *kya*·ve key

chiesa ⓕ *kye*·za church

chilo ⓜ *kee*·lo kilogram

chilometro ⓜ kee·*lo*·me·tro kilometre

chitarra ⓕ kee·*ta*·ra guitar

chiudere *kyoo*·de·re close

chiuso/a ⓜ/ⓕ *kyoo*·zo/a closed • shut • locked

ciascuno/a ⓜ/ⓕ chas·*koo*·no/a each

cibo ⓜ *chee*·bo food
— **da bebè** da be·*be* baby food
ciclismo ⓜ chee·*kleez*·mo cycling
ciclista ⓜ&ⓕ chee·*klee*·sta cyclist
ciclopista ⓕ chee·klo·*pee*·sta bike path
cidì ⓜ chee·*dee* CD
cieco/a ⓜ/ⓕ *chye*·ko/a blind
cielo ⓜ *che*·lo sky
cima ⓕ *chee*·ma peak
cinema ⓜ *chee*·ne·ma cinema
cinghia ⓕ **della ventola** *cheen*·gya de·la *ven*·to·la fanbelt
cintura ⓕ **di sicurezza** cheen·*too*·ra dee see·koo·*re*·tsa seatbelt
cioccolato ⓜ cho·ko·*la*·to chocolate
cipolla ⓕ chee·*po*·la onion
circo ⓜ *cheer*·ko circus
cisti ⓕ **ovarica** *chee*·stee o·*va*·ree·ka ovarian cyst
cistite ⓕ chees·*tee*·te cystitis
città ⓕ chee·*ta* city
cittadinanza ⓕ chee·ta·dee·*nan*·tsa citizenship
ciucciotto ⓜ choo·*cho*·to dummy (pacifier)
classe ⓕ *kla*·se class
— **business** *beez*·nes business class
— **turistica** too·*ree*·stee·ka economy class
classico/a ⓜ/ⓕ *kla*·see·ko/a classical
cliente ⓜ&ⓕ klee·*en*·te client
cocaina ⓕ ko·ka·*ee*·na cocaine
coda ⓕ *ko*·da queue
codice ⓜ **postale** *ko*·dee·che pos·*ta*·le postcode
cognome ⓜ ko·*nyo*·me surname
coincidenza ⓕ ko·een·chee·*den*·tsa coincidence • connection (transport)
collant ⓜ pl ko·*lant* pantyhose
colazione ⓕ ko·la·*tsyo*·ne breakfast
collega ⓜ&ⓕ ko·*le*·ga colleague
collegio ⓜ **universitario** ko·*le*·jo oo·nee·ver·see·*ta*·ryo college

collina ⓕ ko·*lee*·na hill
collirio ⓜ ko·*lee*·ryo eye drops
collo ⓜ *ko*·lo neck
colloquio ⓜ **(selettivo)** ko·*lok*·wyo (se·le·*tee*·vo) interview
colore ⓜ ko·*lo*·re colour
colpa ⓕ *kol*·pa fault (someone's)
colpevole kol·*pe*·vo·le guilty
coltello ⓜ kol·*te*·lo knife
come *ko*·me how
cominciare ko·meen·*cha*·re begin • start
commedia ⓕ ko·*me*·dya play (theatre)
— **comica** ko·mee·ka comedy
commercio ⓜ ko·*mer*·cho trade • business studies
commissione ⓕ ko·mee·*syo*·ne commission
comodo/a ⓜ/ⓕ *ko*·mo·do/a comfortable
compagno/a ⓜ/ⓕ kom·*pa*·nyo/a companion • partner (intimate)
compenso ⓜ kom·*pen*·so fee
compleanno ⓜ kom·ple·*a*·no birthday
complesso ⓜ **rock** kom·*ple*·so rok rock group
completo/a ⓜ/ⓕ kom·*ple*·to/a booked out
comprare kom·*pra*·re buy
compreso/a ⓜ/ⓕ kom·*pre*·zo/a included
computer ⓜ **portatile** kom·*pyoo*·ter por·*ta*·tee·le laptop
comunione ⓕ ko·moo·*nyo*·ne communion
comunista ⓜ&ⓕ ko·moo·*nee*·sta communist
con kon with
— **filtro** ⓜ *feel*·tro filtered
concerto ⓜ kon·*cher*·to concert
condividere kon·dee·*vee*·de·re share (with)
confermare kon·fer·*ma*·re confirm (a booking)

D

confessione ⓕ kon·fe·*syo*·ne confession (religious)

confine ⓜ kon·*fee*·ne border

congelare kon·je·*la*·re freeze

congelato/a ⓜ/ⓕ kon·je·*la*·to/a frozen

coniglio ⓜ ko·*nee*·lyo rabbit

conoscere ko·*no*·she·re know (a person)

conservatore/conservatrice ⓜ/ⓕ kon·ser·va·*to*·re/kon·ser·va·*tree*·che conservative

consigliare kon·see·*lya*·re recommend

consolato ⓜ kon·so·*la*·to consulate

contanti ⓜ pl kon·*tan*·tee count

contare kon·*ta*·re count

conto ⓜ *kon*·to bill (account)

— in banca een *ban*·ka bank account

contraccettivi ⓜ pl kon·tra·che·*tee*·vee contraceptives

contratto ⓜ kon·*tra*·to contract

controllare kon·tro·*la*·re check

controllare kon·tro·*la*·re check

controllore ⓜ kon·tro·*lo*·re ticket collector

convalidare kon·va·lee·*da*·re validate

convento ⓜ kon·*ven*·to convent

coperta ⓕ ko·*per*·ta blanket

coperte ⓕ pl **e lenzuola** ⓕ pl ko·*per*·te e len·*zwo*·la bedding

coperto ⓜ ko·*per*·to cover charge (restaurant)

Coppa ⓕ **del Mondo** *ko*·pa del *mon*·do World Cup

coraggioso/a ⓜ/ⓕ ko·ra·*jo*·zo/a brave

corda ⓕ *kor*·da rope

— del bucato del boo·*ka*·to clothesline

corpo ⓜ *kor*·po body

corrente ⓕ ko·*ren*·te current (electricity)

correre ko·re·re run

corridoio ⓜ ko·ree·*do*·yo aisle (in plane, train)

corrompere ko·*rom*·pe·re bribe

corrotto/a ⓜ/ⓕ ko·ro·to/a corrupt

corsa ⓕ *kor*·sa ride • race

corte ⓕ *kor*·te court (legal)

corto/a ⓜ/ⓕ *kor*·to/a short (length)

cosa ⓕ *ko*·za thing • object • matter

costa ⓕ *kos*·ta coast

costare kos·*ta*·re cost

costruire kos·troo·*ee*·re build

costruttore/costruttrice ⓜ/ⓕ kos·troo·*to*·re/ko·stroo·*tree*·che builder

costume ⓜ **da bagno** kos·*too*·me da *ba*·nyo bathing suit

cotone ⓜ ko·to·ne cotton

cozza ⓕ *ko*·tsa mussel

crema ⓕ *kre*·ma cream

— da barba da *bar*·ba shaving cream

— solare so·*la*·re sunscreen

crescere *kre*·she·re grow

criminalità ⓕ kree·mee·na·lee·*ta* crime (issue)

cristiano/a ⓜ/ⓕ krees·*tya*·no/a Christian

croce ⓕ *kro*·che cross (religious)

crudo/a ⓜ/ⓕ *kroo*·do/a raw

cucchiaino ⓜ koo·kya·*ee*·no teaspoon

cucchiaio ⓜ koo·*kya*·yo spoon

cucciolo ⓜ *koo*·cho·lo puppy

cucina ⓕ koo·*chee*·na kitchen

cucinare koo·chee·*na*·re cook

cucire koo·*chee*·re sew

culla ⓕ *koo*·la cot

cuoco/a ⓜ/ⓕ *kwo*·ko/a cook • chef (restaurant)

cuoio ⓜ *kwo*·yo leather

cuore ⓜ *kwo*·re heart

curare koo·*ra*·re look after

cuscino ⓜ koo·*shee*·no pillow

D

da da from • at • to • since

da solo/a ⓜ/ⓕ da *so*·lo/a alone

danno ⓜ *da*·no damage

D

dare *da*·re give
— **il benvenuto a** eel ben·ve·*noo*·to a welcome
— **un calcio** oon kal·cho kick
data ① *da*·ta date (day)
— **di arrivo** dee a·*ree*·vo date of arrival
— **di nascita** dee *na*·shee·ta date of birth
— **di partenza** dee par·*ten*·tsa date of departure
datore/datrice ⓜ/① **di lavoro** da·*to*·re/da·*tree*·che dee la·*vo*·ro employer
dea ① *de*·a goddess
debole *de*·bo·le weak
degustazione ① **(dei vini)** de·goos·ta·*tsyo*·ne day *vee*·nee (wine) tasting
delitto ⓜ de·*lee*·to crime (infringement)
democrazia ① de·mo·kra·*tsee*·a democracy
denaro ⓜ de·*na*·ro money
dente ⓜ *den*·te tooth (front)
denti ⓜ pl *den*·tee teeth
dentifricio ⓜ den·tee·*free*·cho toothpaste
dentista ⓜ&① den·*tee*·sta dentist
dentro *den*·tro inside
deodorante ⓜ de·o·do·*ran*·te deodorant
deposito ⓜ de·po·*zee*·to deposit (bank)
— **bagagli** ba·*ga*·lyee left luggage (office)
derubare de·roo·*ba*·re rob
desiderare de·see·de·*ra*·re wish • desire
destinazione ① des·tee·na·*tsyo*·ne destination
destra *de*·stra right (direction) • right-wing
detersivo ⓜ de·ter·*see*·vo washing powder
di dee from • by • of
— **andata e ritorno** an·*da*·ta e ree·*tor*·no return (ticket)

— **destra** *de*·stra right-wing
— **fronte a** *fron*·te a opposite
— **lusso** *loo*·so luxurious
— **meno** *me*·no less
— **nuovo** *nwo*·vo again
— **più** pyoo more
— **recente** re·*chen*·te recently
— **seconda mano** se·*kon*·da *ma*·no second-hand
— **sinistra** see·*nee*·stra left-wing
— **solo andata** *so*·lo an·*da*·ta one-way ticket
diabete ⓜ de·a·*be*·te diabetes
diaframma ⓜ dee·a·*fra*·ma diaphragm
diapositiva ① dee·a·po·zee·*tee*·va slide (film)
diarrea ① dee·a·*re*·a diarrhoea
diesel ⓜ *dee*·zel diesel
dieta ① *dye*·ta diet
dietro *dye*·tro behind
difettoso/a ⓜ/① dee·fe·*to*·zo/a faulty
differente (da) dee·fe·*ren*·te (da) different
differenza ① dee·fe·*ren*·tsa difference
— **di fuso orario** dee *foo*·zo o·*ra*·ryo time difference
difficile dee·*fee*·chee·le difficult
digitale dee·jee·*ta*·le digital
dimensioni ① pl dee·men·*syo*·nee size (general)
dimenticare dee·men·tee·*ka*·re forget
dio/dea ⓜ/① *dee*·o/*de*·a god (general)
dipendente ⓜ/① dee·pen·*den*·te addicted • dependant
dipingere dee·*peen*·je·re paint
dire *dee*·re say
diretto/a ⓜ/① dee·*re*·to/a direct
direzione ① dee·*re*·tsyo·ne direction
diritti ⓜ pl **umani** dee·*ree*·tee oo·*ma*·nee human rights
diritto ⓜ dee·*ree*·to/a straight • right (prerogative)
disabile dee·*za*·bee·le disabled

dischetto ⓜ dees·*ke*·to disk (computer)

discriminazione ⓕ dees·kree·mee·na·*tsyo*·ne discrimination

disinfettante ⓜ deez·een·fe·*tan*·te disinfectant

disoccupato/a ⓜ/ⓕ dee·zo·koo·*pa*·to/a unemployed

distributore ⓜ dee·stree·boo·*to*·re petrol/service station

— automatico di biglietti ow·to·*ma*·tee·ko dee bee·*lye*·tee ticket machine

disturbo ⓜ dees·*toor*·bo trouble

disturbi ⓜ pl **da fuso orario** dees·*toor*·bee da *foo*·zo o·*ra*·ryo jet lag

dito ⓜ *dee*·to finger

— del piede del *pye*·de toe

ditta ⓕ *dee*·ta company (firm)

diversi/e ⓜ/ⓕ pl dee·*ver*·see/dee·*ver*·se several

diverso/a dee·*ver*·so/a different • various

divertente dee·ver·*ten*·te funny • entertaining

divertimento ⓜ dee·ver·tee·*men*·to fun

divertirsi dee·ver·*teer*·see enjoy (oneself)

divorziato/a ⓜ/ⓕ dee·vor·*tsya*·to/a divorced

divisa ⓕ dee·*vee*·za uniform

doccia ⓕ *do*·cha shower

documenti ⓜ pl do·koo·*men*·tee papers

documento ⓜ **d'identità** do·koo·*men*·to dee·den·tee·*ta* identification

dogana ⓕ do·*ga*·na customs

dolce ⓜ *dol*·che sweet • dessert

dolce *dol*·che sweet • soft

dolciumi ⓜ pl dol·*choo*·mee candy

dollaro ⓜ *do*·la·ro dollar

dolore ⓜ do·*lo*·re pain

dolori ⓜ pl **mestruali** do·*lo*·ree me·*stroo*·a·lee period pain

doloroso/a ⓜ/ⓕ do·lo·*ro*·zo/a painful • sore

domanda ⓕ do·*man*·da question

domandare do·man·*da*·re ask (a question)

domani do·*ma*·nee tomorrow

— mattina ma·*tee*·na tomorrow morning

— pomeriggio po·me·*ree*·jo tomorrow afternoon

— sera *se*·ra tomorrow evening

donna ⓕ *do*·na woman

— d'affari da·*fa*·ree businesswoman

dopo *do*·po after

dopobarba ⓜ do·po·*bar*·ba aftershave

dopodomani do·po·do·*ma*·nee day after tomorrow

doppio/a ⓜ/ⓕ *do*·pyo/a double

dormire dor·*mee*·re sleep

dose ⓕ *do*·ze dose

— eccessiva e·che·*see*·va overdose

dove *do*·ve where

dozzina ⓕ do·*dzee*·na dozen

dramma ⓜ *dra*·ma drama

droga ⓕ *dro*·ga drug/drugs

drogheria ⓕ dro·ge·*ree*·a grocery

due *doo*·e two

— letti *le*·tee twin/two beds

— volte *vol*·te twice

duomo ⓜ *dwo*·mo cathedral

durante doo·*ran*·te during

duro/a ⓜ/ⓕ *doo*·ro/a hard (not soft)

E

e e and

ebreo/a ⓜ/ⓕ e·*bre*·o/a Jewish

ecografia ⓕ e·ko·gra·*fee*·a ultrasound

economico/a ⓜ/ⓕ e·ko·*no*·mee·ko/a cheap

edicola ⓕ e·*dee*·ko·la newsagency

edificio ⓜ e·dee·*fee*·cho building

egoista ⓜ/ⓕ e·go·ee·*sta* selfish

elenco Ⓜ **telefonico** e·len·ko te·le·fo·nee·ko phone book
elettricista Ⓜ&Ⓕ e·le·tree·chee·sta electrician
elettricità Ⓕ e·le·tree·chee·ta electricity
elezioni Ⓕ pl e·le·tsyo·nee elections • polls
emergenza Ⓕ e·mer·jen·tsa emergency
emicrania Ⓕ e·mee·kra·nya migraine
emotivo/a Ⓜ/Ⓕ e·mo·tee·vo/a emotional
energia Ⓕ **(nucleare)** en·er·jee·a (noo·kle·a·re) (nuclear) energy
enorme e·nor·me huge
entrare en·tra·re enter
entrata Ⓕ en·tra·ta entry
entro (un'ora) en·tro (oon·o·ra) within (an hour)
epatite Ⓕ e·pa·tee·te hepatitis
epilessia Ⓕ e·pee·le·see·a epilepsy
erba Ⓕ er·ba grass • pot (dope)
erbe Ⓕ pl er·be herbs
erborista Ⓜ&Ⓕ er·bo·ree·sta herbalist
eroina Ⓕ e·ro·ee·na heroin
erotico/a Ⓜ/Ⓕ e·ro·tee·ko/a sexy
errore Ⓜ e·ro·re mistake
esame Ⓜ e·za·me test
escluso/a Ⓜ/Ⓕ es·kloo·zo/a excluded
escursione Ⓕ es·koor·syo·ne excursion • trip
— a piedi a pye·dee hike
escursionismo Ⓜ es·koor·syo·neez·mo touring
— a piedi a pye·dee hiking
esecuzione Ⓕ e·se·koo·tsyo·ne performance
esempio Ⓜ e·zem·pyo example
esperienza Ⓕ es·pe·ryen·tsa experience
esperimenti Ⓜ pl **nucleari** es·pe·ree·men·tee noo·kle·a·ree nuclear testing

esposimetro Ⓜ es·po·zee·me·tro light meter
esposizione Ⓕ es·po·zee·tsyo·ne exhibition
espresso/a Ⓜ/Ⓕ es·pre·so/a express
essere e·se·re be
— d'accordo da·kor·do agree
— raffreddato/a Ⓜ/Ⓕ ra·fre·da·to/a have a cold
est Ⓜ est east
estate Ⓕ es·ta·te summer
estetista Ⓜ&Ⓕ es·te·tee·sta beautician
estero/a Ⓜ/Ⓕ es·te·ro/a foreign
età Ⓕ e·ta age
etichetta Ⓕ e·tee·ke·ta luggage tag
etto Ⓜ e·to 100 grams
europeo/a Ⓜ/Ⓕ e·oo·ro·pe·o/a European
eutanasia Ⓕ e·oo·ta·na·zee·a euthanasia

F

fabbrica Ⓕ fa·bree·ka factory
faccia Ⓕ fa·cha face
facile fa·chee·le easy
fagioli Ⓜ pl fa·jo·lee beans
fame Ⓕ fa·me hunger
famiglia Ⓕ fa·mee·lya family
famoso/a Ⓜ/Ⓕ fa·mo·zo/a famous
fango Ⓜ fan·go mud
fantastico/a Ⓜ/Ⓕ fan·tas·tee·ko/a great
fantino Ⓜ fan·tee·no jockey
fare fa·re do • make
— il tifo eel tee·fo support (cheer on)
— l'autostop low·to·stop hitchhike
— la barba la bar·ba shave
— male ma·le hurt
— una camminata oo·na ka·mee·na·ta hike
— una foto oo·na fo·to take a photo
farfalla Ⓕ far·fa·la butterfly
fari Ⓜ pl fa·ree headlights
farina Ⓕ fa·ree·na flour
farmacia Ⓕ far·ma·chee·a pharmacy

farmacista ⓜ&ⓕ far·ma·*chee*·sta chemist

fascia ⓕ *fa*·sha bandage

fatto/a ⓜ/ⓕ *fa*·to/a made

— a mano a *ma*·no handmade

— di (cotone) dee (ko·*to*·ne) made of (cotton)

fattoria ⓕ fa·to·*ree*·a farm

fazzolettini ⓜ pl **di carta** fa·tso·le·*tee*·nee dee *kar*·ta tissues

fazzoletto ⓜ fa·tso·*le*·to handkerchief

febbre ⓕ *fe*·bre temperature (fever)

— da fieno da *fye*·no hay fever

federa ⓕ *fe*·de·ra pillowcase

fegato ⓜ *fe*·ga·to liver

felice ⓜ&ⓕ fe·*lee*·che happy

ferita ⓕ fe·*ree*·ta injury

ferito/a ⓜ/ⓕ fe·*ree*·to/a injured

fermare fer·*ma*·re stop

fermarsi fer·*mar*·see stay (at a hotel)

fermata ⓕ fer·*ma*·ta stop

fermo ⓜ **posta** *fer*·mo *pos*·ta poste restante

ferramenta ⓕ fe·ra·*men*·ta hardware store

ferro ⓜ *fe*·ro iron

— da stiro da *stee*·ro iron (clothes)

festa ⓕ *fes*·ta festival • public holiday • party (celebration)

fetta ⓕ *fe*·ta slice

fiammiferi ⓜ pl tya·*mee*·fe·ree matches

fico ⓜ *fee*·ko fig

fidanzamento ⓜ fee·dan·tsa·*men*·to engagement (couple)

fidanzato/a ⓜ/ⓕ fee·dan·*tsa*·to/a fiance(e)

figlia ⓕ *fee*·lya daughter

figlio ⓜ *fee*·lyo son

film ⓜ feelm movie

filo ⓜ *fee*·lo thread (sewing)

— dentario den·*ta*·ree·o dental floss

fine ⓕ *fee*·ne end

fine settimana ⓜ *fee*·ne se·tee·*ma*·na weekend

finestra ⓕ fee·*nes*·tra window (general)

finestrino ⓜ fee·nes·*tree*·no window (car, plane)

finire fee·*nee*·re end • finish • run out of

finito/a ⓜ/ⓕ fee·*nee*·to finished

fino a (giugno) *fee*·no a (*joo*·nyo) until (June)

fiocchi ⓜ pl **di mais** *fyo*·kee dee *ma*·ees cornflakes

fioraio ⓜ&ⓕ fyo·*ra*·yo florist

fiore ⓜ *fyo*·re flower

firma ⓕ *feer*·ma signature

fiume ⓜ *fyoo*·me river

fluido ⓜ **idratante** floo·*ee*·do ee·dra·*tan*·te hydrating fluid

foglia ⓕ *fo*·lya leaf

fondo ⓜ *fon*·do bottom

fondo/a ⓜ/ⓕ *fon*·do/a deep

footing ⓜ *foo*·*leeng* jogging • running (sport)

forbici ⓕ pl *for*·bee·chee scissors

forchetta ⓕ for·*ke*·ta fork

foresta ⓕ fo·*res*·ta forest

forma ⓕ *for*·ma shape

formaggio ⓜ for·*ma*·jo cheese

— fresco *fres*·ko cream cheese

formica ⓕ for·*mee*·ka ant

forno ⓜ *for*·no oven

— a microonde a mee·kro·*on*·de microwave (oven)

forse *for*·se maybe

forte ⓜ&ⓕ *for*·te strong • loud

fortuna ⓕ for·*too*·na chance • luck

fortunato/a ⓜ/ⓕ for·too·*na*·to/a lucky

forza ⓕ *for*·tsa strength • force

forze ⓕ pl **armate** *for*·tse ar·*ma*·te military

foto ⓕ *fo*·to photo

fotografia ⓕ fo·to·gra·*fee*·a photography

fotografo ⓜ fo·*to*·gra·fo photographer • camera shop

fra fra between
— **poco** po·ko soon
fragile fra·jee·le fragile
fragola ① fra·go·la strawberry
francobollo ⓜ fran·ko·bo·lo stamp
fratello ⓜ fra·te·lo brother
freccia ① fre·cha indicator (car)
freddo/a ⓜ/① fre·do/a cold
freno ⓜ fre·no brake
fresco/a ⓜ/① fres·ko/a fresh
fretta ① fre·ta hurry
friggere free·je·re fry
frigo ⓜ free·go fridge
frigobar ⓜ free·go·bar bar fridge ·
minibar
frigorifero ⓜ free·go·ree·fe·ro
refrigerator
frizione ① free·tsyo·ne clutch
frutta ① froo·ta fruit
— **secca** se·ka dried fruit
fruttivendolo/a ⓜ/①
froo·tee·ven·do·lo/a greengrocer
fumare foo·ma·re smoke
fumato/a ⓜ/① foo·ma·to/a
smoked · stoned (drugged)
funerale ⓜ foo·ne·ra·le funeral
fungo ⓜ foon·go mushroom
funivia ① foo·nee·vee·a cable car
fuoco ⓜ fwo·ko fire
fuori fwo·ree outside
furgone ⓜ foor·go·ne van
futuro ⓜ foo·too·ro future

G

gabinetto ⓜ **(pubblico)** ga·bee·ne·to
(poo·blee·ko) (public) toilet
galleria ① **d'arte** ga·le·ree·a dar·te
art gallery
Galles ⓜ ga·les Wales
gamba ① gam·ba leg (body part)
gambero ⓜ gam·be·ro prawn
gara ⓜ ga·ra race (sport) ·
competition
garage ⓜ ga·raj garage
gas ⓜ gaz gas (for cooking)
gasolio ⓜ ga·zo·lyo diesel

gastroenterite ① gas·tro·en·te·ree·te
gastroenteritis
gattino ⓜ ga·tee·no kitten
gatto ⓜ ga·to cat
gelateria ① je·la·te·ree·a ice-cream
parlour
gelato ⓜ je·la·to ice cream
geloso/a ⓜ/① je·lo·zo/a jealous
gemelli/e ⓜ/① pl je·me·lee/je·me·le
twins
generale je·ne·ra·le general
gengiva ① jen·jee·va gum (mouth)
genitori ⓜ pl je·nee·to·ree parents
gente ① jen·te people
gentile jen·tee·le kind · nice (person)
germogli ⓜ pl **(di soia)** jer·mo·lyee
(dee so·ya) beansprouts
gettone ⓜ je·to·ne token
ghiaccio ⓜ gya·cho ice
già ja already
giacca ① ja·ka jacket
giallo/a ⓜ/① ja·lo/a yellow
Giappone ⓜ ja·po·ne Japan
giardinaggio ⓜ jar·dee·na·jo
gardening
giardino ⓜ jar·dee·no garden
— **zoologico** dzo·o·lo·jee·ko zoo
ginecologo/a ⓜ/① jee·ne·ko·lo·go/a
gynaecologist
ginnastica ① jee·nas·tee·ka
gymnastics
ginocchio ⓜ jee·no·kyo knee
giocare jo·ka·re play
— **a calcio** a kal·cho play soccer
gioco ⓜ jo·ko game (play)
— **elettronico** e·le·tro·nee·ko
computer game
gioielli ⓜ pl jo·ye·lee jewellery
giornale ⓜ jor·na·le newspaper
giornalista ⓜ&① jor·na·lee·sta
journalist
giorno ⓜ jor·no day
giovane jo·va·ne young
girare jee·ra·re turn
gita ① jee·ta tour · trip
giù joo down

giubbotto ⓜ **di salvataggio**
joo·bo·to dee sal·va·ta·jo life jacket

giudice ⓜ joo·dee·che judge

giudò ⓜ joo·do judo

giusto/a ⓜ/ⓕ joo·sto/a right
(correct)

gola ⓕ go·la throat

gomma ⓕ go·ma tyre

— **da masticare** da ma·stee·ka·re
(chewing) gum

gonfiore ⓜ gon·fyo·re swelling

gonna ⓕ go·na skirt

governo ⓜ go·ver·no government

grammi ⓜ pl gra·mee grams

grande gran·de big • large

grande magazzino ⓜ gran·de
ma·ga·dzee·no department store

grandinata ⓕ gran·dee·na·ta
hailstorm

grandine ⓕ gran·dee·ne hail

grasso/a ⓜ/ⓕ gra·so/a fat

gratuito/a ⓜ/ⓕ gra·too·ee·to/a free
(gratis) • complimentary

grigio/a ⓜ/ⓕ gree·jo/a grey

grotta ⓕ gro·ta cave

gruppo ⓜ groo·po band (music)

— **sanguigno** san·gwee·nyo blood
group

guanti ⓜ gwan·tee gloves

guardare gwar·da·re look • watch

— **le vetrine** le ve·tree·ne go window-
shopping

guardaroba ⓜ gwar·da·rro·ba
cloakroom

guastarsi gwas·tar·see break down

guastato/a ⓜ/ⓕ gwas·ta·to/a
broken down

guasto/a ⓜ/ⓕ gwa·sto/a off (food)

guerra ⓕ gwe·ra war

guida ⓕ gwee·da guide (person) •
guidebook

— **agli spettacoli** a·lyee spe·ta·ko·lee
entertainment guide

— **audio** ow·dyo guide (audio)

— **turistica** too·ree·stee·ka
guidebook

guidare gwee·da·re drive

gustoso/a ⓜ/ⓕ goo·sto·zo/a tasty

H   H

halal a·lal halal

hashish ⓜ a·sheesh hash

hockey ⓜ o·kee hockey

— **su ghiaccio** soo gya·cho ice hockey

I

idiota ⓜ&ⓕ ee·dyo·ta idiot

idratante ⓕ ee·dra·tan·te moisturiser

ieri ye·ree yesterday

illegale ee·le·ga·le illegal

imbarazzato/a ⓜ/ⓕ
eem·ba·ra·tsa·to/a embarrassed

imbrogliare eem·bro·lya·re cheat

immersione ⓕ ee·mer·syo·ne
submersion • dive

— **in apnea** een ap·ne·a snorkelling

— **subacquea** soo·ba·kwe·a scuba
diving

immigrazione ⓕ ee·mee·gra·tsyo·ne
immigration

imparare eem·pa·ra·re learn

impermeabile eem·per·mo·a·bee·le
waterproof

impiegato/a ⓜ/ⓕ eem·pye·ga·to/a
employee • office worker

importante eem·por·tan·te important

impossibile eem·po·see·bee·le
impossible

in een in

— **bianco e nero** byan·ko e ne·ro B&W

— **buona salute** bwo·na sa·loo·te in
good health

— **fondo** fon·do at the bottom •
after all

— **fretta** fre·ta in a hurry

— **lista d'attesa** lee·sta da·te·za
standby (ticket)

— **omaggio** o·ma·jo complimentary
(free gift)

— **ritardo** ree·tar·do late

— **salita** sa·lee·ta uphill

— sciopero ⓜ *sho*·pe·ro on strike

— vendita *ven*·dee·ta on sale

inalatore ⓜ ee·na·la·*to*·re inhaler

incidente ⓜ een·chee·*den*·te accident • crash

incinta een·*cheen*·ta pregnant

incontrare een·kon·*tra*·re meet

incrocio ⓜ een·*kro*·cho intersection

indicare een·dee·*ka*·re point

indigestione ⓕ een·dee·je·*styo*·ne indigestion

indirizzo ⓜ een·dee·*ree*·tso address

indossare een·do·*sa*·re wear

indù ⓜ&ⓕ een·*doo* Hindu

industria ⓕ een·*doos*·trya industry

infermiere/a ⓜ/ⓕ een·fer·*mye*·re/a nurse

infezione ⓕ een·fe·*tsyo*·ne infection

infiammazione ⓕ een·fya·ma·*tsyo*·ne inflammation

influenza ⓕ een·floo·*en*·tsa flu • influenza

informatica ⓕ een·for·*ma*·tee·ka IT

informazioni ⓕ pl een·for·ma·*tsyo*·nee information

infortunato/a ⓜ/ⓕ een·for·too·*na*·to/a injured

ingegnere ⓜ&ⓕ een·je·*nye*·re engineer

Inghilterra ⓕ een·geel·*te*·ra England

inglese een·*gle*·ze English

ingorgo ⓜ een·*gor*·go traffic jam

ingrediente ⓜ een·gre·*dyen*·te ingredient

ingresso ⓜ een·*gre*·so cover charge (venue) • entrance

iniezione ⓕ ee·nye·*tsyo*·ne injection

inizio ⓜ ee·*nee*·tsyo start (beginning)

innocente ee·no·*chen*·te innocent

inquinamento ⓜ een·kwee·na·*men*·to pollution

insalata ⓕ een·sa·*la*·ta salad

insegnante ⓜ&ⓕ een·sen·*yan*·te teacher (general)

insetto ⓜ een·*se*·to insect

insieme een·*sye*·me together

insolito/a ⓜ/ⓕ een·*so*·lee·to/a unusual

interessante een·te·re·*san*·te interesting

internazionale een·ter·na·tsyo·*na*·le international

Internet (point) ⓜ *een*·ter·net (poynt) internet (cafe)

interprete ⓜ/ⓕ een·*ter*·pre·te interpreter

interurbano/a ⓜ/ⓕ een·ter·oor·*ba*·no/a long-distance (bus)

intervallo ⓜ een·ter·*va*·lo intermission

intervento ⓜ een·ter·*ven*·to operation (medical) • intervention (police) • speech

intossicazione ⓕ **alimentare** een·to·see·ka·*tsyo*·ne a·lee·men·*ta*·re food poisoning

inverno ⓜ een·*ver*·no winter

invitare een·vee·*ta*·re invite

io *ee*·o I

isola ⓕ *ee*·zo·la island

istruttore/istrutrice ⓜ/ⓕ ee·stroo·*to*·re/ee·stroo·*tree*·che instructor (general)

istruzione ⓕ ees·troo·*tsyo*·ne education

itinerario ⓜ ee·tee·ne·*ra*·ryo itinerary • route

— escursionistico es·koor·syo·*nee*·stee·ko hiking route

IVA ⓕ *ee*·va sales tax

K

kiwi ⓜ *kee*·wee kiwifruit

kosher *ka*·sher kasher

L

là la there

labbra ⓕ pl *la*·bra lips

laboratorio ⓜ la·bo·ra·*to*·ryo workshop

ladro/a ⓜ/ⓕ *la*·dro/a a thief
lago ⓜ *la*·go lake
lamentarsi la·men·*tar*·see complain
lamette ⓕ pl **(da barba)** la·*me*·te (da *bar*·ba) razor blades
lampadina ⓕ lam·pa·*dee*·na light bulb
lampone ⓜ lam·*po*·ne raspberry
lana ⓕ *la*·na wool
lardo ⓜ *lar*·do lard
largo/a ⓜ/ⓕ *lar*·go/a wide
lassativi ⓜ pl la·sa·*tee*·vee laxatives
lato ⓜ *la*·to side
latte ⓜ *la*·te milk
— di soia dee *so*·ya soy milk
— scremato skre·*ma*·to skimmed milk
lattuga ⓕ la·*too*·ga lettuce
lavaggio ⓜ **a secco** la·*va*·jo a se·ko dry cleaning
lavanderia la·van·de *ree*·a laundry (room)
— a gettone je·*to*·ne laundrette
lavare la·*va*·re wash (something)
lavarsi la·*var*·see wash (oneself)
lavatrice ⓕ la·va·*tree*·che washing machine
lavorare la·vo·*ra*·re work
— in proprio een *pro*·pryo (to be) self-employed
lavoratore/lavoratrice ⓜ/ⓕ la·vo·ra·*to*·re/la·vo·ra·*tree*·che worker
lavoro ⓜ la·*vo*·ro job • occupation • work
legale le·*ga*·le legal
legge ⓕ *le*·je law
leggere *le*·je·re read
leggero/a ⓜ/ⓕ le·*je*·ro/a light (not heavy)
legna ⓕ **(da ardere)** *le*·nya (da *ar*·de·re) (fire)wood
legno ⓜ *le*·nyo wood
legume ⓜ le·*goo*·me legume
lei lay she
Lei sg pol lay you
lentamente len·ta·*men*·te slowly

lenti ⓕ pl **a contatto** *len*·tee a kon·*ta*·to contact lenses
lenticchia ⓕ len·*tee*·kya lentil
lento/a ⓜ/ⓕ *len*·to/a slow
lenzuolo ⓜ len·*tswo*·lo sheet (bed)
lesbica ⓕ *lez*·bee·ka lesbian
lettera ⓕ *le*·te·ra letter
letto ⓜ *le*·to bed
— matrimoniale ma·tree·mo·*nya*·le double bed
libero/a ⓜ/ⓕ *lee*·be·ro/a free (not bound) • vacant
libreria ⓕ lee·bre·*ree*·a bookshop
libretto ⓜ lee·*bre*·to booklet
— di circolazione dee cheer·ko·la·*tsyo*·ne car owner's title
libro ⓜ *lee*·bro book
licenza ⓕ lee·*chen*·tsa permit
limetta ⓕ lee·*me*·ta lime (fruit) • nail file
limite ⓜ **di velocità** *lee*·mee·te doo ve·lo·chee·*ta* speed limit
limonata ⓕ lee·mo·*na*·ta lemonade
limone ⓜ lee·mo·ne lemon
linea ⓕ *lee*·ne·a line
— aerea a·e·re·a airline
lingua ⓕ *leen*·gwa tongue • language
lista ⓕ *lee*·sta list
— d'attesa da·*te*·za waiting list
lite ⓕ *lee*·te fight
litigare lee·tee·*ga*·re argue
litro ⓜ *lee*·tro litre
livello ⓜ lee·*ve*·lo level (tier)
livido ⓜ *lee*·vee·do bruise
locale ⓜ lo·*ka*·le bar • venue
locale lo·*ka*·le local
lontano/a ⓜ/ⓕ lon·*ta*·no/a far
loro *lo*·ro they
Loro pl pol *lo*·ro you
lozione ⓕ lo·*tsyo*·ne lotion
— abbronzante a·bron·*dzan*·te tanning lotion
lubrificante ⓜ loo·bree·fee·*kan*·te lubricant
lucchetto ⓜ loo·*ke*·to bike lock • padlock

M

luce ① *loo*·che light
lucertola ① loo·*cher*·to·la lizard
lui ① *loo*·ee he
lumaca ① loo·*ma*·ka snail
luminoso/a ⓜ/① loo·meen·*o*·zo/a light (not dark)
luna ① *loo*·na moon
— di miele dee *mye*·le honeymoon
— piena *pye*·na full moon
lungo/a ⓜ/① *loon*·go/a long
luogo ⓜ *lwo*·go place (location)
— di nascita dee *na*·shee·ta place of birth
lusso ⓜ *loo*·so luxury

M

ma ma but
macchina ① *ma*·kee·na car • machine
— fotografica fo·to·*gra*·fee·ka camera
macelleria ① ma·che·le·*ree*·a butcher's shop
madre ① *ma*·dre mother
maestro/a ⓜ/① ma·*es*·tro/a teacher (primary school or music) • instructor (skiing)
maglietta ① ma·*lye*·ta T-shirt
maglione ⓜ ma·*lyo*·ne jumper • sweater
magro/a ⓜ/① *ma*·gro/a thin • lean
mai mai never
maiale ⓜ ma·*ya*·le pig • pork
maionese ① ma·yo·*ne*·ze mayonnaise
male ⓜ *ma*·le pain • harm • evil
mal ⓜ mal
— di aereo dee a·*e*·re·o travel sickness (air)
— di denti dee *den*·tee toothache
— di macchina dee *ma*·kee·na travel sickness (car)
— di mare dee *ma*·re travel sickness (sea)
— di pancia dee *pan*·cha stomach ache
— di testa dee *tes*·ta headache
malato/a ⓜ/① ma·*la*·to/a ill • sick

malattia ① ma·la·*tee*·a disease
— venerea ve·*ne*·re·a venereal disease
mamma ① *ma*·ma mum
mammografia ① ma·mo·gra·*fee*·a mammogram
mancare man·*ka*·re miss • be lacking
mancia ① *man*·cha tip (gratuity)
mandare man·*da*·re send
mandarino ⓜ man·da·*ree*·no mandarin
mandorla ① *man*·dor·la almond
mangiare man·*ja*·re eat
manifestazione ① ma·ne·fes·ta·*tsyo*·ne demonstration (protest)
mano ① *ma*·no hand
manovale ⓜ&① ma·no·*va*·le manual worker
manuale ma·noo·*a*·le manual
manubrio ⓜ ma·*noo*·bryo handlebars
manzo ⓜ *man*·dzo beef
marciapiede ⓜ mar·cha·*pye*·de footpath
mare ⓜ *ma*·re sea
marea ① ma·*re*·a tide
margarina ① mar·ga·*ree*·na margarine
marito ⓜ ma·*ree*·to husband
marmellata ① mar·me·*la*·ta jam
— d'arance da·*ran*·che marmalade
marmo ⓜ *mar*·mo marble
marrone ⓜ/① ma·*ro*·ne brown
martello ⓜ mar·*te*·lo hammer
massaggio ⓜ ma·*sa*·jo massage
materasso ⓜ ma·te·*ra*·so mattress
matita ① ma·*tee*·ta pencil
matrimonio ⓜ ma·tree·*mo*·nyo marriage
mattina ① ma·*tee*·na morning
mazzuolo ⓜ ma·*tswo*·lo mallet
meccanico ⓜ&① me·*ka*·nee·ko mechanic
medicina ① me·dee·*chee*·na medicine
medicinale ⓜ me·dee·chee·*na*·le drug (medicinal)

medico ⓜ *me·dee·ko* doctor

meditazione ⓕ *me·dee·ta·tsyo·ne* meditation

mela ⓕ *me·*la apple

melanzana ⓕ *me·lan·dza·na* aubergine • eggplant

melodia ⓕ *me·lo·dee·a* tune

melone ⓜ *me·lo·ne* melon

membro ⓜ *mem·*bro member

mendicante ⓜ&ⓕ *men·dee·kan·te* beggar

meno *me·*no less

menù ⓜ *me·noo* menu

meraviglioso/a ⓜ/ⓕ *me·ra·vee·lyo·zo/a* wonderful

mercato ⓜ *mer·ka·to* market

merletto ⓜ *mer·le·to* lace

mescolare *mes·ko·la·re* mix

mese ⓜ *me·ze* month

messa ⓕ *me·sa* Mass

messaggio ⓜ *me·sa·jo* message

mestiere ⓜ *mes·tye·re* craft (trade) • occupation (work)

mestruazione ⓕ *me·stroo·a·tsyo·ne* menstruation

metallo ⓜ *me·ta·lo* metal

metro ⓜ *me·*tro metre (distance)

metropolitana ⓕ *me·tro·po·lee·ta·na* subway

mettere *me·te·re* put

mezzanotte ⓕ *me·dza·no·te* midnight

mezzi ⓜ pl **di comunicazione** *me·tsee dee ko·moo·nee·ka·tsyo·ne* media

mezzo ⓜ *me·dzo* half

mezzogiorno ⓜ *me·dzo·jor·no* noon

microonda ⓕ *mee·kro·on·da* microwave

miele ⓜ *mye·*le honey

migliore *mee·lyo·re* better • best

millimetro ⓜ *mee·lee·me·tro* millimetre

minestra ⓕ *mee·nes·tra* soup

minibar ⓜ *mee·nee·bar* minibar • bar fridge

minuto ⓜ *mee·noo·to* minute

minuto/a ⓜ/ⓕ *mee·noo·to/a* tiny

mobili ⓜ pl *mo·bee·lee* furniture

moda ⓕ *mo·*da fashion

moderno/a ⓜ/ⓕ *mo·der·no/a* modern

moduli ⓜ pl *mo·doo·lee* paperwork

modulo ⓜ *mo·doo·lo* form (paper)

moglie ⓕ *mo·lye* wife

molestia ⓕ *mo·les·tya* harassment

molto *mol·*to very

molto/a ⓜ/ⓕ *mol·to/a* a lot (of) • many

monastero ⓜ *mo·nas·te·ro* monastery

mondo ⓜ *mon·*do world

monete ⓕ pl *mo·ne·te* coins

mononucleosi ⓕ *mo·no·noo·kle·o·zee* glandular fever

montagna ⓕ *mon·ta·nya* mountain

monumento ⓜ *mo·noo·men·to* monument

morbillo ⓜ *mor·bee·lo* measles

morire *mo·ree·re* die

morso ⓜ *mor·*so bite (dog)

morto/a ⓜ/ⓕ *mor·to/a* dead

mosca ⓕ *mos·*ka fly

moschea ⓕ *mos·ke·a* mosque

mostrare *mos·tra·re* show

moto ⓕ *mo·*to motorbike

motore ⓜ *mo·to·re* engine

motoscafo ⓜ *mo·to·ska·fo* motorboat

mucca ⓕ *moo·ka* cow

mughetto ⓜ *moo·ge·to* thrush (medical)

multa ⓕ *mool·*ta fine (payment)

muro ⓜ *moo·*ro wall (outer)

muscolo ⓜ *moo·sko·lo* muscle

museo ⓜ *moo·ze·o* museum

musica ⓕ *moo·zee·ka* music

musicista ⓜ&ⓕ *moo·zee·chee·sta* musician

— di strada *dee stra·*da busker

musulmano/a ⓜ/ⓕ *moo·sool·ma·no/a* Muslim

M

N

N

muta ① **di subacqueo** *moo*·ta dee soo·*ba*·kwe·o wetsuit
muto/a ⑩/① *moo*·to/a mute

narrativa ① na·ra·*tee*·va fiction
naso ⑩ *na*·zo nose
Natale ⑩ na·*ta*·le Christmas
natura ① na·*too*·ra nature
nausea ① *now*·ze·a nausea
— **mattutina** ma·too·*tee*·na morning sickness
nave ① *na*·ve ship • boat
nazionale na·tsyo·*na*·le national
nazionalità ① na·tsyo·na·lee·*ta* nationality
nebbioso/a ⑩/① ne·*byo*·zo/a foggy
necessario/a ⑩/① ne·che·*sa*·ryo/a necessary
negozio ⑩ ne·*go*·tsyo shop
— **da campeggio** da kam·*pe*·jo camping store
— **di abbigliamento** dee a·*bee*·lya·men·to clothing store
— **di articoli sportivi** dee ar·*tee*·ko·lee spor·*tee*·vee sports store
— **di giocattoli** dee jo·*ka*·to·lee toyshop
— **di scarpe** dee *skar*·pe shoe shop
— **di souvenir** dee soo·ve·*neer* souvenir shop
nero/a ⑩/① *ne*·ro/a black
nessuno/a dei due ⑩/① ne·*soo*·no/a day *doo*·e neither
neve ① *ne*·ve snow
nido ⑩ *nee*·do nest • childminding (group)
niente *nyen*·te nothing • none
nipote ⑩&① nee·*po*·te grandchild
no no no
noce ① *no*·che nut • walnut
— **di acagiù** dee a·ka·*joo* cashew
nodulo ⑩ *no*·doo·lo lump
noi noy we
noioso/a ⑩/① no·*yo*·zo/a boring
noleggiare no·le·*ja*·re hire

nome ⑩ *no*·me name
non non no • not
— **ancora** an·*ko*·ra not yet
— **fumatore** foo·ma·*to*·re nonsmoking
— **diretto/a** ⑩/① dee·*re*·to/a nondirect
nonna ① *no*·na grandmother
nonno ⑩ *no*·no grandfather
nord ⑩ nord north
normale nor·*ma*·le regular
notizie ① pl no·*tee*·tsye news
notte ① *no*·te night
nubile ① *noo*·bee·le single (woman)
numero ⑩ *noo*·me·ro number
— **di camera** dee *ka*·me·ra room number
— **di targa** dee *tar*·ga licence plate number
— **di telefono** dee te·*le*·fo·no telephone number
nuotare nwo·*ta*·re swim
nuoto ⑩ *nwo*·to swimming
Nuova Zelanda ① nwo·va dze·*lan*·da New Zealand
nuovo/a ⑩/① *nwo*·vo/a new
nuvola ① *noo*·vo·la cloud
nuvoloso/a ⑩/① noo·vo·*lo*·zo/a cloudy

O

obiettivo ⑩ o·bye·*tee*·vo lens • objective
occhiali ⑩ pl o·*kya*·lee glasses (spectacles)
— **da sci** da shee goggles (skiing)
— **da sole** da *so*·le sunglasses
occhio ⑩ *o*·kyo eye
oceano ⑩ o·*che*·a·no ocean
odore ⑩ o·*do*·re smell
oggetti ⑩ pl o·*je*·tee articles • things
— **d'artigianato** dar·tee·ja·*na*·to handicrafts
— **di valore** dee va·*lo*·re valuables
— **in ceramica** een che·*ra*·mee·ka pottery
oggi o·*jee* today

olio ⓜ *o*·lyo oil
— **d'oliva** do·*lee*·va olive oil
oliva ⓕ o·*lee*·va olive
ombra ⓕ *om*·bra shadow • shade
ombrello ⓜ om·*bre*·lo umbrella
omeopatia ⓕ o·me·o·pa·*tee*·a homeopathy
omosessuale ⓜ&ⓕ o·mo·se·*swa*·le homosexual
onda ⓕ *on*·da wave
opera ⓕ *o*·pe·ra work (of art)
— **lirica** *lee*·ree·ka opera
operaio/a ⓜ/ⓕ o·pe·*ra*·yo/a factory worker
operatore/operatrice ⓜ/ⓕ o·pe·ra·to·re/o·pe·ra·*tree*·che operator
opinione ⓕ o·pee·*nyo*·ne opinion
oppure o·*poo*·re or • otherwise • or else
ora ⓕ *o*·ra hour
orario ⓜ o·*ra*·ryo timetable
— **di apertura** dee a·per·*too*·ra opening hours
— **ridotto** ree·*do*·to part-time
orchestra ⓕ or·*kes*·tra orchestra
ordinare or·dee·*na*·re order
ordinario/a ⓜ/ⓕ or·dee·*na*·ryo/a ordinary
ordine ⓜ *or*·dee·ne order
orecchini ⓜ pl o·re·*kee*·nee earrings
orecchio ⓜ o·*re*·kyo ear
originale ⓜ/ⓕ o·ree·jee·*na*·le original
oro ⓜ *o*·ro gold
orologio ⓜ o·ro·*lo*·jo clock • watch
orrendo/a ⓜ/ⓕ o·*ren*·do/a awful
ospedale ⓜ os·pe·*da*·le hospital
ospitalità ⓕ os·pee·ta·lee·*ta* hospitality
ossigeno ⓜ o·*see*·je·no oxygen
osso ⓜ *o*·so bone
ostello ⓜ **della gioventù** os·*te*·lo *de*·la jo·ven·*too* youth hostel
osteria ⓕ os·te·*ree*·a pub
ostrica ⓕ *o*·stree·ka oyster

ottimo/a ⓜ/ⓕ o·*tee*·mo/a excellent • great
ovest ⓜ *o*·vest west

P

pacchetto ⓜ pa·*ke*·to parcel • packet • package
pace ⓕ *pa*·che peace
padella ⓕ pa·*de*·la frying pan
padre ⓜ *pa*·dre father
padrone/padrona ⓜ/ⓕ **di casa** pa·*dro*·ne/pa·*dro*·na dee *ka*·za landlord/landlady
paese ⓜ pa·*e*·ze country (nation)
Paesi Bassi ⓜ pl pa·*e*·zee *ba*·see Netherlands
pagamento ⓜ pa·ga·*men*·to payment
pagare pa·*ga*·re pay
pagina ⓕ *pa*·jee·na page
paio ⓜ *pa*·yo pair (couple)
palazzo ⓜ pa·*la*·tso palace
palcoscenico ⓜ pal·ko·*she*·nee·ko stage
palestra ⓕ pa·*le*·stra gym
palla ⓕ *pa*·la ball (sports)
pallacanestro ⓕ pa·la·ka·*ne*·stro basketball
pallamuro ⓕ pa·la·*moo*·ro handball
pallavolo ⓕ pa·la·*vo*·lo volleyball
pallone ⓜ pa·*lo*·ne ball (inflated)
pancetta ⓕ pan·*che*·ta bacon
pane ⓜ *pa*·ne bread
— **a pasta acida** a *pas*·ta a·*chee*·da sourdough bread
— **di segala** dee se·*ga*·la rye bread
— **integrale** een·te·*gra*·le wholemeal bread
— **tostato** tos·*ta*·to toast
panetteria ⓕ pa·ne·te·*ree*·a bakery
panino ⓜ pa·*nee*·no roll (bread)
panna ⓕ *pa*·na cream (food)
— **acida** a·*chee*·da sour cream
pannolino ⓜ pa·no·*lee*·no diaper • nappy
pantaloncini ⓜ pl pan·ta·lon·*chee*·nee shorts

pantaloni ⓜ pl pan·ta·lo·nee pants • trousers

pap test ⓜ pap test pap smear

papà ⓜ pa·pa dad

parabrezza ⓜ pa·ra·bre·dza windscreen

parcheggio ⓜ par·ke·jo carpark

parco ⓜ par·ko park

— nazionale na·tsyo·na·le national park

— giochi jo·kee playground

parlamentare ⓜ&ⓕ par·la·men·ta·re member of parliament

parlamento ⓜ par·la·men·to parliament

parlare par·la·re speak • talk

parola ⓕ pa·ro·la word

parrucchiere ⓜ pa·roo·kye·re beauty salon

parrucchiere/a ⓜ/ⓕ pa·roo·kye·re/a hairdresser

parte ⓕ par·te part

partenza ⓕ par·ten·tsa departure

partire par·tee·re depart • leave

partita ⓕ par·tee·ta game • match

partito ⓜ par·tee·to party (politics)

Pasqua ⓕ pas·kwa Easter

passaggio ⓜ pa·sa·jo pass (sport) • passage

passaporto ⓜ pa·sa·por·to passport

passatempo ⓜ pa·sa·tem·po hobby

passato ⓜ pa·sa·to past

passeggero/a ⓜ/ⓕ pa·se·je·ro/a passenger

passeggiata ⓕ pa·se·ja·ta walk

passo ⓜ pa·so pass (mountain)

pasta ⓕ pas·ta pasta • noodles

pasticceria ⓕ pa·stee·che·ree·a cake shop

pasto ⓜ pas·to meal

— freddo fre·do buffet (meal)

patata ⓕ pa·ta·ta potato

paté ⓜ pa·te pate (food)

patente ⓕ **(di guida)** pa·ten·te (dee gwee·da) drivers licence

pavimento ⓜ pa·vee·men·to floor

pazzo/a ⓜ/ⓕ pa·tso/a crazy

pecora ⓕ pe·ko·ra sheep

pedale ⓜ pe·da·le pedal

pedone ⓜ/ⓕ pe·do·ne pedestrian

pelle ⓕ pe·le skin

pellicola ⓕ pe·lee·ko·la film (for camera)

pene ⓜ pe·ne penis

penicillina ⓕ pe·nee·chee·lee·na penicillin

penna ⓕ **(a sfera)** pe·na (a sfe·ra) pen (ballpoint)

pensare pen·sa·re think

pensionato/a ⓜ/ⓕ pen·syo·na·to/a pensioner • retired

pensione ⓕ pen·syo·ne guesthouse • boarding house

pentola ⓕ pen·to·la pan

pepe ⓜ pe·pe pepper

peperoncino ⓜ pe·pe·ron·chee·no chilli

peperone ⓜ pe·pe·ro·ne capsicum

per per for • to • through • by

— esempio e·zem·pyo for example

— sempre sem·pre forever

pera ⓕ pe·ra pear

percentuale ⓕ per·chen·twa·le percentage

perché per·ke why • because

perdere per·de·re lose

perdonare per·do·na·re forgive

pericoloso/a ⓜ/ⓕ pe·ree·ko·lo·zo/a dangerous • unsafe

permanente ⓜ/ⓕ per·ma·nen·te permanent

permesso ⓜ per·me·so permission • permit

perso/a ⓜ/ⓕ per·so/a lost

persona ⓕ per·so·na person

personale ⓜ/ⓕ per·so·na·le personal

pesante pe·zan·te heavy

pesca ⓕ pe·ska fishing • peach

pesce ⓜ pe·she fish (food)

pesce/pesci ⓜ sg/pl pe·she/pe·shee fish (alive)

pescheria ⓕ pe·ske·ree·a fish shop

peso ⓜ *pe*·zo weight
petizione ⓕ pe·tee·*tsyo*·ne petition
pettine ⓜ *pe*·tee·ne comb
petto ⓜ *pe*·to chest
pezzo ⓜ *pe*·tso piece
— di antiquariato dee an·tee·kwa·*rya*·to antique
— d'artigianato dar·tee·ja·*na*·to craft (product)
piacere pya·*che*·re like
pianeta ⓜ pya·*ne*·ta planet
piano ⓜ *pya*·no floor (storey)
pianta ⓕ *pyan*·ta map • plant
piatto ⓜ *pya*·to plate
— fondo *fon*·do bowl
piatto/a ⓜ/ⓕ *pya*·to/a flat
piazza ⓕ *pya*·tsa square (town)
picchetti ⓜ pl pee·*ke*·tee pegs (tent)
piccolo/a ⓜ/ⓕ *pee*·ko·lo/a small
piccone ⓜ pee·*ko*·ne pickaxe
piccozza ⓕ pee·*ko*·tsa ice axe
pidocchi ⓜ pl pee·*do*·kee lice
piede ⓜ *pye*·de foot
pieno/a ⓜ/ⓕ *pye*·no/a full
pietra ⓕ *pye*·tra stone
pignatta ⓕ pee·*nya*·ta pot (ceramics)
pigro/a ⓜ/ⓕ *pee*·gro/a lazy
pila ⓕ *pee*·la battery
pillola ⓕ *pee*·lo·la pill • the Pill
— anticoncezionale an·tee·kon·che·tsyo·*na*·le the Pill
— del mattino dopo del ma·*tee*·no *do*·po morning after pill
ping pong ⓜ *peeng pong* table tennis
pinzette ⓕ pl peen·*tse*·te tweezers
pioggia ⓕ *pyo*·ja rain
piombo ⓜ *pyom*·bo lead
piscina ⓕ pee·*shee*·na swimming pool
pisello ⓜ pee·*ze*·lo pea
pista ⓕ *pee*·sta trail • track (sports) • racetrack • slope
pittore/pittrice ⓜ/ⓕ pee·*to*·re/ pee·*tree*·che painter
pittura ⓕ pee·*too*·ra painting (the art)

più pyoo more
plastica ⓕ *pla*·stee·ka plastic
un po' oon po (a) little
poco/a ⓜ/ⓕ *po*·ko/a few
poesia ⓕ po·e·*zee*·a poetry
politica ⓕ po·*lee*·tee·ka politics
politico ⓜ po·*lee*·tee·ko politician
polizia ⓕ po·lee·*tsee*·a police (civilian)
polline ⓜ *po*·lee·ne pollen
pollo ⓜ *po*·lo chicken
polmoni ⓜ pl pol·*mo*·nee lungs
polso ⓜ *pol*·so wrist
polvere ⓕ *pol*·ve·re powder
pomeriggio ⓜ po·me·*ree*·jo afternoon
pomodoro ⓜ po·mo·*do*·ro tomato
pompa ⓕ *pom*·pa pump
pompelmo ⓜ pom·*pel*·mo grapefruit
ponte ⓜ *pon*·te bridge
popolare po·po·*la*·re popular
porro ⓜ *po*·ro leek
porta ⓕ *por*·ta door
portacenere ⓜ por·ta·*che*·ne·re ashtray
portafoglio ⓜ por·ta·*fo*·lyo wallet
portare por·*ta*·re bring • carry
portatile ⓜ por·ta·*tee*·le laptop
portatile por·ta·*tee*·le portable
porto ⓜ *por*·to harbour • port
posate ⓕ pl po·*za*·te cutlery
possibile po·*see*·bee·le possible
posta ⓕ *pos*·ta mail
— elettronica e·le·*tro*·nee·ka email
— ordinaria or·dee·*na*·rya surface mail
— prioritaria pree·o·ree·*ta*·rya express mail
— raccomandata ⓕ ra·ko·man·*da*·ta registered mail
posteggio ⓜ **di tassì** po·*ste*·jo dee ta·*see* taxi stand
posto ⓜ *pos*·to place • seat
— di polizia dee po·lee·*tsee*·a police station
potabile po·*ta*·bee·le drinkable

potere ⓜ po·*te*·re power (strength)
potere po·*te*·re can
povero/a ⓜ/ⓕ *po*·ve·ro/a poor
povertà ⓕ po·ver·*ta* poverty
pranzo ⓜ *pran*·dzo lunch
praticare pra·tee·*ka*·re play (sport)
— il surf eel soorf surf
prima colazione ⓕ *pree*·ma
ko·la·*tsyo*·ne breakfast
preferire pre·fe·*ree*·re prefer
preferito/a ⓜ/ⓕ pre·fe·*ree*·to/a
favourite
pregare pre·*ga*·re worship (pray)
preghiera ⓕ pre·*gye*·ra prayer
prendere *pren*·de·re take
— in affitto een a·*fee*·to rent
— in prestito een *pres*·tee·to borrow
prenotare pre·no·*ta*·re book (make
a booking)
prenotazione ⓕ pre·no·ta·*tsyo*·ne
reservation
preoccupato/a ⓜ/ⓕ
pre·o·koo·*pa*·to/a worried
preparare pre·pa·*ra*·re prepare
preservativo ⓜ pre·zer·va·*tee*·vo
condom
presidente ⓜ pre·zee·*den*·te
president
pressione ⓕ pre·*syo*·ne pressure
— del sangue del *san*·gwe blood
pressure
presto ⓜ/ⓕ *pres*·to early
prete ⓜ *pre*·te priest
prezioso/a ⓜ/ⓕ pre·*tsyo*·zo/a
valuable
prezzemolo ⓜ pre·*tse*·mo·lo parsley
prezzo ⓜ *pre*·tso price
— d'ingresso deen·*gre*·so admission
price
prigione ⓕ pree·*jo*·ne prison
prigioniero/a ⓜ/ⓕ pree·jo·*nye*·ro/a
prisoner
prima *pree*·ma before
— classe ⓕ *kla*·se first class
— colazione ⓕ ko·la·*tsyo*·ne
breakfast

primavera ⓕ pree·ma·*ve*·ra spring
(season)
primo ministro ⓜ/ⓕ *pree*·mo
mee·*nee*·stro prime minister
primo/a ⓜ/ⓕ *pree*·mo/a first
principale preen·chee·*pa*·le main
privato/a ⓜ/ⓕ pree·*va*·to/a private
problema ⓜ pro·*ble*·ma problem
— cardiaco kar·*dee*·a·ko heart
condition
produrre pro·*doo*·re produce
profesore/profesoressa ⓜ/ⓕ
pro·fe·*so*·re/pro·fe·so·*re*·sa teacher
(general)
profitto ⓜ pro·*fee*·to profit
profondo/a ⓜ/ⓕ pro·*fon*·do/a deep
profumo ⓜ pro·*foo*·mo perfume
programma ⓜ pro·*gra*·ma program
proiettore ⓜ pro·ye·*to*·re projector
promessa ⓕ pro·*me*·sa promise
pronto/a ⓜ/ⓕ *pron*·to/a ready
pronto soccorso ⓜ *pron*·to so·*kor*·so
first-aid
proprietario/a ⓜ/ⓕ
pro·prye·*ta*·ryo/a owner
proroga ⓕ *pro*·ro·ga extension (visa)
prosciutto (cotto) pro·*shoo*·to
(*ko*·to) ham (boiled)
prossimo/a ⓜ/ⓕ *pro*·see·mo/a next
proteggere pro·*te*·je·re protect
protetto/a ⓜ/ⓕ pro·*te*·to/a
protected
protestare pro·tes·*ta*·re protest
provare pro·*va*·re try (attempt)
provviste ⓕ pl pro·*vee*·ste
provisions • supplies
— alimentari a·lee·men·*ta*·ree food
supplies
prugna ⓕ *proo*·nya plum • prune
prurito ⓜ proo·*ree*·to itch
pugilato ⓜ poo·jee·*la*·to boxing
pulce ⓕ *pool*·che flea
pulito/a ⓜ/ⓕ poo·*lee*·to/a clean
pulizia ⓕ poo·lee·*tsee*·a cleaning
pullman ⓜ *pool*·man bus (coach)
punteggio ⓜ poon·*te*·jo score

punto ⓜ *poon*·to point
puntura ⓕ poon·*too*·ra bite (insect)
puro/a ⓜ/ⓕ *poo*·ro/a pure

Q

quaderno ⓜ kwa·*der*·no notebook
quadro ⓜ *kwa*·dro painting (canvas)
qualcosa kwal·*ko*·za something
qualcuno/a ⓜ/ⓕ kwal·*koo*·no/a someone
qualità ⓕ kwa·lee·*ta* quality
quando *kwan*·do when
quantità ⓕ kwan·tee·*ta* amount • quantity
quanto/a ⓜ/ⓕ *kwan*·to/a how much
quarantena ⓕ kwa·ran·*te*·na quarantine
quaresima ⓕ kwa·*re*·zee·ma Lent
quartiere ⓜ kwar·*tye*·re suburb
quarto ⓜ *kwar*·to quarter
questo/a ⓜ/ⓕ *kwe*·sto/a this (one)
questura ⓕ kwes·*too*·ra police headquarters
qui kwee here
quota ⓕ *kwo*·ta altitude

R

racchetta ⓕ ra·*ke*·ta racquet
raccogliere ra·ko·*lye*·re pick (up)
raccomandare ra·ko·man·*da*·re recommend
raccomandata ⓕ ra·ko·man·*da*·ta registered mail
raccontare ra·kon·*ta*·re tell
racconto ⓜ ra·*kon*·to story
radiatore ⓜ ra·dya·*to*·re radiator
rafano ⓜ *ra*·fa·no horseradish
raffreddore ⓜ ra·fre·*do*·re cold (illness)
ragazza ⓕ ra·*ga*·tsa girl(friend)
ragazzo ⓜ ra·*ga*·tso boy(friend)
ragione ⓕ ra·*jo*·ne reason
ragno ⓜ *ra*·nyo spider
rapido/a ⓜ/ⓕ *ra*·pee·do/a quick
rapinare ra·pee·*na*·re rob

rapporti ⓜ pl **protetti** ra·*por*·tee pro·*te*·tee safe sex
rapporto ⓜ ra·*por*·to relationship
raro/a ⓜ/ⓕ *ra*·ro/a rare
rasatura ⓕ ra·za·*too*·ra shave
rasoio ⓜ **(elettrico)** ra·*zo*·yo (e·*le*·tree·ko) razor
ravanello ⓜ ra·va·*ne*·lo radish
razzismo ⓜ ra·*tseez*·mo racism
re ⓜ re king
realistico/a ⓜ/ⓕ re·a·*lee*·stee·ko/a realistic
recente re·*chen*·te recent
recinzione ⓕ re·cheen·*tsyo*·ne fence
regalo ⓜ re·*ga*·lo present (gift)
— di nozze dee *no*·tse wedding present
reggiseno ⓜ re·jee·*se*·no bra
regina ⓕ re·*jee*·na queen
regione ⓕ re·*jo*·ne region
regista ⓜ&ⓕ re·*jee*·sta director (films)
registrazione ⓕ re·jee·stra·*tsyo*·ne check-in (hotel)
regolare re·go·*la*·re regular
regole ⓕ pl *re*·go·le rules
religione ⓕ re·lee·*jo*·ne religion
religioso/a ⓜ/ⓕ re·lee·*jo*·zo/a religious
reliquia ⓕ re·*lee*·kwee·a relic
remoto/a ⓜ/ⓕ re·*mo*·to/a remote
respirare res·pee·*ra*·re breathe
resto ⓜ *res*·to change (money)
rete ⓕ *re*·te net
ricco/a ⓜ/ⓕ *ree*·ko/a rich (wealthy)
ricetta ⓕ ree·*che*·ta prescription
ricevere ree·*che*·ve·re receive
ricevuta ⓕ ree·che·*voo*·ta receipt
richiedere ree·*kye*·de·re ask (for something)
riciclabile ree·chee·*kla*·bee·le recyclable
riciclare ree·chee·*kla*·re recycle
ricordino ⓜ ree·kor·*dee*·no souvenir
ridere *ree*·de·re laugh
rifiutare ree·fyoo·*ta*·re refuse

S

rifugiato/a m/f ree-foo-*gya*-to/a refugee

rifiuti m pl ree-*fyoo*-tee rubbish

rilassarsi ree-la-*sar*-see relax

rimborso m reem-*bor*-so refund

ringraziare reen-gra-*tsya*-re thank

riparare ree-pa-*ra*-re repair

ripido/a m/f ree-*pee*-do/a steep

riposare ree-po-*za*-re rest

riscaldamento m rees-kal-da-*men*-to heating

— centrale chen-*tra*-le central heating

rischio m *rees*-kyo risk

riscuotere un assegno ree-*skwo*-te-re oon a-*se*-nyo cash a cheque

riso m *ree*-zo rice

— integrale een-te-*gra*-le brown rice

risposta f rees-*pos*-ta answer

ristorante m rees-to-*ran*-te restaurant

ritardo m ree-*tar*-do delay

ritiro bagagli ree-*tee*-ro ba-*ga*-lyee baggage claim

ritmo m *reet*-mo rhythm

ritornare ree-tor-*na*-re return

ritorno m ree-*tor*-no return

rivista f ree-*vee*-sta magazine

roba f *ro*-ba stuff (belongings) • dope (drugs)

roccia f *ro*-cha rock • rock climbing

romantico/a m/f ro-*man*-tee-ko/a romantic

romanzo m ro-*man*-dzo novel

rompere *rom*-pe-re break

rosa m/f *ro*-za pink

rossetto m ro-*se*-to lipstick

rosso/a m/f *ro*-so/a red

rotonda f ro-*ton*-da roundabout

rotondo/a m/f ro-*ton*-do/a round

rotto/a m/f *ro*-to/a broken

roulotte f roo-*lot* caravan

rovine f pl ro-*vee*-ne ruins

rubare roo-*ba*-re steal

rubato/a m/f roo-*ba*-to/a stolen

rubinetto m roo-bee-*ne*-to faucet

rullino m roo-*lee*-no film (roll for camera)

rumoroso/a m/f roo-mo-*ro*-zo/a noisy

ruota f *rwo*-ta wheel

ruscello m roo-*she*-lo stream

S

sabato m *sa*-ba-to saturday

sabbia f *sa*-bya sand

sacchetto m sa-*ke*-to bag (shopping)

sacco m *sa*-ko sack • bag

— a pelo a *pe*-lo sleeping bag

sala f *sa*-la room • hall

— di transito dee *tran*-zee-to transit lounge

— d'aspetto das-*pe*-to waiting room

salame m sa-*la*-me salami

salario m sa-*la*-ryo wage

saldi m pl *sal*-dee sales

saldo m *sal*-do balance (account)

sale m *sa*-le salt

salire sa-*lee*-re climb • go up

— su soo board (a plane, ship)

salmone m sal-*mo*-ne salmon

salsa f *sal*-sa sauce

salsiccia f sal-*see*-cha sausage

saltare sal-*ta*-re jump

salumeria f sa-loo-me-*ree*-a delicatessen

salute f sa-*loo*-te health

salva slip m pl *sal*-va sleep panty liners

San Silvestro m san seel-*ves*-tro New Year's Eve

sandali m pl *san*-da-lee sandals

sangue m *san*-gwe blood

santo/a m/f *san*-to/a saint

santuario m san-too-a-*ryo* shrine

sapere sa-*pe*-re know (how to)

sapone m sa-*po*-ne soap

sardine f pl sar-*dee*-ne sardines

sarto/a m/f *sar*-to/a tailor

sauna f *sow*-na sauna

sbagliato/a m/f sba-*lya*-to/a wrong

sbaglio m *sba*-lyo mistake

scacchi m pl *ska*-kee chess

scala ① **mobile** *ska*·la mo·*bee*·le escalator

scalare ska·*la*·re climb

scale ① pl *ska*·le stairway

scanner ⓜ *ska*·ner scanner

scarafaggio ⓜ ska·ra·*fa*·jo cockroach

scarpe ① pl *skar*·pe shoes

scarpette ① pl skar·*pe*·te boots (soccer)

scarponi ⓜ pl skar·*po*·nee boots (hiking, ski)

scatola ① *ska*·to·la box • carton • can • tin

scatoletta ① ska·to·*le*·ta tin • can

scheda ① **telefonica** *ske*·da te·le·*fo*·nee·ka phone card

scherma ① *sker*·ma fencing (sport)

scherzo ⓜ *sker*·tso joke

schiena ① *skye*·na back (body)

sci ⓜ shee skiing • ski(s)

— acquatico a·kwa·*tee*·ko waterskiing

sciare shee·*a*·re ski

sciarpa ① *shar*·pa scarf

scienza ① *shen*·tsa science

sciopero ⓜ *sho*·pe·ro strike

sciovia ① shee·o·*vee*·a ski-lift

sciroppo ⓜ shee·*ro*·po syrup

— per la tosse per la *to*·se cough medicine

scogliera ① sko·*lye*·ra cliff

scommessa ① sko·*me*·sa bet

scomodo/a ⓜ/① *sko*·mo·do/a uncomfortable

sconosciuto/a ⓜ/① sko·no·*shoo*·to/a stranger

sconto ⓜ *skon*·to discount

scorie ① pl *sko*·rye waste (rubbish)

— radioattive ra·dyo·a·*tee*·ve nuclear waste

— tossiche *to*·see·che toxic waste

scottatura ① sko·ta·*too*·ra sunburn

Scozia ① *sko*·tsya Scotland

scrittore/scrittrice ⓜ/① skree·*to*·re/skree·*tree*·che writer

scrivere *skree*·ve·re write

scultura ① skool·*too*·ra sculpture

scuola ① *skwo*·la school

— superiore soo·pe·*ryo*·re high school

scuro/a ⓜ/① *skoo*·ro/a dark

se se if

seccato/a ⓜ/① se·*ka*·to/a cross (angry)

secchio ⓜ *se*·kyo bucket

secco/a ⓜ/① *se*·ko/a dry

seconda classe ① se·*kon*·da *kla*·se second class

(di) seconda mano ⓜ/① (dee) se·*kon*·da *ma*·no secondhand

secondo ⓜ se·*kon*·do second

secondo/a ⓜ/① se·*kon*·do/a second

sedere se·*de*·re sit

sedia ① *se*·dya chair

— a rotelle a ro·*te*·le wheelchair

sedile ⓜ se·*dee*·le seat (chair)

seggiolino ⓜ se·jo·*lee*·no child seat

seggiovia ① se·jo·*vee*·a chairlift (skiing)

segnale ⓜ se·*nya*·le signal • dial tone

— acustico a·*koos*·tee·ko dial tone

segnare se·*nya*·re score

segno ⓜ *se*·nyo sign

segretario/a ⓜ/① se·gre·*ta*·ryo/a secretary

seguire se·*gwee*·re follow

sella ① *se*·la saddle

semaforo ⓜ se·*ma*·fo·ro traffic lights

semplice ⓜ/① *sem*·plee·che simple

sempre *sem*·pre always

senape ① *se*·na·pe mustard

seno ⓜ *se*·no breast

sensuale ⓜ/① sen·soo·*a*·le sensual

sentiero ⓜ sen·*tye*·ro path • track • trail

— di montagna dee mon·*ta*·nya mountain path

sentimenti ⓜ pl sen·tee·*men*·tee feelings

sentire sen·*tee*·re feel • hear

senza *sen*·tsa without

— piombo *pyom*·bo unleaded

senzatetto ⓜ&① sen·tsa·*te*·to homeless

separato/a ⓜ/ⓕ se·pa·ra·to/a separate

sera ⓕ se·ra evening

serie ⓕ **(televisiva)** se·ree·e (te·le·vee·see·va) (TV) series

serio/a ⓜ/ⓕ se·ryo/a serious

serpente ⓜ ser·pen·te snake

serratura ⓕ se·ra·too·ra lock (door)

servizi ⓜ pl **igienici** ser·vee·tse ee·je·nee·chee toilets

servizio ⓜ ser·vee·tsyo service • service-charge

— militare mee·lee·ta·re military service

sessismo ⓜ se·seez·mo sexism

sesso ⓜ se·so sex

seta ⓕ se·ta silk

settimana ⓕ se·tee·ma·na week

— santa san·ta Holy Week

sfogo ⓜ sfo·go rash

— da pannolino da pa·no·lee·no nappy rash

sfruttamento ⓜ sfroo·ta·men·to exploitation

sì see yes

sicuro/a ⓜ/ⓕ see·koo·ro/a safe

sidro ⓜ see·dro cider

sieropositivo/a ⓜ/ⓕ sye·ro·po·zee·tee·vo/a HIV positive

sigaretta ⓕ see·ga·re·ta cigarette

sigaro ⓜ see·ga·ro cigar

simile ⓜ/ⓕ see·mee·le similar

simpatico/a ⓜ/ⓕ seem·pa·tee·ko/a nice (person)

sinagoga ⓕ see·na·go·ga synagogue

sindaco ⓜ seen·da·ko mayor

sinistra ⓕ see·nee·stra left (direction)

sintetico/a ⓜ/ⓕ seen·te·tee·ko/a synthetic

siringa ⓕ see·reen·ga syringe

slitta ⓕ slee·ta sleigh • toboggan

soccorso ⓜ so·kor·so help • aid

socialista ⓜ&ⓕ so·cha·lee·sta socialist

socio/a ⓜ/ⓕ so·cho/a member

soffice ⓜ/ⓕ so·fee·che soft

sognare so·nya·re dream

sogno ⓜ so·nyo dream

soldato ⓜ sol·da·to soldier

soldi ⓜ pl sol·dee money • cash

sole ⓜ so·le sun

soleggiato/a ⓜ/ⓕ so·le·ja·to/a sunny

solo so·lo only

— andata ⓕ an·da·ta one-way

sonniferi ⓜ pl so·nee·fe·ree sleeping pills

sonno ⓜ so·no sleep • sleepiness

sopra so·pra above • over

soprannome ⓜ so·pra·no·me nickname

sordo/a ⓜ/ⓕ sor·do/a deaf

sorella ⓕ so·re·la sister

sorpresa ⓕ sor·pre·sa surprise

sorridere so·ree·de·re smile

sostenitore/sostenitrice ⓜ/ⓕ sos·te·nee·to·re/sos·te·nee·tree·che supporter

sotto so·to below

sottoaceti ⓜ pl so·to·a·che·tee pickles

sottotitoli ⓜ pl so·to·tee·to·lee subtitles

spacciatore/spacciatrice ⓜ/ⓕ spa·cha·to·re/spa·cha·tree·che drug dealer

Spagna ⓕ spa·nya Spain

spago ⓜ spa·go string

spalla ⓕ spa·la shoulder

spazio ⓜ spa·tsyo space

spazzatura ⓕ spa·tsa·too·ra rubbish • garbage

spazzolino ⓜ **da denti** spa·tso·lee·no da den·tee toothbrush

specchio ⓜ spe·kyo mirror

speciale spe·cha·le special

specialista ⓜ&ⓕ spe·cha·lee·sta specialist

specie ⓕ spe·che species • type

— in via di estinzione een vee·a dee es·teen·tsyo·ne endangered species

— **protetta** pro·*te*·ta protected species

spermicida ① sper·mee·*chee*·da spermicide

spesso *spe*·so often

spesso/a ⓜ/① *spe*·so/a thick

spettacolo ⓜ spe·*ta*·ko·lo show • performance

spiaggia ① *spya*·ja beach

spiccioli ⓜ pl *spee*·cho·lee loose change

spina ① *spee*·na plug (electricity)

— **multipla** *mool*·tee·pla adaptor

spinaci ⓜ pl spee·*na*·chee spinach

spingere *speen*·je·re push

spirale ① spee·*ra*·le IUD

spogliatoio ⓜ spo·lya·*to*·yo change room (sport)

sporco/a ⓜ/① *spor*·ko/a dirty

sportivo/a ⓜ/① spor·*tee*·vo/a sportsperson

sposalizio ⓜ spo·za·*lee*·tsyo wedding

sposare spo·*za*·re marry

sposato/a ⓜ/① spo·*za*·to/a married

spremuta ① spre·*moo*·ta fruit juice (fresh)

— **d'arancia** da·*ran*·cha orange juice (fresh)

spuntino ⓜ spoon·*tee*·no snack

squadra ① *skwa*·dra team

stadio ⓜ *sta*·dyo stadium

stagione ① sta·*jo*·ne season

stampante ① stam·*pan*·te printer (computer)

stanco/a ⓜ/① *stan*·ko/a tired

stanza ① *stan*·tsa room

stasera sta·*se*·ra tonight

Stati Uniti d'America ⓜ pl *sta*·tee oo·*nee*·tee da·*me*·ree·ka USA

stato ⓜ **civile** *sta*·to chee·*vee*·le marital status

statua ① *sta*·too·a statue

stazione ① sta·*tsyo*·ne (train) station

— **d'autobus** *dow*·to·boos bus station

— **della metropolitana** *de*·la me·tro·po·lee·*ta*·na metro station

— **di servizio** dee ser·*vee*·tsyo petrol station • service station

— **ferroviaria** fe·ro·*vyar*·ya train station

stelle ① pl *ste*·le stars

stendersi *sten*·der·see lie (not stand)

sterlina ① ster·*lee*·na pound (money)

stesso/a ⓜ/① *ste*·so/a same

stile ⓜ *stee*·le style

stipendio ⓜ stee·*pen*·dyo salary

stitichezza ① stee·tee·*ke*·tsa constipation

stivali ⓜ pl stee·*va*·lee boots

stoffa ① *sto*·fa fabric

stomaco ⓜ *sto*·ma·ko stomach

stordito/a ⓜ/① stor·*dee*·to/a dizzy

storia ① *sto*·rya history • story

storico/a ⓜ/① *sto*·ree·ko/a historical

storta ① *stor*·ta sprain

strada ① *stra*·da road • street

straniero/a ⓜ/① stra·*nye*·ro/a foreign

strano/a ⓜ/① *stra*·no/a strange

strato **d'ozono** *stra*·to do·*dzo*·no ozone layer

stretto/a ⓜ/① *stre*·to/a tight

studente/studentessa ⓜ/① stoo·*den*·te/stoo·den·*te*·sa student

stufa ① *stoo*·fa heater • stove

— **a gas** a gaz gas stove

stupido/a ⓜ/① *stoo*·pee·do/a stupid

stupro ⓜ *stoo*·pro rape

stuzzicadenti ⓜ stoo·tsee·ka·*den*·te toothpick

su soo on · up

succo ⓜ *soo*·ko juice

— **d'arancia** da·*ran*·cha orange juice (bottled)

— **di frutta** dee *froo*·ta fruit juice (bottled)

sud ⓜ sood south

sugo ⓜ *soo*·go sauce

suocera ① *swo*·che·ra mother-in-law

suocero ⓜ *swo*·che·ro father-in-law

suonare (la chitarra) swo·*na*·re (la kee·*ta*·ra) play (guitar)

suora ⓕ *swo*·ra nun

supermercato ⓜ soo·per·mer·*ka*·to supermarket

superstizione ⓕ soo·per·stee·*tsyo*·ne superstition

surf ⓜ **da neve** soorf da *ne*·ve snowboarding

surgelati ⓜ pl soor·je·*la*·tee frozen foods

sussidio ⓜ **di disoccupazione** soo·*see*·dyo dee dee·zo·koo·pa·*tsyo*·ne unemployment benefit

sveglia ⓕ *sve*·lya alarm clock

svegliarsi sve·*lyar*·see wake up

Svizzera ⓕ svee·*tse*·ra Switzerland

T

tabaccheria ⓕ ta·ba·ke·*ree*·a tobacconist

tabacco ⓜ ta·*ba*·ko tobacco

tabellone ⓜ **segnapunti** ta·be·*lo*·ne se·nya·*poon*·tee scoreboard

tacchino ⓜ ta·*kee*·no turkey

tachimetro ⓜ ta·*kee*·me·tro speedometer

taglia ⓕ *ta*·lya size (clothes)

tagliare ta·*lya*·re cut

tagliaunghie ta·lya·*oon*·gye nail clippers

taglio ⓜ **di capelli** *ta*·lyo dee ka·*pe*·lee haircut

tamponi ⓜ pl tam·*po*·nee tampons

tappa ⓕ *ta*·pa leg (in race or journey) • stage (in race)

tappeto ⓜ ta·*pe*·to mat • rug

tappi ⓜ pl **per le orecchie** *ta*·pee per le o·*re*·kye earplugs

tappo ⓜ *ta*·po plug (bath)

tardi *tar*·dee late

targa ⓕ *tar*·ga number plate

tariffa ⓕ **postale** ta·*ree*·fa pos·*ta*·le postage

tasca ⓕ *tas*·ka pocket

tassa ⓕ *ta*·sa tax

tassì ⓜ ta·*see* taxi

tasso ⓜ **di cambio** *ta*·so dee *kam*·byo exchange rate

tastiera ⓕ tas·*tye*·ra keyboard

tavola ⓕ *ta*·vo·la table

— da surf da soorf surfboard

tazza ⓕ *ta*·tsa cup

tè ⓜ te tea

teatro ⓜ te·*a*·tro theatre

— dell'opera del·*o*·per·a opera house

telecomando ⓜ te·le·ko·*man*·do remote control

telefonare te·le·fo·*na*·re telephone

telefonata ⓕ te·le·fo·*na*·ta phone call

telefono ⓜ te·*le*·fo·no telephone

— cellulare che·loo·*la*·re mobile/cell phone

— diretto dee·*re*·to direct-dial

— pubblico *poo*·blee·ko public telephone

telegramma ⓜ te·le·*gra*·ma telegram

telenovela ⓕ te·le·no·*ve*·la soap opera

teleobiettivo ⓜ te·le·o·bye·*tee*·vo telephoto lens

telescopio ⓜ te·le·*sko*·pyo telescope

televisione ⓕ te·le·vee·*zyo*·ne television

temperatura ⓕ tem·pe·ra·*too*·ra temperature (weather)

temperino ⓜ tem·pe·*ree*·no penknife

tempio ⓜ *tem*·pyo temple

tempo ⓜ *tem*·po time • weather

— pieno *pye*·no full-time

temporale ⓜ tem·po·*ra*·le storm

tenda ⓕ *ten*·da tent

tensione ⓕ **premestruale** ten·*syo*·ne pre·me·*stroo*·a·le premenstrual tension

Terra ⓕ *te*·ra Earth

terra ⓕ *te*·ra land

terremoto ⓜ te·re·*mo*·to earthquake

terribile te·*ree*·bee·le terrible

terzo/a ⓜ/ⓕ *ter*·tso/a third

tessera ⓕ *te*·se·ra pass (document)

test ⓜ **di gravidanza** test dee gra·vee·*dan*·tsa pregnancy test kit

testa ⓕ *tes*·ta head
tiepido/a ⓜ/ⓕ *tye*·pee·do/a warm
tifoso/a ⓜ/ⓕ tee·*fo*·zo/a fan
(person) • supporter
timido/a ⓜ/ⓕ *tee*·mee·do/a shy
tipico/a ⓜ/ⓕ *tee*·pee·ko/a typical
tipo ⓜ *tee*·po type
tirare tee·*ra*·re pull
titolo ⓜ *tee*·to·lo title
titoli ⓜ pl **di studio** *tee*·to·lee dee
stoo·dee·o qualifications
toboga ⓜ to·*bo*·ga toboggan • sledge
toccare to·*ka*·re touch
tomba ⓕ *tom*·ba grave
tonno ⓜ *to*·no tuna
topo ⓜ *to*·po mouse (rodent) • rat
torcia ⓕ **elettrica** *tor*·cha e·*le*·tree·ka
torch (flashlight)
torre ⓕ *to*·re tower
torta ⓕ *tor*·ta cake • pie
tossico/a ⓜ/ⓕ *to*·see·ko/a toxic
tossicodipendenza ⓕ
to·see·ko·dee·pen·*den*·tsa drug
addiction
tossire to·*see*·re cough
tostapane ⓜ tos·ta·*pa*·ne toaster
tovaglia ⓕ to·*va*·lya tablecloth
tovagliolo ⓜ to·va·*lyo*·lo napkin
tradurre tra·*doo*·re translate
traffico ⓜ *tra*·fee·ko traffic
traghetto ⓜ tra·*ge*·to ferry
tram ⓜ tram tram
tramezzino ⓜ tra·me·*dzee*·no
sandwich
tramonto ⓜ tra·*mon*·to sunset
tranquillo/a ⓜ/ⓕ tran·*kwee*·lo/a
quiet
trasporto ⓜ tras·*por*·to transport
travestito ⓜ tra·ves·*tee*·to drag queen
treno ⓜ *tre*·no train
triste *tree*·ste sad
troppo (caro/a) *tro*·po (*ka*·ro/a) too
(expensive)
troppo/a ⓜ/ⓕ *tro*·po/a too much •
too many
trovare tro·*va*·re find

trucco ⓜ *troo*·ko make-up
tu inf too you
tubo ⓜ **di scappamento** *too*·bo dee
ska·pa·*men*·to exhaust (car)
tuffi ⓜ pl *too*·fee diving (in pool)
turista ⓜ&ⓕ too·*ree*·sta tourist
tutti/e ⓜ/ⓕ pl *too*·tee/*too*·te all
tutto ⓜ *too*·to everything
tutto/a ⓜ/ⓕ sg *too*·to/a all

U

ubriaco/a ⓜ/ⓕ oo·*bree*·a·ko/a drunk
uccello ⓜ oo·*che*·lo bird
ufficio ⓜ oo·*fee*·cho office
— **del turismo** del too·*reez*·mo tourist
office
— **oggetti smarriti** o·*je*·tee
sma·*ree*·tee lost property office
— **postale** pos·*ta*·le post office
ultimo/a ⓜ/ⓕ *ool*·tee·mo/a last
un po' oon po (a) little
una volta ⓕ oo·na *vol*·ta once
università ⓕ oo·nee·ver·see·*ta*
university
universo ⓜ oo·nee·*ver*·so universe
uomo ⓜ *wo*·mo man
— **d'affari** da·*fa*·ree businessman
uovo ⓜ *wo*·vo egg
urgente ⓜ&ⓕ oor·*jen*·te urgent
urlare oor·*la*·re shout
usare oo·*za*·re use
usa e getta oo·za e *je*·ta disposable
uscire con oo·*shee*·re kon go out
with • date
uscita ⓕ oo·*shee*·ta exit
utile oo·tee·le useful
uva ⓕ pl *oo*·va grapes
— **passa** *pa*·sa raisin

V

vacanza ⓕ va·*kan*·tsa holiday •
vacation
vacanze ⓕ pl va·*kan*·tse holidays
vaccinazione ⓕ va·chee·na·*tsyo*·ne
vaccination

vagone ⓜ va·*go*·ne carriage • wagon
— letto *le*·to sleeping car
valigetta ⓕ va·lee·*je*·ta briefcase
— del pronto soccorso del *pron*·to so·*kor*·so first-aid kit
valigia ⓕ va·*lee*·ja suitcase
valle ⓕ *va*·le valley
valore ⓜ va·*lo*·re value (price)
vanga ⓕ *van*·ga spade
vecchio/a ⓜ/ⓕ ve·*kyo*/a old
vedere ve·*de*·re see
vedovo/a ⓜ/ⓕ ve·*do*·vo/a widower/widow
veduta ⓕ ve·*doo*·ta lookout
vegetariano/a ⓜ/ⓕ ve·je·ta·*rya*·no/a vegetarian
velenoso/a ⓜ/ⓕ ve·le·*no*·zo/a poisonous
veloce ve·*lo*·che fast
velocità ⓕ ve·lo·chee·*ta* speed
vendere *ven*·de·re sell
vendita ⓕ *ven*·dee·ta sale
venire ve·*nee*·re come
ventilatore ⓜ ven·tee·la·*to*·re fan (machine)
vento ⓜ *ven*·to wind
verde *ver*·de green
verdura ⓕ ver·*doo*·ra vegetable
vero/a ⓜ/ⓕ *ve*·ro/a true
vescica ⓕ ve·*shee*·ka blister
vetro ⓜ *ve*·tro glass
via ⓕ *vee*·a way
— aerea a·*e*·re·a airmail
viaggiare vee·a·*ja*·re travel
viaggio ⓜ vee·a·jo trip
— d'affari da·*fa*·ree business trip
viale ⓜ vee·*a*·le avenue
vicino/a ⓜ/ⓕ vee·*chee*·no/a close • nearby
vicino (a) vee·*chee*·no (a) near (to)
vicolo ⓜ *vee*·ko·lo lane
videonastro ⓜ vee·de·o·*nas*·tro video tape
videoregistratore ⓜ vee·de·o·re·jee·stra·*to*·re video
vigna ⓕ *vee*·nya vineyard • wine cellar

vigneto ⓜ vee·*nye*·to vineyard
villaggio ⓜ vee·*la*·jo village
vincere *veen*·che·re win
vincitore/vincitrice ⓜ/ⓕ veen·chee·*to*·re/veen·chee·*tree*·che winner
vino ⓜ *vee*·no wine
— bianco *byan*·ko white wine
— rosso *ro*·so red wine
— spumante spoo·*man*·te sparkling wine
viola vee·*o*·la purple
virus ⓜ *vee*·roos virus
visita ⓕ *vee*·zee·ta visit • tour • medical examination
— guidata gwee·*da*·ta guided tour
vista ⓕ *vee*·sta view
visto ⓜ *vee*·sto visa
vita ⓕ *vee*·ta life
vitamine ⓕ pl vee·ta·*mee*·ne vitamins
vitello ⓜ vee·*te*·lo veal
vitto ⓜ *vee*·to food
vivere *vee*·ve·re live
vocabolarietto ⓜ vo·ka·bo·la·*rye*·to phrasebook
vocabolario ⓜ vo·ka·bo·*la*·ryo dictionary
voce ⓕ *vo*·che voice
volare vo·*la*·re fly
volere vo·*le*·re want
volo ⓜ *vo*·lo flight
volta ⓕ *vol*·ta time • turn
volume ⓜ vo·*loo*·me volume
vomitare vo·mee·*ta*·re vomit
votare vo·*ta*·re vote
vuoto/a ⓜ/ⓕ *vwo*·to/a empty

Z

zaino ⓜ *dzai*·no backpack • knapsack
zanzara ⓕ tsan·*tsa*·ra mosquito
zenzero ⓜ *dzen*·dze·ro ginger
zia ⓕ *tsee*·a aunt
zucca ⓕ *tsoo*·ka pumpkin
zucchero ⓜ *tsoo*·ke·ro sugar

Index

l'indice

For topics that are covered in several sections of this book, we've
indicated the most relevant page number in bold.

10 Ways to Start a Sentence

When's (the next flight)?	A che ora è (il prossimo volo)?	a ke *o*·ra e (eel *pro*·see·mo *vo*·lo)
Where's (the station)?	Dov'è (la stazione)?	*do*·ve (la sta·*tsyo*·ne)
I'm looking for (a hotel).	Sto cercando (un albergo).	sto cher·*kan*·do (oon al·*ber*·go)
Do you have (a map)?	Ha (una pianta)?	a (*oo*·na *pyan*·ta)
Is there (a toilet)?	C'è (un gabinetto)?	che (oon ga·bee·*ne*·to)
I'd like (a coffee).	Vorrei (un caffè).	vo·*ray* (oon ka·*fe*)
I'd like to (hire a car).	Vorrei (noleggiare una macchina).	vo·*ray* (no·le·*ja*·re *oo*·na *ma*·kee·na)
Can I (enter)?	Posso (entrare)?	*po*·so (en·*tra*·re)
Could you please (help me)?	Può (aiutarmi), per favore?	pwo (a·yoo·*tar*·mee) per fa·*vo*·re
Do I have to (book a seat)?	Devo (prenotare un posto)?	*de*·vo (pre·no·*ta*·re oon *po*·sto)